Alternative Business Structures

Other titles available from Law Society Publishing:

COFAs Toolkit (forthcoming, 2012)
Jeremy Black

COLPs Toolkit (forthcoming, 2012)
Michelle Garlick

Outcomes-Focused Regulation
Andrew Hopper QC and Gregory Treverton-Jones QC

The Solicitor's Handbook 2012
Andrew Hopper QC and Gregory Treverton-Jones QC

Titles from Law Society Publishing can be ordered from all good bookshops or direct (telephone 0870 850 1422, email **lawsociety@prolog.uk.com** or visit our online shop at **www.lawsociety.org.uk/bookshop**).

ALTERNATIVE BUSINESS STRUCTURES

The Regulation of Law Firms

Iain Miller and Mark Pardoe

The Law Society

All rights reserved. No part of this publication may be reproduced in any material form, whether by photocopying, scanning, downloading onto computer or otherwise without the written permission of the Law Society except in accordance with the provisions of the Copyright, Designs and Patents Act 1988. Applications should be addressed in the first instance, in writing, to Law Society Publishing. Any unauthorised or restricted act in relation to this publication may result in civil proceedings and/or criminal prosecution.

The authors have asserted the right under the Copyright, Designs and Patents Act 1988 to be identified as authors of this work.

Whilst all reasonable care has been taken in the preparation of this publication, neither the publisher nor the authors can accept any responsibility for any loss occasioned to any person acting or refraining from action as a result of relying upon its contents.

The views expressed in this publication should be taken as those of the authors only unless it is specifically indicated that the Law Society has given its endorsement.

© The Law Society 2012

Crown copyright material is reproduced with the permission of the Controller of Her Majesty's Stationery Office

ISBN-13: 978-1-907698-15-6

Published in 2012 by the Law Society
113 Chancery Lane, London WC2A 1PL

Typeset by Columns Design XML Ltd, Reading
Printed by Hobbs the Printer Ltd, Totton, Hants

The paper used for the text pages of this book is FSC® certified. FSC (the Forest Stewardship Council®) is an international network to promote responsible management of the world's forests.

Contents

Preface vii
Table of cases ix
Table of statutes xi
Table of statutory instruments xv
Table of other enactments xvii
Abbreviations xix

1	**Introduction**		**1**
	1.1	What is an alternative business structure?	1
	1.2	The origins of ABSs and LSA 2007	4
2	**The regulatory boundaries**		**8**
	2.1	Introduction	8
	2.2	The reserved legal activities	10
	2.3	Controlling the perimeter of reserved legal activities	15
	2.4	Regulated but not reserved legal activities	16
	2.5	Unregulated legal activities	18
	2.6	Separate business provisions – the price of being regulated	19
	2.7	Alterations to the reserved legal activities	20
	2.8	Impact of the regulatory boundaries on ABSs	20
3	**Key regulatory concepts**		**21**
	3.1	Ownership regulation	21
	3.2	Regulation of managers and employees	23
	3.3	HOLPs and HOFAs	24
	3.4	Licensing	25
	3.5	The Legal Ombudsman	26
	3.6	Entity regulation	27
4	**Role of the SRA**		**29**
	4.1	What is the SRA?	29
	4.2	The SRA and the new regulatory environment	31

CONTENTS

	4.3	Risk-based regulation	32
5	**Authorisation process**		**35**
	5.1	Application process	35
	5.2	Fees	37
	5.3	Assessing applications	38
	5.4	Business systems and governance	40
	5.5	Approval of owners	40
	5.6	Approval of HOLPs and HOFAs	48
	5.7	Insurance requirements	49
	5.8	Access to justice objective	50
6	**Supervision and enforcement**		**51**
	6.1	SRA enforcement strategy	51
	6.2	Investigatory powers	53
	6.3	Suspension or revocation of a licence	53
	6.4	Enforcement of licence conditions	55
	6.5	Divestiture	55
	6.6	Intervention	56
	6.7	Appeals to the SDT	57

APPENDICES

A	**Legal Services Act 2007 (extracts)**		67
B	**SRA Authorisation Rules for Legal Services Bodies and Licensable Bodies 2011**		140
C	**SRA Practice Framework Rules 2011**		182
D	**SRA Suitability Test 2011**		216
E	**Law Society Practice Notes**		**226**
	E1	Alternative business structures	226
	E2	Compliance officers	235
Index			243

Preface

The provision of regulated legal services has until now been the sole preserve of individuals who have qualified into one of the legal professions. Once an individual was admitted into the profession they were, for the most part, allowed to get on with their professional practice with little interference unless something went wrong.

The Legal Services Act (LSA) 2007 allows new entrants into the legal services market. Any organisation can now provide regulated legal services as long as they comply with the regulatory requirements. These organisations are known as alternative business structures (ABSs). The legal professions no longer have a monopoly on the provision of regulated legal services. These new entrants will change the legal services market.

No one knows how significant an impact ABSs will have. However, they arrive at a time when all law firms are facing a challenging economic climate and they will provide additional competition. There is no reason to think that ABSs will only be limited to the section of the legal services market that relates to consumers. Existing outsourcing organisations will appreciate that this is an opportunity for them as well. It is also likely that ABSs will be a further catalyst to changes that are already taking place such as outsourcing and consolidation.

In enacting LSA 2007, Parliament decided not to wipe the slate clean and start again. Instead ABSs have been grafted on to the existing framework. In many places, such as in relation to appeal mechanisms, the tension between the old and the new is clear and still needs to be resolved. The Solicitors Regulation Authority (SRA) has sought to harmonise the regulation of established law firms and that of the new ABSs. On the surface of its rules the structure is very similar, although there is a lot going on 'under the hood'. It may be that in time the ownership flexibility of ABSs will prove attractive to many established law firms who will conclude that there is little practical difference between the ABS regulatory regime and the regime for established law firms. If this does happen then the ABS will become the dominant provider of legal services.

This book aims to provide an introductory guide to how these new organisations are regulated by the largest legal services regulator, the SRA. It is also possible for an ABS to be licensed by the Council for Licensed Conveyancers. Both the Bar Standards Board and the Intellectual Property Regulation Board have announced that they will apply to regulate ABSs, further widening the choice.

I am very grateful for the assistance of a number of people, not least Mark Pardoe, my co-author, who has done a lot of the heavy lifting in relation to the book's

PREFACE

underlying scheme. I have also been assisted enormously by Andrew Hopper QC both by his advice on certain areas and by his more direct help in relation to **Chapter 6** on supervision and enforcement. I am also very grateful for the tolerance of Janet Noble at Law Society Publishing, who originally approached me with the idea for the book.

The law is stated as at 31 January 2012.

Iain Miller
January 2012

Table of cases

Agassi v. Robinson (Inspector of Taxes) [2005] EWCA Civ 1507; [2006] 1 WLR 2126; [2006] 1 All ER 900 .... 2.2.2
Bank of Scotland v. Whiteside (unreported, Manchester County Court, 21 February 2011) 2.3
Dooley v. The Law Society (unreported, HC, 15 September 2000) 6.6
Holder v. The Law Society [2003] 3 All ER 183; [2003] 1 WLR 1059; [2003] EWCA Civ 39 .... 6.6
Jideofo v. The Law Society [2007] EW Misc 3 (EWLS) 5.5.2
Media Protection Services v. Gilligan (unreported, Liverpool Magistrates Court, 7 September 2011) 2.3
Piper Double Glazing Ltd v. DC Contracts [1994] 1 WLR 777 .... 2.2.2
Sheikh v. The Law Society [2007] 3 All ER 183; [2006] EWCA Civ 1577 .... 6.6

Table of statutes

Access to Justice Act 1999 .... 4.1, 4.2
Administration of Justice Act
    1985 .... 1.2, 3.6, 4.1, 6.7
Charitites Act 1993 .... 5.5.2
Commissioners for Oaths Act
    1889 .... 2.2.6
Commissioners for Oaths Act
    1891 .... 2.2.6
Companies Act 2006 .... 5.5.2
Compensation Act 2006 .... 2.4.2
    Part 2 .... 2.4.2
    s.4(2)(b) 2.4.2
County Courts Act 1984
    s.60A 2.2.1
Courts and Legal Services Act
    1990 .... 4.1, 4.2
    s.119(1) 2.2.2
Financial Services and Markets
    Act 2000 .... 2.6, 3.5, 4.1
    Part XVI 3.5
Immigration and Asylum Act
    1999 .... 2.4.1
    s.84 .... 2.4.1
Insolvency Act 1986 .... 2.4.3
    s.390(2) 2.4.3
    s.391 .... 2.4.3
    s.392 .... 2.4.3
Land Registration Act 2002 .... 2.2.3
Legal Services Act 2007 .... 1.1, 1.2, 2.1,
        2.2.1, 2.2.2, 2.2.3, 2.2.4,
        2.2.5, 2.2.6, 2.3, 2.4, 2.4.1,
        2.5, 3.1, 3.2, 3.3, 3.5, 4.1,
        5.3, 5.4, 5.5.1, 5.5.2
    Part 1
        s.1 .... 3.1
        (1)–(3) 4.3
        (1)(a) 5.4
        (c) 5.8
        (d) 5.4
    Part 3 .... **App.A**
    s.12 .... 2.2.2, 5.7

s.12(1) 2.2, 2.7
    (a) 2.2.1
    (b) 2.2.2
    (c) 2.2.3
    (d) 2.2.4
    (e) 2.2.5
    (f) 2.2.6
    (3) 2.7
s.14 .... 2.3
s.15 .... 2.3
    (5) 2.3
    (9) 2.3
s.16 .... 2.3
s.18 .... 2.1
s.20 .... 1.2
    (5) 2.1
s.24(1)–(5) 2.7
s.26 .... 2.7
Part 4
s.28 .... 4.3
    (3) 4.3
s.29(1) 4.1
    (2) 4.1
s.30(1) 4.1
Part 5 .... 1.1, 6.7.7, **App.A**
s.83 .... 5.1
    (5)(b) 5.8
    (d), (e) 5.7
s.90 .... 2.1, 3.2, 5.5.1, 6.3
s.91 .... 3.3
    (1) 5.6
    (3) 5.6
    (4) 5.5.1
s.92 .... 3.3, 5.6
s.93 .... 6.2
s.94 .... 6.2
s.95 .... 3.2, 6.1
s.97(5)(b) 2.2.2
s.99 .... 3.2, 6.1
s.101 .... 6.3
s.111(1) 2.1

TABLE OF STATUTES

Legal Services Act 2007 – *continued*
  Part 5 – *continued*
    s.113(2), (3) 3.5
  Part 6 .... 3.5
    s.127(2) 3.5
  Part 8
    s.176 .... 2.1, 5.5.1, 6.3
    s.191 .... 2.2.1
    s.192(1) 2.2.1
      (2) 2.2.1
      (3) 2.2.1
  Part 9
    s.207(1) 1.1, 3.2
  Sched.2 .... 2.2, **App.A**
    para.3 .... 2.2.1
    para.4 .... 2.2.2
      (1) 2.2.2
        (b) 2.2.2
    para.5(1) 2.2.3
      (2) 2.2.3
    para.6 .... 2.2.4
    para.7 .... 2.2.5
    para.8 .... 2.2.6
  Sched.3 .... **App.A**
    para.3(5), (6) 2.2.3
      (9) 2.2.3
      (10) 2.2.3
    para.5(2) 2.2.5
      (3) 2.2.5
      (4) 2.2.5
  Sched.4 ..... 1.2, 2.2.1, 2.2.2, 2.2.3,
                2.2.4, 2.2.5, 2.2.6
    Part 1 .... **App.A**
  Sched.5
    Part 1
      para.1 .... 2.2.1, 2.2.2, 2.2.3,
                2.2.4, 2.2.5, 2.2.6
    Part 2 . 2.2.1, 2.2.2, 2.2.3, 2.2.4,
                  2.2.5. 2.2.6
  Sched.11 .... 5.1, **App.A**
    paras.11–14 .... 3.3
    para.11 .... 5.6
      (3) 3.3
        (a) 5.6
        (b) 2.1, 5.6
    para.12 .... 5.6
    para.13 .... 5.6
      (3)(a) 5.6
    para.14 .... 5.6
    para.24 .... 6.3
  Sched.12 .... **App.A**

Sched.13 .... **App.A**
  Part 1
    para.1(1) 5.5.1
    para.2 .... 3.1, 5.5.1
    para.3 .... 1.1, 3.1, 5.5.1
      (3) 5.5.1
    para.4 .... 5.5.1
    para.5 .... 3.1, 5.5.1
    para.6 .... 5.5.1
      (1) 3.1
      (3) 3.1
      (c) 3.1, 5.5.1
    para.8 .... 6.7.2
  Part 2
    para.10 .... 3.1, 5.5.1
    para.11 .... 3.1
    para.17 .... 3.1, 6.3
      (1) 6.7.2
      (3)–(5) 3.1
    para.19(1) 6.7.2
      (2)–(4) 3.1
  Part 3
    para.21 .... 3.1
    para.22 .... 3.1
    para.24(1) 6.3, 6.5
    para.28 .... 3.1, 6.3
      (1) 6.7.2
      (3)–(6) 3.1
      (4) 3.1
    para.31(1) 6.7.2
      (2)–(5) 3.1
      (3) 3.1
    para.33 .... 3.1, 6.3
      (1) 6.7.2
    para.36 .... 3.1
      (1) 6.7.2
  Part 4
    para.38 .... 3.1
  Part 5 .... 5.5.1
    paras.41–45 .... 6.5
    para.43 .... 3.1
    para.44 .... 6.5
    para.45 .... 6.5
      (5) 6.5
    para.46 .... 6.4
      (5) 6.4
    para.49(2) 6.7.2
Sched.14 .... 6.6, **App.A**
    para.1(1) 6.6
      (2) 6.6
      (4) 6.6
    para.3(7) 6.6
    para.10(5) 6.6

Sched.16 .... 1.2
Sched.17 .... 1.2
Sched.18 .... 2.4.1
Public Notaries Act 1801 .... 2.2.5
Solicitors Act 1974 ...... 1.2, 3.5, 4.1, 6.7
    s.20 .... 2.2.2
        (1) 2.2.2
    ss.21–25 .... 2.2.2
    s.22(1) 2.2.2

s.43 .... 3.2, 5.5.2
s.44B 6.2
s.44BA 6.2
s.47(2)(g) 5.5.2
Sched.1 .... 6.6
Sched.1A 3.5
Stamp Duties Management Act 1891
    s.24 .... 2.2.6

Table of statutory instruments

Civil Procedure Rules 1998, SI 1998/3132
    rule 67.4 .... 6.6
European Communities (Lawyer's Practice) Regulations 2000, SI 2000/1119
    reg.17 .... 5.6
Legal Services Act 2007 (Appeals from Licensing Authority Decisions) (No.2)
    Order 2011, SI 2011/2863 .... 6.7, 6.7.7
    art.5(3) 6.7.7
Legal Services Act 2007 (Licensing Authorities) (Maximum Penalty) Rules
    2011, SI 2011/1659 .... 6.1
Solicitors (Disciplinary Proceedings) Rules 2007, SI 2007/3588 .... 6.7, 6.7.1, 6.7.5
    rule 2(1) 6.7.1
    rule 4 .... 6.7.1
Solicitors Disciplinary Tribunal (Appeals) (Amendment) Rules 2011,
    SI 2011/3070 .... 6.7
Solicitors Disciplinary Tribunal (Appeals and Amendment) Rules 2011,
    SI 2011/2346 .... 6.7, 6.7.1
    rule 3 .... 6.7.1
    rule 5(1), (3), (4) 6.7.1
    rule 6(1), (4)–(7) 6.7.2
    rule 7(1)–(7) 6.7.2
    rule 8(1), (2), (4)–(7) 6.7.2
    rule 9 .... 6.7.1
        (1)–(3) 6.7.3
    rule 11 .... 6.7.1
        (1)–(3) 6.7.3
    rule 12(2)(a)–(c) 6.7.5
        (4)–(6) 6.7.5
    rule 13 .... 6.7.1, 6.7.3
    rule 14 .... 6.7.1, 6.7.4
    rule 15 .... 6.7.1, 6.7.3
    rule 16 .... 6.7.1
        (1)–(4) 6.7.5
    rule 17 .... 6.7.5
    rule 18 .... 6.7.1
    rule 19(1) 6.7.1, 6.7.3
        (2)(a)(b) 6.7.3
        (3) 6.7.1
    rule 20(1), (2), (5) 6.7.3
    rule 21(1) 6.7.5
    rule 22 .... 6.7.5
    rule 23(1)–(6) 6.7.4

TABLE OF STATUTORY INSTRUMENTS

Solicitors Disciplinary Tribunal (Appeals and Amendment) Rules 2011,
SI 2011/2346 – *continued*
    rule 25 .... 6.7.5
    rule 28 .... 6.7.5
    rule 29 .... 6.7.6

Table of other enactments

Internal Governance Rules
 2009 .... 4.1
Legal Ombudsman Scheme
 Rules 2010
  rule 2.1 .... 3.5
Ownership of Licensed Bodies:
 Schedule 13 – Prescribed
 Rules 6.4
Rules on the Prescribed Period
 for the Making of Appeals
 Against Decisions of a
 Licensing Authority
 Regarding Ownership of
 Licensed Bodies 6.7.2
  rule 6 .... 6.7.7
Solicitors' Code of Conduct
 2007 .... 3.6, 4.2
  rule 13 .... 2.3
SRA Accounts Rules 2011............... 3.3
  rule 31 .... 6.2
SRA Authorisation Rules for
 Legal Services Bodies and
 Licensable Bodies 2011 .. 3.3, 4.2, 5.1,
   5.2, 6.3. 6.7, **App.B**
 Part 1
  rules 2–15 .... 5.4
  rule 2 .... 5.1
 Part 2
  rule 5
   5.1 .... 5.1
   5.2 .... 5.1
   5.3 .... 5.1
   5.4 .... 5.1
   5.5 .... 5.1
   note (iii) 5.1
  rule 6 .... 5.3, 6.3
   6.1 .... 5.1, 5.3, 5.8
   6.2 .... 5.3
   6.3 .... 5.3
    (f) 5.8
   6.4 .... 5.3

Part 3
 rule 8
  8.3 .... 5.2
  8.5 .... 3.3, 5.3, 5.6
   (b) 5.6
   (c)(i)(B) 3.3
    (C) 3.3
   (ii) 3.3
   (d) 5.6
   (e)(i)–(iii) 3.3
   (g)(ii) 5.6
   note (x) 3.3
  8.6 .... 5.3, 5.5.2
   (a) 5.5.2
   (d) 5.5.2
   (e) 5.5.2
 rule 9 .... 5.5.2
Part 4 .... 1.1, 3.2, 5.3, 5.5.2, 5.6
 rule 13
  13.2 .... 3.2, 5.5.2
 rule 14 .... 3.2, 5.1, 5.5.2
  14.4 .... 5.5.2
  14.5 .... 5.5.2
  14.6 .... 5.5.2, 5.6
  14.7 .... 5.5.2, 5.6
  14.8 .... 5.5.2
 rule 15 .... 5.5.2
  15.1 .... 3.2
 rule 16 .... 5.5.2
 rule 17 .... 5.1, 5.5.2
 rule 18 .... 5.1, 5.6
Part 5
 rule 19
  19.1 .... 5.1
  19.2 .... 5.1
  19.3 .... 5.1
  19.4 .... 5.1
 rule 20 .... 5.1
 rule 21
  21.1 .... 5.1
  21.2 .... 5.1

TABLE OF OTHER ENACTMENTS

SRA Authorisation Rules for Legal
   Services Bodies and Licensable Bodies
   2011 – *continued*
      Part 5 – *continued*
         rule 21.3 .... 5.1
         rule 22 .... 5.1, 6.3
            22.1 .... 6.3
            22.2 .... 6.3
            note (iv) 6.3
      Part 6 .... 5.1
      Part 8
         rule 31 .... 6.7
      Part 9
         rule 34
            34.1 .... 5.1
            34.2 .... 5.1
            34.3 .... 5.1
         rule 35 .... 5.1
SRA Code of Conduct 2011
   Chapter 3
      O(3.4) 4.1
   Chapter 10 .... 6.2
      O(10.6)–(10.10) 6.2
   Chapter 12 .... 2.6
      O(12.1) 2.6
      O(12.2) 2.6
      O(12.3) 2.6
      O(12.5) 2.6
      O(12.6) 2.6
   Chapter 14 .... 1.1, 3.2
SRA Compensation Fund Rules
   2011 .... 5.2, 5.3, 5.4, 5.7
      rule 2.7 .... 5.7
SRA Disciplinary Procedure
   Rules 2011 .... 6.1

SRA Indemnity Insurance Rules
   2011 .... 5.3, 5.4, 5.7
      App.1 .... 5.7
      App.4 .... 5.7
SRA Practice Framework Rules
   2011 .... **App.C**
      rule 4 .... 2.3
      rule 12 .... 5.3
      rule 14 .... 5.3
      rule 15 .... 5.3
      rule 16 .... 5.3
SRA Suitability Test 2011.. 3.1, 5.4, 5.5.2,
                                    5.6, **App.D**
      O(SB1.1) 5.5.2
      O(SB1.2) 5.5.2
      O(SB1.3) 5.5.2
      Part 1 .... 5.5.2
         para.1
            1.1 .... 5.5.2
            1.2 .... 5.5.2
            1.3 .... 5.5.2
         para.2
            2.1 .... 5.5.2
         para.3
            3.1 .... 5.5.2
         para.4 .... 5.5.2
         para.5
            5.1 .... 5.5.2
            5.2 .... 5.5.2
         para.6
            6.1 .... 5.5.2
            6.2 .... 5.5.2
      Part 2 .... 3.1, 5.5.2
         para.10 .... 5.5.2
            10.1(h) 3.1

Abbreviations

ABS	alternative business structure
AJA 1985	Administration of Justice Act 1985
ARP	Assigned Risks Pool
CLC	Council for Licensed Conveyancers
COFA	compliance officer for finance and administration
COLP	compliance officer for legal practice
HOFA	head of finance and administration
HOLP	head of legal practice
LDP	legal disciplinary practice
LeO	Legal Ombudsman
LLP	limited liability partnership
LSA 2007	Legal Services Act 2007
LSB	Legal Services Board
MDP	multi-disciplinary practice
OFT	Office of Fair Trading
OLC	Office for Legal Complaints
SDT	Solicitors Disciplinary Tribunal
SRA	Solicitors Regulation Authority

CHAPTER 1

Introduction

1.1 WHAT IS AN ALTERNATIVE BUSINESS STRUCTURE?

'Alternative business structure' (ABS) is a term used to describe an organisation: (1) that is licensed to carry on one or more of the specific legal activities that are regulated by the Legal Services Act (LSA) 2007; and (2) whose owners and/or managers include individuals or entities who are not qualified lawyers. The term was used in Sir David Clementi's *Review of the Regulatory Framework for Legal Services in England and Wales – Final Report* (December 2004), known as the 'Clementi report', and has been used since then to describe these new types of organisations. However, although 'Alternative Business Structures' appears as a heading at LSA 2007, Part 5, the term has no statutory meaning.

An ABS is defined by its non-lawyer or external participation, but the term does not apply to all firms with external ownership or management. The term 'manager' is defined in Chapter 14 of the SRA Code of Conduct as:

(i) a member of an LLP;
(ii) a director of a company;
(iii) a partner in a partnership; or
(iv) in relation to any other body, a member of its governing body.

See also **3.2** and the definition in LSA 2007, s.207(1).

Whilst a member of a limited liability partnership (LLP) or a partner will clearly have some level of 'ownership', a director or member of a governing body (such as a board or management committee) may not. It is therefore possible for an LLP with a non-lawyer management team to remain a traditional law firm. To this extent, the use of the term 'manager' is less than clear. In addition, ownership of a body by a non-lawyer only becomes 'material' if it, in broad terms, exceeds 10 per cent. (See LSA 2007, Sched.13, para.3 and the SRA Authorisation Rules 2011, Part 4.)

The Solicitors Regulation Authority (SRA) in its consultation paper 'Regulating Alternative Business Structures' (1 June 2009) describes an ABS in the following way (at paras.3.1 and 3.2):

> Very broadly, ABSs will enable lawyers and non-lawyers to share the management and control of a business which provides reserved legal services to the public. ABSs will allow external investment and ownership of law firms.

The minimum requirements for an ABS are that
- it must have at least one 'manager' who is authorised to provide the reserved legal activity delivered by the ABS, and
- it must have at least one non-lawyer 'manager' or owner.

The paper sets out three broad types of models for ABSs:

1. Firms that are like traditional law firms or legal disciplinary practices (LDPs) but have at least one non-lawyer manager, and which have no external ownership and provide solicitor-type services only.
2. Entities that have complete or partial external ownership, with the legal services being operated through a ring-fenced entity.
3. The multi-disciplinary practice (MDP) model where combinations of different services are provided by one entity, for example, the provision of legal services via lawyers in an entity with accountants or even estate agents.

The SRA then considers potential models for ABSs at Appendix A of the paper:

Model 1 – LDP plus

- LDP comprising three lawyer and one non-lawyer 'manager'
- No external ownership

All existing LDPs with a non-lawyer 'manager' will need to become an ABS. The sort of practice this model might apply to would be, for example, a firm which has taken on as a 'manager' its former HR head, IT head or head of finance.

Model 2 – Totally externally owned; owner has no interest in supply of ABSs' services

- 100 per cent external ownership of ABS
- External owner has a commercial interest only in the ABS – i.e. although the external owner has a commercial interest in the financial fortunes of the ABS, it has no interest in supplying products through it (for example, litigation funding,) to clients of the ABS

The ABS would be a ring-fenced legal services arm of the parent external owner. The ABS could take advantage of the parent's corporate brand (e.g. 'Nike Law' or 'Fortnum and Mason Law').

Model 3 – totally externally owned; owner has an interest in supply of ABSs' services

- 100 per cent external ownership of ABS
- External owner has interest in legal services provided by the ABS to clients.

The ABS would be ring-fenced and branded as in Model 2. The parent external owner may have an interest in, for example, cross-selling insurance products, litigation funding and other financial or other services to clients of the ABS as a component part of the legal service supplied to clients. The external owner may be regulated by a regulator from a different sector (for example, the FSA in the case of banks or other financial service/insurance providers, or the Ministry of Justice in the case of claims management companies) – for example, 'HSBC Law'. Or there could be no specific sector regulator in the case of, for example, a motoring organisation or an estate agency. In both cases, there is an assumption that these offer no other services requiring regulation. A fictional example might be 'Motoring Law'.

Model 4 – Multidisciplinary practice (MDP)

- A one stop shop comprising 'managers' from legal and other professions providing legal and other services to clients
- No external ownership

The ABS would be a joint practice of lawyers and non-lawyers who would share the fees received for the delivery of legal and non-legal services to clients. This could be, for example, a niche property practice with surveyors, architects, town planners, property managers, builders, decorators, furniture removers and conveyancers. The SRA would regulate only the legal services; other professionals would be regulated by their own regulators.

Model 5 – Co-op model (external ownership, legal and non-legal services)

Using a corporate brand, for example, one firm provides funeral services, will-writing services and probate services; or the ABS could provide a mixture of social welfare advice, administration, and legal services.
 The SRA might license the body but regulate only the legal services.

Model 6 – Private equity investment

- Legal services firm with partial private equity ownership.

Representatives of the private equity house might become members of the ABS incorporated practice, and the private equity company may hold shares in the ABS.

Model 7 – Floated company

The ABS firm might be floated on AIM/stock market subject to stock market/corporate governance rules.

Model 8 – Hub and spoke

Non-licensed hub – an administration company for 'back office' services (such as changing documentation), but could include some intellectual services. The hub would receive a service charge from the regulated spokes which provide the legal services – could be national franchise or network arrangement.

- Firms can outsource work now, such as accounts, IT, typing
- Hub could be licensed, and may need to be in some cases.

Model 9

Model 2 or Model 3 with more than one ring-fenced company.

- (100 per cent external ownership).
- External owner owns more than one ring-fenced law firm.
- Need to manage conflicts of interest.

Model 10

Not for profit organisations providing legal services (e.g. charities, Citizens Advice Bureaus).

Model 11

In-house teams expanding into the market (e.g. local authorities).

No one knows which, if any, of these models are likely to become commonplace within the legal services market. With the possible exception of Australia, no other country has liberalised the ownership of law firms to such an extent.

1.2 THE ORIGINS OF ABSs AND LSA 2007

The market for legal services is substantial. At the end of 2011 it was estimated to be worth £28.6bn (*The Legal Services Market: The Race is On*, Espirito Santo Bank, October 2011). References to legal services are normally to the two largest and most established legal professions, solicitors and barristers. There are however several other regulated providers of legal services. These are notaries, trade mark and patent attorneys, legal executives, licensed conveyancers and law costs draftsmen.

Until the implementation of LSA 2007, the regulatory landscape for the wider legal profession had certain common features:

- Regulation was primarily directed at individuals – there was little in the overall structure to recognise firms or entities.
- The members of each profession were, for the most part, required to practise independently of each other. So, for example, solicitors and barristers could not practise in partnership together.
- Each regulatory scheme was self-contained and there was no oversight of the regulators except to the limited extent provided by the court by way of appeal from regulatory and disciplinary decisions and by the Legal Services Ombudsman in relation to, primarily, complaints.
- Non-lawyers could not own a share in law firms.
- The regulator combined the role of regulation and representation.
- Each regulatory body dealt with complaints about its particular profession.

(A notable exception to some of these general points is the Council for Licensed Conveyancers. This is a statutory body established by the Administration of Justice Act (AJA)1985 to reduce the then monopoly of solicitors over conveyancing. As a statutory body, the Council for Licensed Conveyancers does not a have a representative function and AJA 1985 provided for an element of external ownership.)

The restrictive nature of these arrangements led to a level of dissatisfaction about the complex nature of legal regulation and the level of consumer complaints, particularly in relation to solicitors. In 2001 a report by the Office of Fair Trading

(OFT) entitled *Competition in Professions – A report by the Director General of Fair Trading* (March 2001) identified a number of anti-competitive restrictions imposed on professional bodies, namely by the Law Society and General Council of the Bar rules, such as a ban on partnerships between different types of lawyers and on MDPs.

The report concluded that a change in legislation was needed to open up the legal market and to allow regulatory bodies such as the Law Society to regulate non-solicitor partners. OFT press release 10/01, 'Reform for competition needed in professions' (7 March 2001), announced the publication of the report and stated:

> Competition brings consumers lower prices, more choice and new services. The law to combat restrictions on competition should apply as widely as possible and the scope to exclude professional rules from competition law should be removed. There remain numerous restrictions on competition in the professions. Apart from those shown to be necessary for economic efficiency and consumer benefits, restrictions on competition should go.

The government's response to the OFT report, from the then Lord Chancellor's Department (subsequently Department for Constitutional Affairs, now Ministry of Justice), was in the form of a consultation paper entitled 'In the Public Interest' (July 2002), which raised a number of concerns about legal regulation and called for a review.

In 2003 a report by the then Department for Constitutional Affairs, *Competition and Regulation in the Legal Services Market* (July 2003), proposed setting up a review of the regulation of legal services. On 24 July 2003, the government commissioned Sir David Clementi to conduct a full review of legal services regulation. The terms of reference of this review were wide and of particular relevance to ABSs. They were:

> To consider what regulatory framework would best promote competition, innovation and the public and consumer interest in an efficient, effective and independent legal sector.
> To recommend a framework which will be independent in representing the public and consumer interest, comprehensive, accountable, consistent, flexible, transparent, and no more restrictive or burdensome than is clearly justified.

The resulting Clementi report (December 2004) concluded that the framework for the provision of legal services in England and Wales was outdated. Clementi stated (at para.32 of the Foreword):

> Whilst some lawyers will continue to argue that the current system 'ain't broke', I believe there is strong evidence of the need for major reform . . . to the types of business structures permitted to provide legal services to the consumer, . . .

Clementi felt that the restrictive practices regarding the structures in which lawyers could work could no longer be justified as being in the public interest. The report identified three key areas that needed to be addressed. First, the regulatory structure itself was outmoded as it had at its heart a fundamental conflict between the roles of the regulator and the representative body. These functions should be separated and that separation should be overseen by a new oversight body, the Legal Services Board (LSB). Second, complaints should be taken away from front-line regulators altogether and placed in the hands of a new statutory body, the Office for Legal Complaints (OLC).

The third area was in relation to law firm ownership. Clementi's proposal was the establishment of ABSs, which would bring together lawyers from different professional bodies such as solicitors and barristers and also permit non-lawyers to be involved in the management and ownership of such practices. Notably Clementi did not favour the establishment of MDPs or firms where the external owners were not themselves managers of the business. He thought the freeing up of the market should proceed in incremental steps.

However, the then government took the view that it would legislate for such wider ownership. The government's White Paper, *The Future of Legal Services: Putting Consumers First* (Cm 6679, 2005), set out the agenda for reform of the regulation and delivery of legal services. The White Paper extolled the benefits of ABSs, which the government viewed as extensive, and listed at pp.40–41:

Potential benefits for consumers:

- more choice: consumers will have greater flexibility in deciding from where to obtain legal and some non-legal services.
- reduced prices: consumers should be able to purchase some legal services more cheaply. This should arise where ABS firms realise savings through economies of scale and reduce transaction costs where different types of legal professionals are part of the same firm.
- better access to justice: ABS firms might find it easier to provide services in rural areas or to less mobile consumers.
- improved consumer service: consumers may benefit from a better service where ABS firms are able to access external finance and specialist non-legal expertise.
- greater convenience: ABS firms can provide one-stop-shopping for related services, for example car insurance and legal services for accident claims.
- increased consumer confidence: higher consumer protection levels and an increase in the quality of legal services could flow from ABS firms which have a good reputation in providing non-legal services. These firms will have a strong incentive to keep that reputation when providing legal services.

Potential benefits for legal service providers:

- increased access to finance: at present, providers can face constraints on the amount of equity, mainly debt equity, they can raise. Allowing alternative business structures will facilitate expansion by firms (including into international markets) and investment in large-scale capital projects that increase efficiency.
- better spread of risk: a firm could spread its risk more effectively among shareholders. This will lower the required rate of return on any investment, facilitate investment and could deliver lower prices.
- increased flexibility: non-legal firms such as insurance companies, banks and estate agents will have the freedom to realise synergies with legal firms by forming ABS firms and offering integrated legal and associated services.
- easier to hire and retain high-quality non-legal staff: ABS firms will be able to reward non-legal staff in the same way as lawyers.

- more choice for new legal professionals: ABS firms could contribute to greater diversity by offering those who are currently under-represented more opportunities to enter and remain within the profession.

The White Paper proposed legislation for the introduction of ABSs as well as an ABS licensing regime. The government's view of ABSs was that they would provide greater consumer choice and flexibility in legal services by removing disproportionate restrictions on business structures, allowing lawyers and non-lawyers to set up business together for the first time ever, and enabling services to develop in new, consumer-friendly ways.

The White Paper led in due course to the Legal Services Bill, which was published on 24 May 2006, and LSA 2007 received royal assent on 30 October 2007.

The key features of LSA 2007 are:

- the creation of the LSB as a single supervisory body to oversee the approved regulators under LSA 2007, being the Law Society, the General Council of the Bar, the Master of the Faculties, the Institute of Legal Executives, the Council for Licensed Conveyancers, the Chartered Institute of Patent Attorneys, the Institute of Trade Mark Attorneys and the Association of Law Costs Draftsmen (see LSA 2007, s.20 and Sched.4);
- the creation of the OLC, a single point of contact for all consumer complaints concerning the provision of regulated legal services. The OLC oversees the running of the Legal Ombudsman;
- the requirement for professional bodies such as the Law Society and the General Council of the Bar to separate their regulatory and representative functions. This led to the establishment of the SRA and the Bar Standards Board;
- the introduction of a self-contained regulatory structure to regulate the provision of reserved legal activities to members of the public by organisations that are owned and/or managed by non-lawyers.

However, LSA 2007 does not create a new comprehensive structure for the regulation of the legal professions. Instead, it grafts the above provisions on to the existing statutory and non-statutory structures. Therefore, the pre-existing statutory schemes for the regulation of solicitors under the Solicitors Act 1974 (as amended) and licensed conveyancers under AJA 1985 remain, albeit with substantial amendment by LSA 2007, Scheds.16 and 17. The effect is that ABSs have a self-contained regulatory framework under LSA 2007, but compete with established law firms whose regulatory structures derive from other statutes. One of the great challenges for regulators is to level the playing field for legal services providers operating under these separate regulatory frameworks. To a large extent this has been achieved, but occasionally the cracks show.

CHAPTER 2

The regulatory boundaries

2.1 INTRODUCTION

LSA 2007 has had a profound impact upon the regulatory landscape for the provision of legal services. Until the advent of ABSs, the regulation of the legal professions had been primarily based upon two pillars. First, individuals were approved as being suitable by admission to the profession. They were then regulated as individuals throughout their professional life. Second, only members of the profession could own or manage law firms. Traditionally, a consumer knew that to obtain legal advice they should go to a solicitor, who may in turn refer them to a barrister. This meant that the ability to describe oneself as a solicitor or barrister was the most important aspect of attracting work. The use of the title 'solicitor' was and remains controlled by statute and it is a criminal offence to use the term when not entitled to do so (Solicitors Act 1974, s.21). However, the terms 'lawyer' or 'law firm' are not protected and any organisation is able to use these titles. Until recently, though, their use was not very common.

A secondary mechanism of control was that some narrow aspects of the legal work of solicitors and barristers (known as 'reserved legal activities' under LSA 2007) were controlled by and reserved to the legal professions.

Widening the scope of ownership and control of law firms means that it is no longer possible to base regulation on the simple mechanism of membership of a profession. In future, a bank or an insurance company will be able to provide reserved legal activities. What this means in practice is that the main mechanism of regulation has shifted from the requirement that an individual belongs to a profession and is able to use a title to the requirement that an organisation is able to provide reserved legal activities.

The reserved legal activities are therefore hugely important; they are the fundamental building blocks of LSA 2007. For example, they are pivotal to:

- the definition of 'authorised persons' (s.18);
- the designation of a regulator as an approved regulator (s.20(5));
- the grant of licences to ABSs (s.111(1));
- the appointment of a head of legal practice (Sched.11, para.11(3)(b)).

Importantly, LSA 2007 also extends the scope of the regulation to include individuals who are not themselves authorised persons, but who are managers or employees of an ABS, or have an interest (including an indirect or material interest) in an ABS. Section 90 states that such non-authorised persons:

> must not do anything which causes or substantially contributes to a breach by –
> (a) the licensed body, or
> (b) an employee or manager of the licensed body who is an authorised person in relation to an activity which is a reserved legal activity,
>
> of the duties imposed on them by section 176.

These obligations arise as a direct consequence of the reserved legal activities being carried out by the ABS.

An ABS will only be able to undertake those reserved legal activities that its relevant licensing or regulatory body is authorised to license. For example, if the licensing body is the SRA, solicitors and therefore the ABS can perform all reserved legal activities, apart from some notarial activities. By contrast, the Council for Licensed Conveyancers (CLC) is an approved regulator only in relation to certain reserved legal activities and hence ABSs regulated by the CLC are more limited in the scope of activities they can undertake. (At the time of writing the CLC has an application before the LSB to become an approved regulator of advocacy and litigation.)

Despite the fact that these reserved legal activities are of fundamental importance to LSA 2007 in terms of approach to the regulatory framework, the Act makes no material changes to the definitions of reserved legal activities that previously existed in the regulatory regime based around professional title. The effect of this is that the regulation of legal services now rests upon a series of regulated activities that are narrow in their scope.

An ABS (or indeed any law firm) will be authorised to carry out one or more of the reserved legal activities. In being so regulated it will also be regulated as to the manner in which it provides more general legal advice and assistance which would of itself not be regulated. Conversely, it is possible to have a 'law firm' that provides non-reserved legal activities and therefore does not need to be regulated. This type of organisation may confine itself to legal advice or advocacy in, say, the employment tribunal, which is unregulated. Under the previous framework this organisation would have been at a disadvantage as it was competing with organisations that described themselves as solicitors. Now it may be less clear in the minds of consumers as to which organisations are providing regulated legal services and which are not. It is therefore of fundamental significance that any prospective ABS understands whether it wants or needs to be regulated and what the consequences of regulation are for the scope of its legal practice.

2.2 THE RESERVED LEGAL ACTIVITIES

There are six legal activities which are currently reserved and therefore (subject to exemptions) can only be carried out by appropriately authorised persons. These reserved legal activities, set out in LSA 2007, s.12(1) and defined in Sched.2, are described below.

In its comprehensive paper *The Regulation of Legal Services: Reserved Legal Activities – History and Rationale* (2010), the Legal Services Institute sets out the historical origins of the reserved legal activities. In its conclusion, the paper states (at p.35):

> ... the origins of many of the reservations of legal activities are remarkably obscure. We consider that the often non-existent, and sometimes limited, evidence of Parliamentary consideration and debate at the time the reservations were created or confirmed provides little basis for suggesting a common policy rationale that justifies their existence.

2.2.1 Exercise of a right of audience

The meaning of a 'right of audience' is given in LSA 2007, Sched.2, para.3 as the right to appear before and address a court, including the right to call and examine witnesses. However, it does not include a right to appear in relation to any particular court or proceedings where prior to LSA 2007 coming into force there was no restriction placed on a person exercising that right.

LSA 2007, s.12(1)(a) provides that the exercise of a right of audience is a reserved legal activity. Schedule 4 confirms that the existing regulators, all of whom, except the Master of the Faculties and the CLC, are approved in relation to rights of audience (and at the time of writing, the CLC had applied to the LSB to become an approved regulator in relation to rights of audience). In addition, LSA 2007 provides for continuity of these rights (Sched.5, para.1), and makes transitional provisions (Sched.5, Part 2). Rights of audience are also granted to employees of housing management bodies in respect of certain housing proceedings in a county court before a district judge by way of the addition of s.60A to the County Courts Act 1984 (LSA 2007, s.191).

The 'right' of audience is not a universal concept in the sense that there is not one right of audience but a number of rights depending upon the profession and qualifications of the individual concerned. For example, barristers have a right of audience in all courts. Solicitors have a right of audience in county courts and certain hearings in magistrates' courts but do not normally have a right of audience in the High Court or Crown Court unless they have obtained a separate qualification of higher rights of audience.

LSA 2007 contains a number of exemptions. However, anyone who appears before a court for a fee will normally need to be qualified. Courts will continue to be able to allow someone to be represented where they consider it appropriate.

The Act also retains the power of 'any court in any proceedings to refuse to hear a person (for reasons which apply to that person as an individual) who would otherwise have a right of audience before the court in relation to those proceedings' (s.192(1)). If it does so it must give its reasons for refusing (s.192(2)). Where a court does not permit the appearance of advocates, or does so only with leave, the existence of rights of audience under LSA 2007 does not entitle an advocate to appear in that court (s.192(3)).

2.2.2 The conduct of litigation

LSA 2007, Sched.2, para.4 defines the 'conduct of litigation' as the issuing of proceedings before any court in England and Wales, the commencement, prosecution and defence of such proceedings, and the performance of any ancillary functions (such as entering appearances to actions) in relation to such proceedings. It does not include any such activity in relation to any particular court or proceedings where prior to LSA 2007 coming into force there was no restriction placed on a person entitled to carry on that activity.

The conduct of litigation has traditionally been the preserve of solicitors. Curiously, LSA 2007 adds to the definition of the conduct of litigation contained in existing legislation. Before it was amended by LSA 2007, the Courts and Legal Services Act 1990, s.119(1) defined the 'right to conduct litigation' as the right:

(a) to issue proceedings before any court; and
(b) to perform any ancillary functions in relation to proceedings (such as entering appearances to actions).

The definition of 'conduct of litigation' in LSA 2007, Sched.2, para.4(1) is similar but includes at subsection (b) 'the commencement, prosecution and defence of such proceedings' (and LSA 2007, s.97(5)(b) inserts a similarly worded subsection, (aa), into the definition of the 'right to conduct litigation' in s.119(1) of the Courts and Legal Services Act 1990). This is interesting because the general intention appears to have been for LSA 2007 to re-enact the previous statutory provisions. Indeed, para.65 of the explanatory notes to the Act states:

> The 'reserved legal activities' defined by section 12 are all activities that were regulated under previously enacted legislation.

The answer may be that the parliamentary draftsman intended to incorporate the slightly different wording previously contained in the Solicitors Act 1974, s.20(1), which relates to unqualified persons acting as solicitors:

> No unqualified person shall –
>
> (a) act as a solicitor, or as such issue any writ or process, or commence, prosecute or defend any action, suit or other proceeding, in his own name or in the name of any other person, in any court of civil or criminal jurisdiction

By LSA 2007, s.12(1)(b) the conduct of litigation is made a reserved legal activity. Schedule 4 confirms that the existing regulators, all of whom, except the Master of the Faculties, the Institute of Legal Executives and the CLC, are approved in relation to the conduct of litigation (and at the time of writing the CLC has applied to the LSB to become an approved regulator for the conduct of litigation). In addition, LSA 2007 provides for continuity of these rights (Sched.5, para.1), and makes transitional provisions (Sched.5, Part 2).

The leading authority on the meaning of the conduct of litigation is *Agassi* v. *Robinson (Inspector of Taxes)* [2005] EWCA Civ 1507. In that case, the Court of Appeal agreed with the decision of Mr Justice Potter in *Piper Double Glazing Ltd* v. *DC Contracts* [1994] 1 WLR 777, who held that the words 'acting as a solicitor' in the Solicitors Act 1974, ss.21 to 25:

> ... are limited to the doing of acts which only a solicitor may perform and/or the doing of acts by a person pretending or holding himself out to be a solicitor. Such acts are not to be confused with the doing of acts of a kind commonly done by solicitors, but which involve no representation that the actor is acting as such (at p.786).

In *Agassi*, Lord Justice Dyson held (at [57]):

> A person who does not have a current practising certificate and who is not an authorised litigator ... acts as a solicitor in breach of section 20(1) of the 1974 Act at least if he: (a) issues proceedings; (b) performs any ancillary functions in relation to proceedings; or (c) draws or prepares an instrument relating to legal proceedings contrary to section 22(1) of the 1974 Act.

As a breach of the Solicitors Act 1974, s.20 is a criminal offence, the court thought that the section ought to be narrowly construed. Many activities that might be considered by some to be litigation are ancillary to the conduct of litigation – such as taking a statement from a witness, or dealing with correspondence from the other party – and consequently do not fall within the meaning of conduct of litigation. Lord Justice Dyson stated (at [56]):

> The word 'ancillary' [in the Courts and Legal Services Act 1990, s.119(1)] indicates that it is not all functions in relation to proceedings that are comprised in the 'right to conduct litigation'. The usual meaning of 'ancillary' is 'subordinate'. A clue to what was intended lies in the words in brackets '(such as entering appearances to actions)'. These words show that it must have been intended that the ancillary functions would be formal steps required in the conduct of litigation. These would include drawing or preparing instruments within the meaning of section 22 of the 1974 Act and other formal steps.

2.2.3 Reserved instrument activities

'Reserved instrument activities' means preparing any instrument of transfer or charge for the purposes of the Land Registration Act 2002, making an application or lodging a document for registration under the Land Registration Act 2002, and preparing any other instrument relating to real or personal estate for the purposes of the law of England and Wales, or instrument relating to court proceedings within England and Wales (LSA 2007, Sched.2, para.5(1)). There are savings in respect of instrument activities for which there were no restrictions before LSA 2007 came into force, but only those instrument activities related to particular court proceedings (Sched.2, para.5(2)).

This is the most opaque reserved legal activity. In *The Regulation of Legal Services: Reserved Legal Activities – History and Rationale* (2010), the Legal Services Institute describes it in the following way (at p.19):

> The expression 'reserved instrument activities' is not a familiar one – even to lawyers. For many, it is synonymous with 'conveyancing'. However, this would (paradoxically) be both an unduly restrictive as well as a generous interpretation. It is restrictive because the definition in the Act encompasses activities that are not related to conveyancing (such as the transfer of personal property). It is generous because many of the activities carried out as part of a conveyancing transaction do not fall within the definition.

By LSA 2007, s.12(1)(c), reserved instrument activities are made a reserved legal activity. Schedule 4 confirms that the existing regulators, all of whom, except the Institute of Legal Executives and the Association of Law Costs Draftsmen, are approved in relation to reserved instrument activities. In addition, LSA 2007 provides for continuity of these rights (Sched.5, para.1), and makes transitional provisions (Sched.5, Part 2).

The following are not included within the definition:

(a) the preparation of farm business tenancies where the activity is carried out by a Fellow of the Central Association of Agricultural Valuers or a Member of Fellow of the Royal Institution of Chartered Surveyors (Sched.3, para.3(5) and (6));
(b) where the activity is carried out by a person employed merely to engross the instrument or application (Sched.3, para.3(9)); and
(c) where the activity is carried out by an individual who carries on the activity otherwise than for, or in expectation of, any fee, gain or reward (Sched.3, para.3(10)).

2.2.4 Probate activities

'Probate activities' means preparing any probate papers for the purposes of the law of England and Wales or in relation to any proceedings in England and Wales. Probate papers are defined as papers on which to found or oppose a grant of probate or a grant of letters of administration (LSA 2007, Sched.2, para.6).

By LSA 2007, s.12(1)(d) probate activities are made a reserved legal activity. Schedule 4 confirms that the existing regulators, all of whom, except the Institute of Legal Executives, the Chartered Institute of Patent Attorneys, the Institute of Trade Mark Attorneys and the Association of Law Costs Draftsmen are approved in relation to probate activities. In addition the LSA 2007 provides for continuity of these rights (Sched.5, para.1), and makes transitional provisions (Sched.5, Part 2).

The Institute of Chartered Accountants of Scotland and the Association of Chartered Certified Accountants have been approved by the LSB as regulators in relation to probate activities since LSA 2007 came into force. However, they have not yet authorised their members to carry out such activities.

The narrow scope of probate activities is a contentious issue. It includes only the taking out of a grant of probate (or letters of administration), not the administration of an estate or the drawing up of a will, and there seems no logical basis for such limitation.

2.2.5 Notarial activities

By LSA 2007, Sched.2, para.7(1), 'notorial activities' means activities which, immediately before LSA 2007 came into force, were customarily carried on by notaries in accordance with the Public Notaries Act 1801. This definition does not include activities carried on in relation to reserved instrument activities or probate activities or the administration of oaths.

On its website at **www.thenotariessociety.org.uk/what-a-notary-does** the Notaries Society describes the work of notaries as follows:

WHAT A NOTARY DOES

Many notaries provide a service for commercial firms engaged in international trade, and for private individuals. The most common tasks are:
- Preparing and witnessing powers of attorney for use overseas
- Dealing with purchase or sale of land and property abroad
- Providing documents to deal with the administration of the estates of people who are abroad, or owning property abroad
- Authenticating personal documents and information for immigration or emigration purposes, or to apply to marry or to work abroad
- Authenticating company and business documents and transactions

What else can Notaries do?

Most notaries act in that capacity to provide the sort of services already described, but they can also provide authentication and a secure record for almost any sort of transaction, document or event.

Also as a member of the oldest legal profession in England and Wales. a notary can do any form of legal work for you except for taking cases to court.

Most notaries are also solicitors and do their general legal work in that capacity and under the regulation of the Solicitors Regulation Authority. Others (including the Scrivener notaries in London) practice only as notaries doing commercial and property work (including conveyancing) and family and private client work (including wills, probate and the administration of estates).

By LSA 2007, s.12(1)(e), notarial activities are made a reserved legal activity. Schedule 4 confirms that the existing regulator, the Master of the Faculties, is the only approved regulator in relation to notarial activities. In addition, LSA 2007 provides for continuity of these rights (Sched.5, para.1), and makes transitional provisions (Sched.5, Part 2).

There are also exemptions in respect of persons who otherwise have statutory authority to carry on notarial activities (LSA 2007, Sched.3, para.5(2)), and individuals who carry on those activities otherwise than for, or in expectation of, any fee, gain or reward (Sched.3, para.5(4)). Certain exemptions in relation to the Public Notaries Act 1801, s.14 are also continued (Sched.3, para.5(3)).

2.2.6 Administration of oaths

The 'administration of oaths' means the exercise of the powers conferred on a commissioner for oaths by the Commissioners for Oaths Acts 1889 and 1891 and the Stamp Duties Management Act 1891, s.24 (LSA 2007, Sched.2, para.8).

By LSA 2007, s.12(1)(f), administration of oaths is made a reserved legal activity. Schedule 4 confirms that all the existing approved regulators are approved in relation to the administration of oaths. In addition, LSA 2007 provides for continuity of these rights (Sched.5, para.1), and makes transitional provisions (Sched.5, Part 2).

2.3 CONTROLLING THE PERIMETER OF RESERVED LEGAL ACTIVITIES

As the undertaking of reserved legal activities is what separates those organisations that need to be regulated from those that do not, it is reasonable to expect that in due course breaches of this perimeter will be carefully monitored and penalties enforced. It is a criminal offence under LSA 2007, s.14 to carry on a reserved legal activity unless entitled to do so. At present, it is not clear as to which organisation actually has the responsibility to monitor breaches. Each individual approved regulator or licensing authority does not have a strategic interest in the overall position and it appears that it may fall to the LSB.

The status of the conduct of litigation as a reserved legal activity has already led to concern in the civil and criminal courts (although, it appears, not among the regulators). In *Bank of Scotland* v. *Whiteside* (unreported, Manchester County Court, 21 February 2011), His Honour Judge Holman criticised a debt recovery firm, Henderson Booth and Snell Ltd (HBS), which was acting in relation to litigation in the county court when not authorised to do so. His judgment concludes:

> The information provided clearly shows that HBS is, and has been, undertaking these activities on a regular and widespread basis. There would appear, therefore, to have been a wholesale disregard for the provisions of the Legal Services Act 2007 (and indeed its predecessor).

In the criminal sphere, difficulties arose in relation to a company that brings prosecutions for breaches of intellectual property rights on behalf of the Premier

League. In *Media Protection Services* v. *Gilligan* (unreported, Liverpool Magistrates Court, 7 September 2011), District Judge Sanders expressed concern as to whether such an unregulated organisation is able to do this for commercial reward.

Further practical difficulties are caused by LSA 2007, s.15. The main purpose of this section is to control unregulated entities that employ authorised persons and to prevent those authorised persons providing reserved legal activities to members of the public or sections of the public, with or without a view to profit. Section 16 makes it an offence for the employer to carry on reserved legal activities through such an employee. Whilst it is sensible to have such a provision to control the perimeter, the section does have some unintended consequences for in-house lawyers. Clearly there is no problem when an in-house lawyer provides reserved legal activities to his employer. However, there are some long-established provisions, which were until recently contained in rule 13 of the Solicitors' Code of Conduct 2007 and are now contained in rule 4 of the SRA Practice Framework Rules 2011, that permit in-house lawyers to provide such services to persons other than their employer in particular circumstances. Lawyers to whom they apply include lawyers acting for members of an association where they are employed by the association and also lawyers acting for insurers and the insured when employed by the insurer. Whilst such arrangements have until now been permissible, they may be contrary to LSA 2007, s.15 as the lawyer could be said to be providing reserved legal activities to the public or a section of the public. The SRA is alive to the problem and has produced guidance on the subject (see 'In-house lawyers, regulation and the Legal Services Act 2007' (SRA, 17 October 2011)). As the guidance makes clear, the question of whether s.15 is breached is fact-sensitive. However, this uncertainty may be a further reason for membership associations and others to carefully consider whether to become an ABS.

An additional problem is that s.15(5) seems to prevent in-house lawyers undertaking pro bono work as part of their employer's corporate and social responsibility programme, as this would form part of the employer's business. Under s.15(9), the Lord Chancellor can make provision for what does or does not fall within s.15(5) and pro bono work as part of this kind of programme would seem to be a candidate for such provision.

2.4 REGULATED BUT NOT RESERVED LEGAL ACTIVITIES

Although LSA 2007 specifically defines the six reserved legal activities, a further complication arises in that some legal activities that do not fall within this definition are nevertheless regulated by statute. These activities – immigration advice and services, claims management services and insolvency work – are described below.

2.4.1 Immigration advice and services

The provision of immigration advice and services is currently regulated by the Immigration and Asylum Act 1999, s.84. This is despite the provision of immigration services being included in the draft list of legal activities governed by statute in the government's White Paper, *The Future of Legal Services: Putting Consumers First* (Cm 6679, 2005), with the expectation being that it would be included as a reserved legal activity.

Immigration advice and services are dealt with in Sched.18 to LSA 2007. This designates the Law Society, the General Council of the Bar and the Institute of Legal Executives as qualifying regulators for the purposes of authorising solicitors, barristers and legal executives to provide immigration advice and services under the Immigration and Asylum Act 1999.

From 1 April 2011, responsibility for the oversight of the regulation of immigration advice and services authorised by these three qualified regulators under LSA 2007 transferred to the LSB from the Office of the Immigration Services Commissioner. Schedule 18 to LSA 2007 also allows other approved regulators to apply to the LSB to become qualified regulators of immigration advice and services.

Schedule 18 only applies to approved regulators under LSA 2007. The Office of the Immigration Services Commissioner will continue to regulate those individuals providing immigration advice and services who are directly regulated by it.

The regulation of immigration advice and services does not sit happily within the overall scheme of LSA 2007. The regulation of reserved legal activities is concerned with function, while the regulation of immigration advice and services is concerned with the subject of the advice. As such the provision of immigration advice and services overlaps with some of the reserved legal activities such as rights of audience and conduct of litigation.

2.4.2 Claims management services

The Ministry of Justice has been responsible for directly regulating the activities of businesses providing claims management services since April 2007 under Part 2 of the Compensation Act 2006. The Compensation Act 2006, s.4(2)(b) defines claims management services as 'advice or other services in relation to the making of a claim'. Secondary legislation defines the scope of regulation, including the regulated sectors and the regulated activities subject to the authorisation regime.

Any business providing regulated claims management services in England and Wales is, unless exempt, required to be authorised irrespective of its registered address or the location of the business. Exemptions include those already regulated (for example, solicitors and insurers) and independent trade unions. Businesses authorised under the Compensation Act 2006 are subject to a range of statutory conditions, including compliance with conduct rules geared firmly towards the provision of consumer information and safeguards.

2.4.3 Insolvency work

Currently the Association of Certified Chartered Accountants, the Institute of Chartered Accountants in England and Wales, the Institute of Chartered Accountants in Ireland, the Institute of Chartered Accountants in Scotland, the Insolvency Practitioners Association, the SRA, the Law Society of Scotland and the Secretary of State are the only bodies recognised by orders made under the Insolvency Act 1986 as being able to grant the right to practise insolvency work.

The provision of insolvency work is regulated by the Insolvency Act 1986, and in order to act as an insolvency practitioner an individual needs to be specifically authorised. By the Insolvency Act 1986, s.390(2), this authorisation is conferred either through membership of a professional body recognised under the Act (s.391) or by permission of a competent authority (s.392).

2.5 UNREGULATED LEGAL ACTIVITIES

There are a number of legal activities – such as will-writing, advice and assistance at a police station, non-contentious employment advice (including advice on discrimination) and mental health advice – which are not reserved legal activities under LSA 2007, nor are they regulated by other statutory provisions. The consequence of this is that those services can be provided by non-authorised persons who are not subject to regulation.

Currently many of these unregulated legal activities are undertaken by solicitors and are therefore regulated by the SRA. However, where consumers procure unregulated activities from non-authorised persons, they will not have any regulatory protection.

As can be seen above, many of the unregulated legal activities are those which can have a serious impact upon an individual's life and where the consequences of incorrect advice can significantly and adversely affect an individual.

For example, advice and assistance at a police station is not a regulated activity unless carried out by someone who is legally qualified and therefore regulated as an individual practitioner. If incorrect advice is given at a police station, the consequences for the individual concerned could be grave.

The Clementi report (December 2004) stated (Chapter E, para.38):

> within the appropriate legislative framework, it is for Government to decide which legal services should be reserved, after appropriate consultation, in particular with the Regulator. Whereas there should not be a gap in regulation once it is determined that something is within the regulatory net, there are asymmetries in the regulatory system of which the Regulator should take note. Any changes to the regulatory net to deal with such matters should be subject to careful cost/benefit analysis.

2.6 SEPARATE BUSINESS PROVISIONS – THE PRICE OF BEING REGULATED

Chapter 12 of the SRA Code of Conduct 2011 sets out provisions to limit the way in which an organisation providing reserved legal activities can hive off its non-reserved legal activities. The chapter starts:

> The purpose of this chapter is to ensure clients are protected when they obtain mainstream legal services from a firm regulated by the SRA. This is accomplished by restricting the services that can be provided through a separate business that is not authorised by the SRA or another approved regulator.

The chapter outlines two types of services: 'prohibited separate business activities' and 'permitted separate business'. The prohibited separate business activities closely resemble the reserved legal activities but include drafting wills and immigration work. More significantly they include 'providing legal advice or drafting legal documents ... where such activity is not provided as a subsidiary but necessary part of some other service which is one of the main services of the separate business' (i.e. the non-authorised business). Permitted separate business includes alternative dispute resolution, financial services, estate agency, management consultancy and 'providing legal advice or drafting legal documents ... where such activity is provided as a subsidiary but necessary part of some other service which is one of the main services of the separate business'.

Outcomes 12.1 and 12.2 provide that a regulated individual or body should not own, have a significant interest in, actively participate in, be owned by or be connected with a separate business which conducts prohibited separate business activities. Outcome 12.3 provides that where there is a similar relationship with a permitted separate business then there need to be safeguards in place to ensure that clients are not misled about the extent to which the services of both the authorised body and the separate business are regulated. Outcome 12.5 provides that a regulated individual or body must be 'only connected with reputable separate businesses'.

The effect of these provisions is that there should be no difficulty in a multi-disciplinary professional firm being licensed to provide reserved legal activities as part of its overall practice, as long as clients are fully informed as to what services are and are not regulated for that purpose. The same considerations will apply to a financial services firm, save that outcome 12.6 provides that a regulated individual or body must be 'only connected with a permitted separate business which is an appointed representative if it is an appointed representative of an independent financial adviser', where 'appointed representative' has the meaning given in the Financial Services and Markets Act 2000.

However, the Chapter 12 provisions do prevent an ABS hiving off unregulated legal activities provided by non-authorised persons, such as will-writing, into a separate unregulated entity. It is unlikely that consumers will make any distinction between reserved and non-reserved legal activities, or more broadly, regulated and unregulated legal activities. Without this protection, there is a risk that consumers will assume that if an ABS is regulated for the provision of reserved legal activities it is also regulated for the provision of non-reserved legal activities by non-authorised persons.

The LSB in its consultation paper 'Alternative Business Structures: Approaches to Licensing' (18 November 2009) expressed the view that the terms of an ABS licence can contain conditions as to non-reserved legal activities that an ABS may or may not undertake.

2.7 ALTERATIONS TO THE RESERVED LEGAL ACTIVITIES

As mentioned, there are currently six reserved legal activities specified in LSA 2007, s.12(1).

Under LSA 2007, s.24(1), the Lord Chancellor can extend the reserved legal activities by order. The activity must first satisfy the definition of 'legal activity' in s.12(3) before it can become reserved. The power to extend the reserved legal activities can only be exercised on the recommendation of the LSB (s.24(2)); the process for making recommendations is set out in Sched.6 (s.24(3)). The Lord Chancellor, upon receipt of a report containing the recommendation in relation to an activity, has 90 days to consider the report (s.24(4)). If the Lord Chancellor decides not to make an order in respect of an activity, he must state the reasons for that decision (s.24(5)). Further, the LSB has the power to recommend that an activity should cease to be a reserved legal activity (s.26).

The scope of the reserved legal activities is the subject of further work by the LSB, which published two consultation papers on the topic during 2011: 'Enhancing Consumer Protection, Reducing Regulatory Restrictions' (28 July 2011) and 'Call for Evidence: Investigation into Will-Writing, Estate Administration and Probate Activities' (5 September 2011). As the existing framework is subjected to proper scrutiny to determine where the public interest lies, it is likely that the scope of the reserved legal activities will change in the future.

2.8 IMPACT OF THE REGULATORY BOUNDARIES ON ABSs

An ABS will need to consider whether it needs to be regulated. In some cases, it may be that its business model does not require it to be regulated. Instead, it can take advantage of the blurred distinction between traditional law firms, ABSs and unregulated entities. In other cases, where reserved legal activities are a necessary part of its business or the ABS intends to acquire or invest in an existing solicitors' practice, different considerations apply.

CHAPTER 3

Key regulatory concepts

The purpose of this chapter is to identify and explain certain key concepts that underpin the regulatory framework for ABSs.

3.1 OWNERSHIP REGULATION

LSA 2007 regulates ownership of an ABS by a non-authorised person where that person holds a restricted interest in the ABS. A restricted interest includes a material interest, which is, broadly, where the non-authorised person holds at least 10 per cent of the shares in the ABS (or equivalent) or at least 10 per cent of the shares in the parent of the ABS, or is able to exercise significant influence in the management of the ABS or its parent by virtue of the shareholding (LSA 2007, Sched.13, paras.2 and 3).

The licensing authority must be satisfied that the non-authorised person holding a restricted interest in the ABS does not compromise the regulatory objectives set out in LSA 2007, s.1, or the ability of authorised persons employed by the ABS to comply with regulatory requirements; and that the person is otherwise a fit and proper person to hold that interest (Sched.13, para.6(1)). In determining whether it is satisfied as to the above matters, the licensing authority must have regard to: the non-authorised person's probity and financial position; whether the person is disqualified from acting as a head of legal practice (HOLP) or head of finance and administration (HOFA) of a licensed body or being a manager or employee of a licensed body, or is included on the list of persons subject to objections and conditions relating to ownership notified to the LSB by licensing authorities; and the person's associates (Sched.13, para.6(3)). Where an ABS is owned by one or more non-authorised persons who have a less than 10 per cent interest in the ABS, these persons will not be subject to the same controls.

Where the licensing authority is the SRA, the SRA Suitability Test 2011 will be applied to interest holders as it is to non-lawyer owners or managers, and this is essentially the same test as that which applies to those seeking admission to the solicitors' profession (see **5.5.2**). It is entirely logical that the character and suitability requirements for non-lawyers who have a material interest in a regulated body should be identical to those applied to the lawyers. In some respects, the test may need to be more onerous. For example, LSA 2007 clearly includes the consideration of the associates of the non-authorised person as part of the approval process for ownership of licensed bodies (Sched.13, para.6(3)(c)). 'Associates' is widely defined to include family members and other businesses related directly or indirectly to the non-authorised person (LSA 2007, Sched.13, para.5). There is no equivalent requirement for admission to one of the legal professions. However, Part 2 of the SRA Suitability Test 2011, which applies to those seeking to become authorised role holders within ABSs (including interest holders), does include a reference to the relevance of evidence reflecting on the honesty and integrity of a person the applicant is related to, affiliated with, or acts together with, where there is reason for the SRA to believe that that person has influence over the way in which the applicant will exercise the authorised role (SRA Suitability Test 2011, para.10.1(h)).

There is a requirement to identify any non-authorised person who has or is expected to have a restricted interest in an ABS in the application for a licence (LSA 2007, Sched.13, para.10). There is also a requirement to inform the licensing authority when a non-authorised person proposes to acquire or acquires a restricted interest in a licensed ABS (Sched.13, para.21). Failure to comply with either of these requirements is a criminal offence (Sched.13, paras.11 and 22). The licensing authority may impose conditions on the approval of the non-authorised person, either in the context of an application (a notified interest) or when notification is made of a new interest in an existing licensed body (a notifiable interest) (Sched.13, paras.17 and 28). If the licensing authority proposes to do so it must give a warning notice as to the proposed conditions and the reasons for imposing them, and permit representations to be made before a final decision is made (Sched.13, paras.17(3)–(5) and 28(3)–(6)). The licensing authority may also object altogether to the non-authorised person's interest in the ABS, with the same limitations (Sched.13, paras.19(2)–(4) and 31(2)–(5)). Where the conditions or objections relate to a notifiable interest, the warning notice and the opportunity for representations may be dispensed with if it is necessary or desirable to do so for the purpose of protecting any of the regulatory objectives (Sched.13, paras.28(4) and 31(3)).

It is also possible for the licensing authority to impose conditions or further conditions on an existing interest holder, or to raise an objection to an existing interest holder, with the same limitations and exceptions (Sched.13, paras.33 and 36). There is a right of appeal to the Solicitors Disciplinary Tribunal (if the licensing authority is the SRA) against such decisions. There is of course no indication at present as to what conditions could sensibly be imposed on an interest holder if in all respects he is a suitable person to hold the interest.

LSA 2007, Sched.13, para.38 allows licensing rules to make general provision for the limitation of the level of the shareholding, control or voting rights of non-authorised persons. The SRA Authorisation Rules 2011 do not expressly provide for this, but the same effect can be achieved by imposing conditions on a case-by-case basis. There is no restriction in LSA 2007 as to the number of ABSs in which a non-authorised person can take an interest. If a non-authorised person continues to hold an interest in an ABS in breach of conditions or despite objection, the licensing authority may apply to the High Court for an order that the person be divested of the interest (Sched.13, para.43).

3.2 REGULATION OF MANAGERS AND EMPLOYEES

Historically, the regulation of employees of solicitors' practices has been limited to the Law Society (now the SRA) or the Solicitors Disciplinary Tribunal making an order under the Solicitors Act 1974, s.43. An employee who is the subject of such an order cannot be employed by a solicitor's practice without the permission of the SRA. Such an order can only be made where an employee is convicted of a criminal offence or

> ... has, in the opinion of the Society, occasioned or been a party to, with or without the connivance of a solicitor, an act or default in relation to a legal practice which involved conduct on his part of such a nature that in the opinion of the Society it would be undesirable for him to be involved in a legal practice ...

LSA 2007 changes this narrow form of regulation for employees. Under LSA 2007, s.95, employees (and managers) of an ABS can have a financial penalty imposed upon them. The current maximum level of the fine is £250 million. Both employees and managers of a licensed body have a duty under LSA 2007, s.90 to not do anything that causes or substantially contributes to a breach by the licensed body, or an authorised person who is an employee or a manager of the licensed body, of the duties imposed on them by the licensed body's regulator. Under LSA 2007, s.99, an employee can be disqualified from being employed by a licensed body where he (intentionally or through neglect) breaches this duty, or causes or substantially contributes to a significant breach of the terms of the licensed body's licence. A manager can also be disqualified from being a manager of a licensed body under s.99 for the same reasons.

There is also an additional regulatory layer relating to managers. The term 'manager' has a very specific meaning under LSA 2007. Under s.207(1) a manager is defined as a person who:

(a) if the body is a body corporate whose affairs are managed by its members, is a member of the body,
(b) if the body is a body corporate and paragraph (a) does not apply, is a director of the body,
(c) if the body is a partnership, is a partner, and
(d) if the body is an unincorporated body (other than a partnership), is a member of its governing body

This definition is reflected in Chapter 14 of the SRA Code of Conduct 2011, which deals with interpretation (see **1.1**).

If an organisation has a manager who is not an authorised person then it is required to be an ABS. Like owners, managers need to be approved by the SRA (except if they are already authorised persons). In some cases, managers will also be employees and in other cases they will also be owners. The definition is not entirely satisfactory because an LLP could have a chief executive who is not a member and therefore does not need to be approved by the SRA. However, if the same organisation was a company that person would need the SRA's approval, as he would almost certainly be a director.

The provisions for approval of managers are set out in Part 4 of the SRA Authorisation Rules 2011. Rule 13.2 provides that a solicitor or an authorised body is deemed to be approved as suitable to be a manager. The test for approval is based upon the SRA Suitability Test (rule 15.1) and the SRA can give approval with or without conditions (rule 14).

3.3 HOLPs AND HOFAs

Under LSA 2007, Sched.11, paras.11–14, every ABS is required to have a head of legal practice (HOLP) and a head of finance and administration (HOFA).

The HOLP must be an authorised person in relation to one or more reserved legal activities (Sched.11, para.11(3)). Section 91 of LSA 2007 sets out the duties of the HOLP, which can be broadly summarised as taking all reasonable steps to ensure:

- compliance with the terms of the ABS's licence and to report to the licensing authority as soon as reasonably practicable any failure to comply with the licence;
- that the licensed body and any employees or managers who are authorised persons comply with their duty to comply with the regulatory arrangements of the licensing authority and to report as soon as reasonably practicable any failures so to comply;
- that non-authorised persons who are employees or managers or who have an interest in the ABS do not do anything that causes or substantially contributes to a breach of the licensed body's or authorised persons' duties to comply with the regulatory arrangements of the licensed body and to report as soon as reasonably practical any failures so to comply.

The obligations of the HOFA are more limited and are set out in LSA 2007, s.92. These are to take all reasonable steps to ensure compliance with the obligations in relation to accounts under the licensing rules and to report any breach of these rules to the licensing authority as soon as reasonably practical. There is no requirement for the HOFA to be an authorised person.

These formal roles are new to legal services regulation and had no equivalent provisions in the existing framework. In its consultation paper 'Alternative Business Structures: Approaches to Licensing' (18 November 2009) the LSB described the roles in the following terms (at para.271):

KEY REGULATORY CONCEPTS

These two functions are therefore very important in ensuring that lawyers' compliance with their professional principles is not compromised and that consumers are properly protected and receive good quality legal advice.

These statutory roles have been adapted by the SRA for application across all of the firms it regulates, including established law firms. To reflect this wider application the SRA has renamed the roles 'compliance officer for legal practice' (COLP) and 'compliance officer for finance and administration' (COFA). The responsibilities of COLPs and COFAs under the SRA's regulatory framework can be found at rule 8.5 of the SRA Authorisation Rules 2011.

The obligations of a COLP under the SRA Authorisation Rules 2011 are wider than those of a HOLP under LSA 2007. In particular, in addition to ensuring compliance with the SRA's regulatory requirements (except the SRA Accounts Rules), there is an obligation under rule 8.5(c)(i)(B) for the COLP to 'ensure compliance with *any statutory obligations* of the body, its managers, employees or interest holders in relation to the body's carrying on of authorised activities' (emphasis added). The COLP must record any failure so to comply and make such records available to the SRA on request (rule 8.5(c)(i)(C)), and report any non-material failure to comply in the annual report to the SRA and any material failure to comply as soon as reasonably practicable (rule 8.5(c)(ii)).

Under the SRA Authorisation Rules 2011, the COFA must take all reasonable steps to ensure that the body and its employees and managers comply with any obligations imposed on them by the SRA Accounts Rules (rule 8.5(e)(i)). Like the COLP, the COFA must record any failure so to comply and make such records available to the SRA on request (rule 8.5(e)(ii)), and report any non-material failure to comply in the annual report to the SRA and any material failure to comply as soon as reasonably practicable (rule 8.5(e)(iii)).

Guidance note (x) to rule 8 states that in determining whether a failure is material, the COLP or COFA needs to take account of factors such as:

(a) the detriment, or risk of detriment, to clients
(b) the extent of any risk of loss of confidence in the firm or in the provision of legal services
(c) the scale of the issue
(d) the overall impact on the firm, its clients and third parties.

The roles of HOLP and HOFA will clearly be important for both the ABS and the regulator.

3.4 LICENSING

At the heart of the regulation of ABSs are licences. An ABS wishing to be regulated by the SRA must apply to the SRA for authorisation. The SRA will then consider whether to authorise it and therefore grant it a licence, which will be subject to conditions. Some of these conditions will be standard, while others may address the particular features of the ABS. The licence will be issued for an undefined period. The licensing (or authorisation) process is discussed in **Chapter 5**.

3.5 THE LEGAL OMBUDSMAN

Complaints concerning services provided to clients by all legal professionals are dealt with by the Legal Ombudsman (LeO), which is the brand adopted by the Office for Legal Complaints (OLC), a body corporate established under LSA 2007.

Prior to LSA 2007, complaints against legal professionals were dealt with by each profession's regulator. The Law Society had a statutory power to award compensation to clients under the Solicitors Act 1974, Sched.1A, which addressed inadequate professional service. This power was latterly exercised by the Legal Complaints Service as a complaints-handling arm of the Law Society. Criticism of the Law Society's operation of the inadequate professional service jurisdiction – most notably and consistently made by the Legal Services Ombudsman – brought the previous statutory scheme to an end. The death knell for the Solicitors Act 1974 scheme can now be seen to have been the Clementi report (December 2004). Sir David Clementi quoted a submission made by the Legal Services Ombudsman to the effect that professional bodies handling complaints against their own members was an idea that 'has lost any legitimacy – consumer culture has moved on' and concluded that a single independent complaints organisation (the name proposed was the OLC) should be formed covering all front-line legal regulatory bodies.

Clementi proposed that the OLC should provide quick and fair redress to consumers in whatever form may be appropriate, and 'without undue reference' to the classification of the complaint into one of inadequate professional service, one of misconduct or one of negligence. The complaint would be determined by reference to what, in the OLC's opinion, was fair and reasonable in the circumstances of the case. The OLC should have the power to award redress to the consumer, which might include powers to require an apology, order a reduction in fees, require work to be re-done, and make an order for redress up to a prescribed limit.

If, when considering the complaint, the OLC was of the view that there had been some element of professional misconduct by the practitioner, it should refer that aspect to the relevant front-line regulator to be considered and dealt with, but redress to the consumer should not be delayed pending the outcome of any disciplinary hearing.

Clementi expressed no view as to what procedure there should be for appeals from a decision of the OLC, but hoped that a fair process of appeal could be achieved without the introduction of elaborate appeal mechanisms, which would prolong the uncertainty of outcome for the parties and would run contrary to the objective of providing quick and appropriate redress with the minimum of formality.

KEY REGULATORY CONCEPTS

The proposals in the Clementi report in relation to complaints handling were incorporated into Part 6 of LSA 2007. It should be noted that the LeO's scheme set out in Part 6 is very similar to that which governs the Financial Ombudsman Service as provided for in Part XVI of the Financial Services and Markets Act 2000. Consequently any court decisions concerning the Financial Services and Markets Act 2000 scheme are likely to be extremely persuasive when a court has to consider what is essentially the same scheme under LSA 2007.

It is important to note that LSA 2007 provides for a division of responsibility between redress for complaints (which is the responsibility of the LeO) and sanction for misconduct (which is the responsibility of the approved regulator). Thus, under the scheme, redress may be given to the complainant but no disciplinary action may be taken against the respondent (LSA 2007, s.113(2)), and the regulatory arrangements of an approved regulator must not include any provision relating to redress in respect of acts or omissions of authorised persons (s.113(3)). On the other hand, the scheme rules 'may not make provision excluding a complaint from the jurisdiction of the ombudsman scheme on the ground that it relates to a matter which has been or could be dealt with under the disciplinary arrangements of the respondent's relevant authorising body' (s.127(2)).

The jurisdiction of the LeO is limited in the following way (rule 2.1 of the Legal Ombudsman Scheme Rules 2010, which are available on the LeO website at **www.legalombudsman.org.uk**):

The complainant must be an individual or:

(a) a micro-enterprise;
(b) a charity with an annual income of less than £1 million;
(c) a club, association or society with annual income of less than £1 million;
(d) a trustee of a trust with a net asset value of less than £1 million; or
(e) a personal representative or residuary beneficiary of an estate where a person with a complaint died before referring it to the LeO.

Therefore the direct impact of the LeO on an ABS's business will depend on the nature of its client base. It is beyond the scope of this book to describe the LeO's complaints procedure in detail but this is dealt with in *The Solicitor's Handbook 2012* (Andrew Hopper QC and Gregory Treverton-Jones QC, Law Society, 2012).

3.6 ENTITY REGULATION

Historically, the regulation of solicitors has been based on solicitors as individuals rather than on the organisations they work within. Even if a solicitor was a partner in a firm, disciplinary proceedings were taken against the individual partner(s) responsible rather than the firm as a whole. This approach continued notwithstanding AJA 1985, which permitted the Law Society to regulate entities.

However, the individual-based regulatory structure does not fit with the concept of ABSs, where the entity is licensed to provide reserved legal activities rather than the individuals within it, few of whom may be solicitors.

As a consequence of this change the SRA has adopted entity-based or, as it calls it, firm-based regulation. This change has a number of consequences. First, it is more likely that in future enforcement action will be taken against the entity rather than against individuals within the entity.

Second, the SRA's considerations when deciding whether to take enforcement action against an entity may differ from those when deciding to take action against an individual. The traditional approach to professional discipline of individual solicitors has been based around concepts such as moral culpability or conduct unbefitting. Whilst in more recent years, particularly after the introduction of the Solicitors' Code of Conduct 2007, the focus shifted towards rule breaches, these concepts still had a place. However, considerations about personal culpability have no place in determining whether to take enforcement action against an entity. In the case of an entity, the approach will be to consider whether it has complied with the SRA's principles (see **4.2**). If it has not, then what risks are posed by that failure? In many cases the risks can be adequately addressed by making improvements to the firm's processes and no enforcement action will need to be taken. There will of course be cases where enforcement action is still necessary to address the identified risks or to act as a deterrent.

Third, the SRA's dealings with the entity will be with those within it who are responsible for compliance, particularly the COLP.

CHAPTER 4

Role of the SRA

4.1 WHAT IS THE SRA?

As observed at **1.2** above, LSA 2007 preserves the status of the existing regulators whilst providing for a separation of the representative and regulatory functions. As a consequence, the Law Society remains an approved regulator under LSA 2007.

The Law Society itself is incorporated by Royal Charter. The current Charter was granted in 1845, since when there have been four supplementary charters (1872, 1903, 1909 and 1954). Although incorporated by Charter, the Law Society has also been given statutory powers for the regulation of solicitors, law firms and certain other legal practitioners in more recent times under the provisions of the Solicitors Act 1974, AJA 1985, the Financial Services and Markets Act 2000, the Courts and Legal Services Act 1990, the Access to Justice Act 1999 and LSA 2007. The Law Society has a governing council which discharges the Law Society's functions through a series of boards and committees.

Although there had been a separate regulatory arm of the Law Society which dealt with regulation and discipline in the form of the Office for the Supervision of Solicitors, and before that the Solicitors Complaints Bureau, in January 2006 and anticipating the reforms heralded by the Clementi report (December 2004), the Law Society formally split its representative and regulatory functions, creating the SRA, which is governed by its own separate board.

The separation of representative and regulatory functions of approved regulators is an important statutory objective of LSA 2007. For example, although under LSA 2007, s.29(1) the LSB is not authorised to exercise its functions in respect of the representative functions of an approved regulator, under s.29(2) it is made clear that s.29(1) does not prevent the LSB from exercising its functions for the purpose of ensuring 'that decisions relating to the exercise of an approved regulator's regulatory functions are, so far as reasonably practicable, taken independently from decisions relating to the exercise of its representative functions'. Similarly, under s.30(1), the LSB must make rules ('internal governance rules') setting out requirements to be met by approved regulators for the purpose of ensuring:

(a) that the exercise of an approved regulator's regulatory functions is not prejudiced by its representative functions, and
(b) that decisions relating to the exercise of an approved regulator's regulatory

functions are so far as reasonably practicable taken independently from decisions relating to the exercise of its representative functions.

Under LSA 2007, the Law Society, as an approved regulator, is responsible for proper discharge of the regulatory functions and objectives specified in the Act. The Law Society has overall responsibility for ensuring the regulatory responsibilities are carried out effectively as well as being directly responsible for promoting the interests of the profession and law reform. However, the Law Society's regulatory powers (both statutory and non-statutory) are delegated by the council (the Law Society's ultimate governing body) to, and exercised by, the SRA. While the Law Society remains a single legal entity, both the Law Society and the SRA have their own chief executive and no individual may be a member of the council of the Law Society and of a regulatory board at the same time. As noted above, LSA 2007 places a duty on the LSB to make rules to ensure separation between an approved regulator's representative functions and its regulatory responsibilities. The Internal Governance Rules 2009 were made by the LSB on 9 December 2009. They are binding on the Law Society, as an approved regulator, and on the SRA as the Law Society's independent regulatory arm. In June 2010, the Law Society and the SRA jointly certified that they had governance arrangements in place which complied with the Internal Governance Rules 2009 save for one exception – namely that the SRA board had a solicitor majority whereas the Internal Governance Rules 2009 require a regulatory board to have a lay person majority. This issue has since been resolved.

The SRA is a board within the Law Society. Its terms of reference are set out in the Law Society's General Regulations, reg.26 and the SRA exercises all monitoring, regulatory, investigative, adjudication, disciplinary, intervention, prosecution, enforcement, civil litigation and costs recovery powers vested in the Law Society or its council. The SRA also, amongst other things, exercises the regulatory powers vested in the Law Society by setting the standards for entry to the profession and the education and training of solicitors and dealing with all matters relating to the setting and maintenance of ethical, conduct and quality standards of solicitors.

The SRA is responsible pursuant to its delegated authority under reg.26 for carrying out investigations in relation to the conduct of solicitors and their employees and, in the light the outcome of any such investigation, deciding what (if any) further regulatory or disciplinary action needs to be taken. In carrying out its functions the SRA operates separately from the Law Society, which carries out a representative function on behalf of solicitors, in accordance with the statutory purposes and objectives of LSA 2007. Except for some shared services, the SRA operates from separate premises from the Law Society; the SRA's premises are currently in Redditch and Leamington Spa with a small office in the City, with a total staff employed of approximately 600. The SRA has announced that it will move to a single site in central Birmingham during 2012.

On 10 November 2011, the Law Society and the SRA announced new arrangements for the governance of the relationship between the two organisations. The agreement permanently resolves how the relationship between the regulator and the Law Society should be managed and will reinforce the SRA's operational independence.

As part of the arrangements, it was agreed that a new business and oversight board would be established, with equal representation from the Law Society and the SRA together with three independent members, which would be responsible for advising the council on the oversight of the SRA and the delivery of shared services functions to both the SRA and the Law Society. The director of organisation services for shared services functions will report directly to the new board. The new arrangements make no change to the SRA board's functions.

4.2 THE SRA AND THE NEW REGULATORY ENVIRONMENT

Historically the legal profession has existed in its own regulatory silo. Any regulatory oversight was primarily provided by the court. Whilst the Legal Services Ombudsman was created by the Courts and Legal Services Act 1990 and the role of the Legal Services Complaints Commissioner was added by the Access to Justice Act 1999, these two statutory posts were generally limited to individual cases rather than providing strategic oversight and were primarily directed at complaints handling.

The regulation of solicitors and other legal professions was primarily rules based. The Solicitors' Code of Conduct 2007, which arrived shortly after the SRA came into being, was intended to provide a complete guide as to how solicitors should act in particular situations. Regulation itself was also rules based. The SRA (and its predecessors) would receive complaints or other intelligence and form a view as to whether a rule had been breached and if so whether disciplinary proceedings should be issued. The SRA held very little information as to how law firms operated and whether they presented a risk until the risk had materialised.

It is difficult to overstate the change to the regulatory landscape by the creation of the LSB as an oversight regulator. The LSB has formed the view that the scheme of regulation based around rules is not appropriate in a modern regulatory setting. As a result it has encouraged approved regulators and licensed bodies to adopt outcomes-focused regulation. Since the LSB approves any changes to the regulatory arrangements of approved regulators, this approach carries significant if not overwhelming weight.

The SRA has adapted its regulatory framework to an outcomes-focused approach. The Solicitors' Code of Conduct 2007 has been replaced by the shorter SRA Code of Conduct 2011, which has at its heart 10 overarching principles, set out below.

You must:
1. uphold the rule of law and the proper administration of justice;
2. act with integrity;

3. not allow your independence to be compromised;
4. act in the best interests of each client;
5. provide a proper standard of service to your clients;
6. behave in a way that maintains the trust the public places in you and in the provision of legal services;
7. comply with your legal and regulatory obligations and deal with your regulators and ombudsmen in an open, timely and co-operative manner;
8. run your business or carry out your role in the business effectively and in accordance with proper governance and sound financial and risk management principles;
9. run your business or carry out your role in the business in a way that encourages equality of opportunity and respect for diversity;
10. protect client money and assets.

In addition to the principles the SRA Code of Conduct 2011 sets out a series of outcomes that should be achieved in certain situations. So, for example, in relation to conflicts, outcome 3.4 is: 'you do not act if there is an own interest conflict or a significant risk of an own interest conflict'. What the outcomes do not do is prescribe how they are to be achieved – the entire basis of outcomes-focused regulation is that the regulated entity can form a view as to how best to achieve the outcome. However, the SRA has included a further layer in the form of indicative behaviours which, whilst not mandatory, are intended to assist in achieving the outcomes. It is fair to say that, in a profession whose existence is based on interpreting rules, this new approach is radical.

4.3 RISK-BASED REGULATION

The second limb of outcomes-focused regulation relates to the way in which the regulator regulates. The core of this approach is the identification and management of risk. In future the SRA will obtain more information from firms and will process that information to establish whether a firm presents a risk. Where firms are thought to be high risk they will be more closely monitored.

To enable this change of approach, the pre-existing structure of the SRA has been swept away and replaced by three main areas of work: authorisation, supervision and enforcement. The SRA no longer wishes to simply be a reactive regulator (although it will still respond to reported events); instead it will now focus much more on relationships with firms and proactive regulation.

Historically the SRA's work has been focused on smaller firms. This is for two reasons: first, their client base tended to result in a higher level of complaints; and second, because they were perceived to pose the greatest risk to the Solicitors' Compensation Fund. However, pursuant to LSA 2007, s.28, the SRA is required to act, so far as is reasonably practicable, in a way that is compatible with the regulatory objectives. These are set out in LSA 2007, s.1(1):

(a) protecting and promoting the public interest;
(b) supporting the constitutional principle of the rule of law;

(c) improving access to justice;
(d) protecting and promoting the interests of consumers;
(e) promoting competition in the provision of services within subsection (2) [legal services by authorised persons];
(f) encouraging an independent, strong, diverse and effective legal profession;
(g) increasing public understanding of the citizen's legal rights and duties;
(h) promoting and maintaining adherence to the professional principles [which are set out in s.1(3)].

In addition, s.28(3) requires approved regulators to have regard to:

(a) the principles under which regulatory activities should be transparent, accountable, proportionate, consistent and targeted only at cases in which action is needed, and
(b) any other principle appearing to it to represent the best regulatory practice.

A risk-based approach is therefore more consistent with the statutory requirement. However, such an approach is likely to see a shift of focus towards larger organisations as they by size alone present a greater risk. This now means that the largest firms (those with the biggest possible impact) may attract greater attention from the SRA.

Risk assessment is dealt with by the SRA's risk centre, which assesses:

- the risk presented by events reported to the SRA;
- the risks inherent in an individual firm;
- the thematic risks that affect groups of firms or sectors of the legal services market;
- the risks presented by the SRA's own operations.

4.3.1 Risks presented by reported events

Reported events (approximately 1,000 per month) are subject to a standardised system which scores them on a sliding scale resulting in a score of low, medium or high risk. Part of the process involves an evaluation of the quality and reliability of the evidence received.

Where appropriate, the event is then referred to the supervision division of the SRA for further action (very serious events like fraud will bypass supervision and will be referred immediately to enforcement). If considered necessary, a member of the supervision division will then make contact with the firm or individual to see if the reported event can be resolved through active engagement, i.e. non-disciplinary measures. It's entirely possible that a reported event with a low risk score (particularly one which falls outside the SRA's published areas of interest) will warrant no further action.

If active engagement doesn't resolve the issue then the supervision division will refer the matter to the enforcement division. Enforcement action is taken in accordance with the SRA's published policy, and is dealt with in more detail in **Chapter 6**.

Where information is received from a member of the public, the SRA simply acknowledges receipt of the information and does not normally involve the informant any further. The SRA specifically refers to such persons as 'informants' not 'complainants' – a use of language that seeks to manage the expectations of those providing information.

4.3.2 Risks inherent in individual firms

The risk centre also deals with risks inherent in individual firms. All firms (including one-person entities) are subject to a risk analysis that examines the potential impact of significant failure in a firm on the eight regulatory objectives and the probability of that failure occurring. The approach of supervision for a particular firm will be allocated by assessing the potential impact that firm's failure may have on the objectives, which is measured with reference to the size of the firm (in terms of turnover, number of employees, annexes, etc.), vulnerability of the firm's client base and the amount of client money held by the firm. Client vulnerability is measured by examining both information asymmetry and actual vulnerability (measured as a proxy depending on the service provided, e.g. family, mental health and criminal clients are more vulnerable than city or commercial clients). Once a firm has been allocated an approach to supervision, the SRA assesses the probability of that firm's failure occurring across key risk categories, including fraud and dishonesty, financial difficulty and instability, operational risks, and fitness and propriety. These risk categories are not static and will evolve over time, e.g. flotation on the stock market is likely to be an additional risk category.

This approach means that when addressing impact of failure and probability of failure, the SRA will be impact-led: impact of failure drives the SRA's approach to supervision, while the probability of failure drives the intensity of that supervision. Given the very big firms will always have higher potential impact, they will attract close supervision. If they have good systems in place that mitigate the risks, the probability of failure will be lower, so the intensity of supervision will be lower.

A high risk firm will be assigned a 'relationship manager' who will work closely with the firm on a variety of issues. There will be close contact over the phone and in person. Medium and low risk firms will receive more 'desk-based' supervision.

4.3.3 Thematic risks

The risk centre will also monitor thematic risks, which are risks caused by the behaviour of groups of firms or arising from a particular category of service. Firms involved in such thematic activity are likely to be from across the risk spectrum.

It is likely that all ABSs that form part of the first wave of licences will attract a high risk categorisation. This is because the risks presented by ABSs are not yet well understood.

CHAPTER 5

Authorisation process

5.1 APPLICATION PROCESS

Pursuant to LSA 2007, s.83 and Sched.11, a licensing authority is required to set out within rules a procedure by which entities can apply to the licensing authority for authorisation. The SRA's authorisation process is prescribed in the SRA Authorisation Rules 2011.

The SRA Authorisation Rules 2011 govern not only licensed bodies but also legal services bodies, which are essentially traditional law firms that do not have external ownership or management. That ABSs are not treated differently from other providers of reserved legal activities is an example of the overall regulatory intention to eliminate distinction between the two types of entities.

Under rule 2 of the SRA Authorisation Rules 2011, an application for authorisation must be submitted using the prescribed form, correctly completed. Application forms and guidance notes are found on the SRA website: **www.sra.org.uk**. The application must also include the application fees, such specified additional information, documents and references which the SRA considers necessary, and any additional information and documentation which the SRA may reasonably require.

The SRA must decide an authorisation application, notify the applicant body of its decision, and (if it decides to refuse the application) set out in the notice the reasons for the refusal within a period of six months beginning with the day on which the application was made (rules 5.1 and 5.2 of the SRA Authorisation Rules 2011). Under rule 5.3 the SRA may (on one occasion) give the applicant body an 'extension notice' extending the decision period. This must be given before the original six-month decision period expires, and must set out the reasons for the extension. The total decision period must not exceed nine months (rules 5.4 and 5.5). Guidance note (iii) to rule 5 clarifies that the means of notice or notification can include any form of written electronic communication normally used for business purposes, such as emails.

Rule 14 deals with the process for approval of individuals (see **5.5.2**).

Pursuant to rules 19.1 and 19.2, the SRA must notify its decision and reasons in writing to the applicant body or authorised body and (where appropriate) to the candidate concerned when it: refuses an application; grants an application subject to a condition; refuses a permission required under a condition on a body's authorisation; or withdraws its approval of a candidate under rules 17 and 18. Under rule 19.3, the SRA must give 28 days' written notice, with reasons, to: the authorised body when the SRA decides to impose a condition on that body's authorisation at any time after the grant of the authorisation; or to the entity and individual concerned, when the SRA decides to withdraw an approval under rules 17 and 18. However, the SRA may shorten or dispense with this 28-day period if it is satisfied that it is in the public interest to do so (rule 19.4).

Rule 20 provides for the notification of certain other third parties where the SRA considers it in the public interest to do so.

The grant of authorisation takes effect from the date of the decision and continues in force unless it ceases to have effect in accordance with rule 21.3 (rules 21.1 and 21.2). Rule 21.3 provides that authorisation ceases:

- when it is revoked by the SRA under rule 22;
- at any time during which the authorisation is suspended;
- subject to Part 6 (changes in partnership), if the body is wound up or for any other reason ceases to exist; or
- if it is a licensed body, it is issued with a licence by another approved regulator.

The SRA will keep a register of all entities that it authorises (rule 34.1). Rule 34.2 sets out the information that will be kept on the register for each authorised body. The register will be available for inspection by members of the public (rule 34.3).

Where a body is granted an authorisation, then under rule 35, the SRA must issue a certificate of authorisation which will state:

- whether it is a licence or a certificate of recognition;
- the name and number under which the body is authorised;
- its registered office (if applicable);
- its main practising address in England and Wales;
- whether it is a partnership, an LLP or a company;
- if it is a company, whether it is: limited by shares; limited by guarantee; an unlimited company; an overseas company registered in England and Wales, Scotland or Northern Ireland; or a societas Europaea;
- the date from which authorisation is granted;
- the terms and conditions to which the body's authorisation is subject.

If a licence is granted subject to conditions, the conditions will logically be linked to the perceived risk areas for the ABS. These conditions could be for example:

- a limitation on the types of reserved activities delivered;
- conditions on a non-authorised person's material interest holding;
- conditions on a HOLP or HOFA;
- a condition to provide specific information.

As mentioned above, the licence will not be time-bound but be valid from the date of issue, although subject to an annual licence fee (see **5.2**).

AUTHORISATION PROCESS

The factors taken into account by the SRA in determining applications for authorisation are set out in detail elsewhere. These include:

- risks inherent in the licensable body (see **4.3.2**);
- approval of non-lawyer managers or owners (see **5.5.2**);
- approval of COLPs and COFAs (see **5.6**);
- whether the licensable body is compatible with the regulatory objectives including the objective of improving access to justice (see **5.8** and rule 6.1 of the SRA Authorisation Rules 2011).

5.2 FEES

Rule 8.3 of the SRA Authorisation Rules 2011 provides that every authorised body must pay to the SRA the prescribed periodical fees applicable to that body by the prescribed date.

In 2010, following the introduction in 2009 of firm-based regulation for traditional firms, the SRA adopted a new fee structure. The SRA noted in its fee policy for 2010/2011 that one of the objectives of the new fee structure was to make it more compatible with ABSs. The key change to the fee structure was that the general cost of regulation was allocated to both regulated individuals and firms rather than being allocated only to individuals. The firm fees are based on turnover, which supports the principle that the fee structure takes account of ability to pay.

The SRA's proposals in its 2011/2012 fee policy are set out below.

Regulated individuals will pay:

- a practising fee of £328; and
- a Compensation Fund fee of £60 irrespective of whether they hold client money.

For regulated firms (not licensed bodies) the SRA will use the 2010 turnover figures provided by a firm to the SRA to determine that firm's practising fee for 2011. Firm fees are calculated using a banded turnover table and the following formula:

$(T - C) \times B + D$

> Where:
> T = turnover
> B = pay percent of turnover within band
> C = minimum turnover in band
> D = minimum fee in band

A Compensation Fund fee of £772 is also payable by firms holding client money.

As noted above, the new fee structure was developed with ABSs in mind. In its consultation paper 'Alternative Business Structures Fee Structure' (3 May 2011), the SRA stated that the starting assumptions for the ABS fee structure were that the ongoing cost of regulation of an ABS will be broadly the same as the cost of regulation of an equivalent traditional firm, and that the same general principals can underpin the fee structure for both. The relevant principles are that the fee structure should:

- Be fair to fee payers
- Be efficient and economical to administer
- Ensure a predictable income to meet the costs of regulation
- Be stable – charges should not vary considerably year on year
- Be as simple as possible – to enable the regulated community to predict likely fees
- Be based on data that can be verified
- Ensure that – wherever possible – costs of particular processes that are not of general application should be borne by those making such applications on, as far as possible, a cost recovery basis
- Take some account of ability to pay, in particular in relation to small and new businesses – fees should not be a deterrent to new entrants.

The paper proposed that the annual periodical fee payable by ABSs should be calculated on the same basis as that for traditional firms, based on banded turnover as outlined above. The SRA Authorisation Rules 2011 provide that turnover will be the basis of charging the periodical fee.

Charging a periodical fee based on turnover for an existing ongoing traditional firm is relatively straightforward, and using historic turnover figures permits the SRA to base calculations on verifiable figures. However, such a calculation is not possible for the initial periodical fee payable on authorisation for an ABS. In its fee policy for 2011/2012 the SRA proposes that the initial periodical fee for an ABS will be calculated based on the ABS's estimated turnover for the first 12 months of business, using the turnover table set out for traditional firms. The definition of turnover for ABSs will be slightly different from that for traditional firms, and will relate to regulated legal activities only. ABSs will also have to pay an application fee to cover the cost of the authorisation process.

The SRA Compensation Fund Rules 2011 have also been adapted to apply to ABSs and the SRA proposes that contributions payable by ABSs should be calculated on the same basis as for traditional firms.

5.3 ASSESSING APPLICATIONS

The introduction to the SRA Handbook states that the SRA's 'modern outcomes-focused, risk-based approach to authorisation' will promote adherence to the professional principles set out in LSA 2007. Rule 6 of the SRA Authorisation Rules 2011 sets out the procedure for determination of authorisation applications.

Rule 6.1 confirms that the SRA will determine applications, so far as is reasonably practicable, in a way that is compatible with the regulatory objectives set out in LSA 2007 (including the objective of improving access to justice) and that the SRA considers most appropriate for the purpose of meeting those objectives.

Under rule 6.2, in relation to ABSs, the SRA may only grant an application for a licence if the applicant entity is a 'licensable body' (which means a body that meets the criteria in rule 14 of the SRA Practice Framework Rules 2011) and the SRA is satisfied that upon authorisation the entity will be in compliance with:

- SRA Indemnity Insurance Rules 2011;
- SRA Compensation Fund Rules 2011;
- rule 8.5 (compliance officers) and rule 8.6 (management and control) of the SRA Authorisation Rules 2011, including any necessary approval of a candidate under Part 4;
- rule 12 (persons who must be 'qualified to supervise'), rule 15 (formation, registered office and practising address) and rule 16 (composition of an authorised body) of the SRA Practice Framework Rules 2011.

Rule 6.3 of the SRA Authorisation Rules 2011 provides that, notwithstanding that the applicant entity meets the conditions set out above, the SRA may refuse an application for authorisation if:

- it is not satisfied that the proposed entity's managers and interest holders are suitable, as a group, to operate or control a business providing regulated legal services;
- it is not satisfied that the proposed entity's management or governance arrangements are adequate to safeguard the regulatory objectives of LSA 2007;
- it is not satisfied that if authorisation is granted, the applicant entity will comply with the SRA's regulatory arrangements (including any conditions imposed on the authorisation);
- the applicant entity has provided inaccurate or misleading information in its application or in response to any requests by the SRA for information;
- the entity has failed to notify the SRA of any changes in the information provided in the application; or
- if, for any other reason, the SRA considers that it would be against the public interest or otherwise inconsistent with the regulatory objectives to grant authorisation.

In reaching a decision as to whether or not to grant authorisation, the SRA will take into account all the circumstances it considers to be relevant, including: any relevant information regarding a manager, employee or interest holder of the applicant entity, any persons with whom they are affiliated if there is reason to believe that such persons may have an influence over the manager, employee or interest holder; and any failure to disclose, or attempts to conceal relevant information (rule 6.4).

The guidance notes to rule 6 clarify that the SRA will take account of 'a broad range of factors' including the applicant entity's business and governance proposals, and advise applicant entities to view the forms, SRA Suitability Test (see **5.5.2**) and the 'decision making criteria'.

5.4 BUSINESS SYSTEMS AND GOVERNANCE

Pursuant to the regulatory objectives of LSA 2007 and in particular the protection and promotion of the public interest and the interests of consumers (s.1(1)(a) and (d)), ABSs need to provide assurances as to equivalent competence and standards that the public would expect from other legal services providers to ensure consumer and public confidence is maintained in the industry. The applicant ABS must provide sufficient information about its business systems and governance in order to enable the licensing authority to make an appropriate judgement concerning whether to authorise or to continue to authorise it.

The SRA's relevant provisions are set out in rules 2 to 15 of the SRA Authorisation Rules 2011. The information or evidence that the SRA will require to assist its determination of an ABS's application as referred to in these rules includes that relating to:

- compliance with regulatory arrangements;
- compliance with the SRA Indemnity Insurance Rules 2011 and the SRA Compensation Fund Rules 2011;
- the ABS's compliance plan, which should give details of clearly defined governance arrangements, appropriate accounting procedures, a system for monitoring, reviewing and managing risks and a system for supporting the development and training of staff;
- approval of the COLP and COFA, who are essential to the ABS's compliance, governance and administrative arrangements;
- approval of managers and owners, including information pertaining to the SRA Suitability Test 2011, i.e. issues of honesty and integrity.

5.5 APPROVAL OF OWNERS

5.5.1 LSA 2007 ownership tests

In its consultation paper 'Alternative Business Structures: Approaches to Licensing' (18 November 2009), the LSB states that consumer confidence in ABSs should be at least as high as that in other law firms. With the advent of non-lawyer owners it is of paramount importance that improper influence is not exercised over the ABS or its lawyer staff, so as to prevent firms from delivering legal services in accordance with regulatory requirements and the rule of law. In order to establish this confidence, under LSA 2007 owners of ABSs are required to be subject to tests for assessing their fitness to own. The LSB considers that these tests should be consistent across licensing authorities, and should be proportionate to identify and manage risk.

Under LSA 2007, Sched.13, para.1(1), a non-authorised person may hold a restricted interest in a licensed body only with the approval of the relevant licensing authority. A 'restricted interest' is defined by Sched.13, para.2 as either:

- a 'material interest', i.e. ownership of at least 10 per cent of the shares in a licensed body or a body which controls a licensed body. LSA 2007 enables licensing authorities to reduce this threshold if they so wish (Sched.13, para.3); or
- a 'controlled interest', which is not specified by LSA 2007 (it is to be specified by the licensing authority's licensing rules) but is deemed to be ownership of more than 10 per cent of the shares in a licensed body or a body which controls a licensed body (Sched.13, para.4).

In the consultation paper, the LSB sets out three tests under LSA 2007 that a non-authorised person must pass to hold a restricted interest in a licensed body. These are based on the approval requirements set out in LSA 2007, Sched.13, para.6.

- Regulatory objectives test: the holding does not compromise the regulatory objectives of LSA 2007.
- Regulated persons test: the holding does not compromise the ability of any employee or manager of the ABS who is an authorised person to comply with the licensing authority's code of conduct or rules.
- Fitness to own test: that the person is otherwise 'fit and proper' to hold that interest.

Regulatory objectives test

As part of a licence application, licensing authorities must require those applying for a licence to identify issues which are contrary to the regulatory objectives. For example, if a non-lawyer owner of an ABS holds a material interest and is subject to other duties which conflict with the regulatory objectives, the ABS must satisfy the licensing authority about what steps that owner has taken to avoid a material conflict of interest.

Regulated persons test

The requirements in LSA 2007, Sched.13, para.6 provide protection for a manager or employee of an ABS who is an authorised person from any potential non-lawyer owner who seeks to influence or cause that manager or employee to breach his professional duties or principles or the licensing rules. In addition, LSA 2007, s.90 creates a duty for non-lawyer owners of an ABS to 'not do anything which causes or substantially contributes to a breach' by an employee or manager of the ABS who is an authorised person of their duties under s.176 to comply with the regulatory arrangements of the ABS's licensing authority. The ABS's HOLP has a statutory duty under s.91(4) to report to the licensing authority any failure of a non-lawyer owner to comply with his duties under s.90. Also, an owner's shareholding can be divested if he is no longer deemed to be fit to own an ABS, and he can be placed on the LSB's list of persons who are subject to objections and conditions on ownership

(LSA 2007, Sched.13, Part 5). The LSB feels that these regulatory provisions will help to mitigate the risk of an owner trying to inappropriately influence any of an ABS's employees.

In the consultation paper the LSB suggested that an ABS should have a constitutional document outlining the hierarchy of regulatory duties that apply to its commercial activities. The governing principle in this respect, as suggested by the LSB, is that a duty to a shareholder does not override or indeed compromise a duty to a lawyer's client or to a court. The LSB also gave an example of a sanction which it considered may be appropriate in the UK (at para.86):

> In Australia, further protection was afforded to Slater and Gordon (a law firm that floated on the Australian stock exchange) by introducing into its constitution a condition that, in appropriate circumstances, a shareholder's shares were to be redeemed by the company for the price they were originally purchased if that shareholder was deemed not fit to own. This measure ensured that divestiture could happen easily; it may be appropriate to introduce a similar sanction for ABS.

Fitness to own test

The fitness to own test for owners is an essential part of ensuring consumer confidence in all forms of ABSs. In its consultation paper, the LSB recommends that the test for fitness should be consistent across all licensing authorities to ensure that an ABS regulated by one licensing authority is not perceived to be riskier than an ABS regulated by another licensing authority.

Based on the responses to that consultation paper, the LSB issued 'Guidance to Licensing Authorities on the Content of Licensing Rules' (March 2010) in which it considers that it is appropriate that a 'fit and proper' test should be applied to both lawyer and non-lawyer owners and should require disclosure of the following information (at para.114):

- any criminal charges or convictions (including spent convictions and cautions) or cases pending in the UK or elsewhere;
- any previous disciplinary action taken by a professional or regulatory body in the UK or elsewhere, whether concluded or not;
- whether the person has ever been disqualified as a director;
- whether the person has ever been declared bankrupt (and whether or not this has been discharged) or entered into an Individual Voluntary Arrangement; and
- any other material information that could reasonably be expected to have a bearing on their fitness to be an owner of a licensed body.

As the test is predicated on the voluntary disclosure of information, systems will need to be in place so that the veracity of the information provided to the licensing authority, such as that pertaining to criminal convictions or disciplinary action, can be checked with other bodies. Licensing authorities therefore need to establish information-sharing powers between themselves, other regulatory bodies and indeed law enforcement agencies. This is of course workable in jurisdictions where these centralised bodies exist and where information is available and reliable;

however, there are many jurisdictions where this is simply not the case, so frameworks in the form of Memoranda of Understanding will need to be established both within England and Wales and internationally. Although the ABS must have a practising address in England and Wales there is nothing to stop individuals from overseas owning an interest in an ABS in this jurisdiction.

The LSB does not require licensing authorities to carry out annual checks on ABS owners, but, as an additional protection, licensing authorities may consider requiring ABSs to notify them of any material changes in the character and suitability of owners subject to the test. If an owner notified of a change of circumstances such as a recent conviction, then the 'fit and proper' test and the resultant regulatory process would need to re-establish 'fitness to own'. It is felt by the LSB that the licensing authority's ability to impose financial penalties and, ultimately, to revoke an ABS's licence is likely to act as a significant deterrent to failing to provide information on a change in an owner's circumstances.

If any adverse information arises from disclosure by the individual owner as part of the test, the licensing authority will assess this information against the individual's role in the ABS. The LSB considers that licensing authorities should have the flexibility to disregard, for example, minor convictions. In other cases, licence conditions rather than disqualification may be appropriate. In cases where false, misleading or insufficient information is supplied, the LSB considers it reasonable for a licensing authority to refuse a licence application.

Under LSA 2007, Sched.13, para.10, in an ABS's application for a licence it must identify any non-authorised person who holds a restricted interest in the ABS, and by Sched.13, para.3(3) this includes any of the person's associates who hold a material interest, or any of the person's associates where the person together with that associate would hold a material interest. 'Associate' is defined in Sched.13, para.5 as including:

- the person's spouse, civil partner, child or stepchild;
- a trustee of a settlement under which the person has a life interest in possession;
- an undertaking of which the person is a director;
- the person's employee or partner;
- if the person has with any other person an agreement or arrangement with respect to the acquisition, holding or disposal of shares or other interests, or under which they act together in exercising their voting power, that other person.

The rationale for including the non-authorised person's associates is to ensure that the full chain of ownership is captured. Further regulatory risk arises from an associate who may seek to or indeed exert inappropriate influence over the non-authorised person by virtue of their relationship.

For the avoidance of doubt, only a person who has a shareholding or voting power in a licensed body can have an associate. An employer will not be subject to the fitness to own test simply because some of its employees, if their shares were combined, would have a material interest.

In its consultation paper, the LSB noted that one possible interpretation of this part of LSA 2007 is that the ownership test itself only ever applies to the non-authorised owner rather than to them and to every one of their associates.

On a more restrictive reading of the Act, however, the LSB said it is arguable that many associates could fall within this definition. A consequence of this is that associate companies will have to ask employees about their shareholdings. The process of identifying the associates and of notifying the licensing authority before a change of control could be very time consuming and burdensome for some businesses. In many instances, the ongoing exercise of identifying all employees and undertakings and employees of undertakings who buy shares in the licensed body (or who propose to buy shares in the licensed body when the body is first licensed) may be complicated, expensive and disproportionate. However, it is more practicable for a business to make such a declaration than for a licensing authority to undertake an investigation before granting a licence.

Nevertheless, LSA 2007, Sched.13, para.6(3)(c) requires a licensing authority to 'have regard to' associates when determining whether a person is a fit and proper person to hold a restricted interest and therefore consideration needs to be given to such associates upon an ABS's application for a licence. The LSB considered the regulatory burden if the licensing authority were to require information about every associate caught by the definition and concluded that the impact on partnerships and private companies with a complicated group structure and/or large membership could be high. A balancing act therefore needs to be struck between encouraging as full a disclosure as possible about associates without over-burdening the ABS. Applicant education is important, as is the knowledge that a negligent or false declaration by an applicant may lead to cancellation of a licence. The LSB's consultation paper makes clear the need to have a balanced approach.

5.5.2 SRA ownership test

The SRA has aligned its own 'fit and proper' test in respect of owners, managers, compliance officers of ABSs, and those seeking admission to the solicitors' profession – the SRA Suitability Test 2011 – with the tests under LSA 2007. This is in keeping with the LSB's vision for the provision of such tests. The SRA Suitability Test is referred to in rule 15 of the SRA Authorisation Rules 2011 and set out separately in the SRA Handbook. It is reproduced at **Appendix D**.

Under para.2.1 of the SRA Suitability Test 2011, candidates must disclose all material information relevant to their application. This will mean owners of an ABS applying for a licence must declare information such as whether they have any criminal convictions, whether there is or has been disciplinary action against them, whether they have been disqualified as directors, whether they are or have been bankrupt, and anything else that is relevant to the question of fitness. The burden of satisfying suitability is on the individual and there is a positive obligation on that individual to provide relevant information. Such an application will need to be supported by independent evidence such as a Criminal Records Bureau report.

The test is designed to ensure that any individual seeking admission as a solicitor or any legally qualified or non-legally qualified applicant for an authorised role in an authorised body has and maintains the honesty, integrity and the level of professionalism expected by the public and other stakeholders and professionals, and does not pose a risk to the public or the profession. The test makes it clear what is required in terms of character, suitability, fitness and propriety; the starting principle is that no applicant has the automatic right of admission or authorisation and it will always be for the individual applicant to discharge the burden of satisfying suitability under the test.

Consistent with the premise of outcomes-focused regulation, the test sets out the SRA's principles (see **4.2**) that apply to all regulated individuals whether they are working at traditional solicitors' firms, in-house, or within an ABS. To train, transfer or to be admitted as a solicitor, or to make a successful application for admission or authorisation as an authorised role holder, an individual must adhere to these principles. The test then sets out the applicable outcomes, which are that:

- solicitors are of the required standard of character and suitability (O(SB1));
- authorised role holders, i.e. COLPs, COFAs, owners or managers, within authorised legal service providers are fit and proper to hold those roles (O(SB2));
- clients, and the wider public, will have confidence that O(SB1) has been demonstrated (O(SB3)).

There is an ongoing obligation to continue to demonstrate these outcomes for those seeking to be regulated persons or authorised role holders.

The test states that, unless there are exceptional circumstances, the SRA will refuse approval of an authorised role holder if:

- the candidate has been convicted by a court of certain criminal offences as set out at para.1.1. Note also that under para.1.2 the SRA is 'more likely than not' to refuse the application in the cases of certain other criminal convictions or cautions not falling within para.1.1, and may refuse the application in other, more minor cases (para.1.3);
- the candidate has been responsible for behaviour which is dishonest, violent, or where there is evidence of discrimination towards others; has misused his position to obtain pecuniary advantage; or has misused his position of trust in relation to vulnerable people (para.3.1);
- the candidate has committed and/or has been adjudged by an education establishment to have committed a deliberate assessment offence which amounts to plagiarism or cheating to gain an advantage for himself or others (para.4);
- there is evidence that the candidate cannot manage his finances properly and carefully, or has deliberately sought to avoid responsibility for his debts and/or there is evidence of dishonesty in relation to the management of his finances (para.5.1). Note also that under para.5.2 if the candidate has been declared

bankrupt, entered into an individual voluntary arrangement or had a county court judgment issued against him there will be a presumption of evidence that he cannot manage his finances properly or carefully;
- the candidate has been made the subject of a serious disciplinary finding, sanction or action by a regulatory body or any court or other body hearing appeals in relation to disciplinary or regulatory findings; has failed to disclose information to a regulatory body when required to do so, or has provided false or misleading information; has significantly breached the requirements of a regulatory body; has been refused registration by a regulatory body; or has failed to comply with the reasonable requests of a regulatory body (para.6.1). Note also that the SRA may refuse the application if the applicant has been rebuked, reprimanded or received a warning about his conduct from a regulatory body under para.6.2.

In addition to the above requirements – taken from Part 1 of the test – applicants seeking to become authorised role holders must meet the requirements set out in Part 2, which states at para.10 that unless there are exceptional circumstances, the SRA may refuse an application for approval if:

- the applicant has been removed from the office of trustee for a charity by an order imposed by the Charities Act 1993;
- the applicant has been removed and/or disqualified as a company director;
- any body corporate of which the applicant is or was a manager or owner has been the subject of a winding up order, an administration order or an administrative receivership, or has otherwise been wound up or put into administration in circumstances of insolvency;
- the applicant has a previous conviction which is now spent for a criminal offence relating to bankruptcy, individual voluntary arrangements or other circumstances of insolvency;
- the applicant is a corporate person or entity subject to a relevant insolvency event;
- the applicant is a corporate person or entity and other matters that call its fitness and propriety into questions are disclosed or come to light;
- the applicant has committed an offence under the Companies Act 2006;
- the SRA has evidence reflecting on the honesty and integrity of a person the applicant is related to, affiliated with, or acts together with, where the SRA has reason to believe that the person may have an influence over the way in which the applicant will exercise his authorised role.

The SRA Suitability Test reflects the leading judgment of the test for character and suitability for solicitors which is found in *Jideofo* v. *The Law Society* [2007] EW Misc 3 (EWLS) where the then Master of the Rolls Lord Clarke stated that:

- the test for character and suitability is a necessarily high test;

- the test for character and suitability is not concerned with 'punishment', 'reward' or 'redemption', but with whether there is a risk to the public or a risk that there may be damage to the reputation of the profession; and
- no one has the right to be admitted as a solicitor and it is for the applicant to discharge the burden of satisfying the test of character and suitability.

Under rule 8.6(a) of the SRA Authorisation Rules 2011, an authorised body must ensure that any manager or owner of the authorised body (or any manager of a body corporate which is a manager or owner of the authorised body) has been approved by the SRA. Further, no licensed body (rule 8.6(d)) or recognised body (rule 8.6(e)) may, except with the written permission of the SRA, permit an individual to be a manager or owner of the body if:

(i) that individual's name has been struck off the roll;
(ii) that individual is suspended from practising as a solicitor;
(iii) that individual's practising certificate has been suspended whilst he is an undischarged bankrupt;
(iv) there is a direction in force in respect of that individual under s.47(2)(g) of the Solicitors Act 1974; or
(v) there is an order in force in respect of that individual under s.43 of the Solicitors Act 1974.

Part 4 of the SRA Authorisation Rules 2011 (rules 13–18) governs the procedure for approval of owners, managers and compliance officers for the purposes of rule 8.6.

Under rule 13.2, as long as the SRA is notified in advance, a solicitor who holds a current practising certificate or is an 'authorised body' is deemed to be approved as a manager or owner of an authorised body, unless there is a condition upon that person's practising certificate or authorisation preventing him from being a manager, owner or interest holder or being a sole practitioner, or the SRA has withdrawn its approval of that person to be a manager or owner.

In all other cases, when considering whether to approve a candidate as a lay manager or owner (or compliance officer), under rule 15 the SRA will consider the criteria set out in its Suitability Test and any other relevant information.

Rule 14 sets out the procedure for approval of non-lawyer managers and owners and compliance officers. The SRA's decision to approve or refuse to approve the candidate must be notified in writing to the applicant body or authorised body and separately to the candidate as soon as possible (rule 14.4). The SRA can, when granting approval or subsequently, make its approval of an owner or manager of an authorised body subject to conditions on the body's authorisation as it considers appropriate (rule 14.5). (For circumstances when it would be appropriate to impose conditions, see rule 9.) If the SRA proposes to object to a candidate becoming an owner of an authorised body (or to approve such a person becoming an owner subject to conditions), it must give the candidate and applicant body a warning notice and consider any representations made by them to the SRA within the prescribed period, unless it considers that it is necessary or desirable to dispense

ALTERNATIVE BUSINESS STRUCTURES

with the warning notice in order to protect the regulatory objectives (rules 14.6 and 14.7). Under rule 14.8, the SRA may at any time require the production of information or documentation from a person who has been approved as an owner or manager (or compliance officer), or from the authorised body, in order to satisfy the SRA that the person met, meets or continues to meet the criteria for approval.

Under rule 16, approval of an owner or manager (or compliance officer) continues until it is withdrawn by the SRA or the approved person ceases to hold office. Under rule 17, the SRA can subsequently withdraw approval of an owner or manager (or compliance officer) if:

(a) it is not satisfied that an approved person met or meets the criteria for approval in Rule 15;
(b) it is satisfied that a condition imposed on the body's authorisation under Rule 14.5 has not been, or is not being complied with;
(c) it is satisfied that the approved person has breached a duty or obligation imposed upon them in or under the SRA's regulatory arrangements or any enactments; or
(d) information or documentation is not promptly supplied in response to a request made under Rule 14.8.

5.6 APPROVAL OF HOLPs AND HOFAs

Paragraphs 11 and 13 of Sched.11 to LSA 2007 provide that a licensed body must at all times have an individual designated as the HOLP and an individual designated as the HOFA whose designations are approved by the licensing authority.

An ABS's HOLP must be an authorised person in relation to at least one of the licensed activities (LSA 2007, Sched.11, para.11(3)(b)). He must take all reasonable steps to ensure compliance with the terms of the ABS's licence and has a duty to report non-compliance with any of the licence terms to the relevant licensing authority (s.91(1)). In addition, the HOLP must oversee the individual lawyers within the firm to ensure that they comply with their professional obligations (s.91(3)). The HOFA of an ABS is responsible for ensuring compliance with the accounts rules and for reporting breaches of those rules to the relevant licensing authority (LSA 2007, s.92).

It is possible for a HOLP and HOFA to be one and the same person. The HOLP or HOFA must consent to his designation of that role (Sched.11, paras.11(3)(a) and 13(3)(a)). In the same way as they do for an owner of an ABS, licensing rules must make provision about criteria to be applied to determine whether a HOLP or HOFA is a 'fit and proper person' (LSA 2007, Sched.11, paras.12 and 14).

An SRA-regulated ABS must at all times have an individual designated as the COLP and an individual designated as the COFA (the SRA equivalent of HOLPs and HOFAs, see **3.3** above). The same person can hold both roles. In each case that individual must be (by rule 8.5(b) and (d) of the SRA Authorisation Rules 2011):

- a manager or an employee of the ABS;

- of sufficient seniority and in a position of sufficient responsibility to fulfil the role; and
- approved as a COLP or COFA by the SRA.

Under rule 8.5(g)(ii) of the SRA Authorisation Rules 2011 the COLP must also be a lawyer of England and Wales, a registered European lawyer or registered with the Bar Standards Board under reg.17 of the European Communities (Lawyer's Practice) Regulations 2000, SI 2000/1119.

The duties of COLPs and COFAs are outlined at rule 8.5 (see also **3.3** above).

Except for rules 14.6 and 14.7 (which apply to owners only), the procedure for approval of a COLP or COFA is the same as that for approval of non-lawyer owners and managers contained in Part 4 (rules 13–18) of the SRA Authorisation Rules 2011. Readers are therefore referred to **5.5.2** above, which discusses the procedure in relation to owners.

In addition, rule 18 deals with the temporary approval (initially for 28 days pending submission of a substantive application) of a COLP or COFA where the authorised body ceases to have a COLP or COFA.

Again, like non-lawyer owners and managers of an ABS, COLPs and COFAs must meet the criteria set out in the SRA Suitability Test 2011 for authorised role holders (see **5.5.2**).

5.7 INSURANCE REQUIREMENTS

Section 83(5)(d) and (e) of LSA 2007 stipulates that licensing rules must contain appropriate indemnification and compensation arrangements. Professional indemnity insurance cover is therefore a mandatory requirement of a licensed body being granted a licence. An ABS must provide adequate levels of redress and protection for consumers of legal services against such things as negligence and fraud. The levels of cover must be the equivalent of what is in place for traditional law firms.

From 1 October 2011, SRA-regulated firms are required to take out professional indemnity insurance pursuant to the SRA Indemnity Insurance Rules 2011 with one or more qualifying insurers in respect of their regulated activities, which include not only reserved legal activities but also other legal activities defined by LSA 2007, s.12 (see Appendix 4 to the SRA Indemnity Insurance Rules). The SRA operates an open-market approach to solicitors' and ultimately ABSs' insurance, with individual firms taking out insurance subject to it being provided by a qualifying insurer and on the minimum terms and conditions set by the SRA. Minimum cover under the SRA's minimum terms is £2 million or in the case of incorporated firms (including ABSs), £3 million. If a firm is unable to procure insurance through the open market, and it is an 'eligible firm', then insurance cover is provided through the Assigned Risks Pool (ARP) but at increased premium rates. If it is not an eligible firm it must cease to practise.

A firm will also need to procure 'run-off' insurance cover for a period of six years after it has ceased to exist. However, if a successor takes over the original firm, the successor will inherit any previous claims that relate to that original firm.

Appendix 1 to the SRA Indemnity Insurance Rules 2011 sets out the SRA minimum terms and conditions of professional indemnity insurance, including the scope of cover, limit of cover, excesses, special conditions, run-off cover, exclusions and general conditions.

The SRA also maintains the Solicitors' Compensation Fund, which makes grants in respect of compensation claims in the event of dishonesty or failure to account on behalf of regulated persons. Each solicitors' firm currently pays £772 into the Compensation Fund, unless the firm does not hold client money, in which case it pays a reduced amount. Under rule 2.7 of the SRA Compensation Fund Rules 2011, ABSs must contribute to this fund as prescribed by the SRA.

5.8 ACCESS TO JUSTICE OBJECTIVE

One of the regulatory objectives of LSA 2007 is improving access to justice (s.1(1)(c)). Licensing authorities must only license bodies which are compatible with this objective; s.83(5)(b) provides that a licensing authority's licensing rules must contain provision as to how the licensing authority, in connection with an application for a licence, should take account of this objective.

An ABS applying to become a licensed body will therefore be required to provide an access to justice statement setting out how it will improve the public's access to justice by recognising and responding to the needs of consumers and offering different ways of delivering legal services. If the licensing authority is the SRA, such a statement will allow the SRA to assess the application in accordance with rule 6.1 of the SRA Authorisation Rules 2011. It will be up to the ABS to demonstrate how it will achieve this objective, but it may be achieved by allowing for different methods of delivery of legal services, such as online or telephone conferencing as well as the more traditional face-to-face method, looking at non-traditional methods of working, or opening at hours outside traditional business hours. Information provided by the ABS to the licensing authority will form an evidence base to determine if the introduction of the ABS is likely to deliver the desired improvements in access to justice. Only in exceptional circumstances would an application be refused because of access to justice implications.

Rule 6.1 of the SRA Authorisation Rules 2011 specifically provides that the SRA will determine applications for authorisation in a way 'which is compatible with the regulatory objectives including the objective of improving access to justice'. Pursuant to rule 6.3(f) the SRA can refuse an application if 'the SRA considers that it would be against the public interest or otherwise inconsistent with the regulatory objectives to grant authorisation'.

CHAPTER 6

Supervision and enforcement

This chapter deals with the relevant framework for when things go wrong. The SRA separates the supervision and enforcement functions in its internal structure, but where there are potential issues then it will be the supervision function that will investigate and consider matters before passing the matter over to the enforcement function. However, clearly quite a large part of supervision in the sense of monitoring risk does not lead to the consideration or carrying out of discipline and enforcement procedures. How the SRA's supervision function goes about monitoring risk is dealt with at **4.3** above.

6.1 SRA ENFORCEMENT STRATEGY

The SRA's approach to enforcement is set out in its enforcement strategy (13 January 2011). This seeks to achieve the following outcomes:

(a) credible deterrence of behaviours that breach the core principles,
(b) the encouragement and facilitation of compliance with the core principles and other regulatory requirements,
(c) control of firms that represent a risk to the public or the core principles,
(d) removal of those who represent a serious risk to the public.

It is clear from the enforcement strategy that enforcement action is only one tool available to the SRA. It aims to encourage compliance with constructive engagement, relationship management and supervision. In deciding an appropriate response after the identification of a possible breach, the factors that the SRA will consider include:

15.1 The number of clients or others affected and the impact on them;
15.2 The impact or risk to public confidence in the administration of justice arising from the firm's conduct;
15.3 Whether the firm accepts promptly and genuinely that it has acted incorrectly, including whether it has reported the circumstances to us itself;
15.4 Whether the firm genuinely accepts the underlying principles applicable to its behaviour and that it will apply them in future in other, perhaps factually different, situations;
15.5 What the firm has done and is going to do to correct the situation;

15.6 Whether the behaviour:

15.6.1 formed or forms part of a pattern of, or repeated, misconduct or other regulatory failure;
15.6.2 continued for an unreasonable period taking into account its seriousness;
15.6.3 persisted after the regulated person realised or should have realised that it was improper;
15.6.4 affected or had the potential to affect a vulnerable person or child;
15.6.5 affected or had the potential to affect a substantial, high-value or high-profile matter;

15.7 The usual factors relevant to regulatory decisions – such as previous regulatory history, evidence of deliberate intent, recklessness or dishonesty, and personal mitigation.

A further factor that the SRA will need to consider is whether enforcement action should be taken against the firm, against an individual, or against both. This is a significant departure from the SRA's previous approach, which focused on individual solicitor regulation. This new approach to enforcement is likely to raise new issues, including:

- How far will the SRA be able to 'track' individuals who move from one entity to another? A solicitor may be responsible for a breach and then leave the firm before it is discovered. If the resulting enforcement action is taken against the firm, will that leave the individual free from any formal record of his involvement?
- A breach may only concern a small part of a much larger organisation yet the enforcement action will be against the entity as a whole. Such an approach is commonplace within the financial services market. However, law firms are structurally different; they tend to be a coalition of partners. It is not unusual for partners and teams to move from one firm to another, and enforcement action may precipitate this and cause substantial damage to the practice.
- A financial penalty may fall on the firm at the time of an order being made by the SRA, which may be several months or years after the breach. However, the breach may relate to actions by partners who have left or there may be partners who were not partners at the time of the breach. The SRA may not be concerned about such matters but the firm may need to ensure that it is able to recoup losses from those who have left.

For SRA-regulated ABSs, the SRA, as the licensing authority, is responsible for disciplinary as well as licensing decisions, with the Solicitors Disciplinary Tribunal (SDT) taking on the role of an appellate body.

It is the SRA (not the SDT) which has the power to fine an ABS, its managers and employees (LSA 2007, s.95) and the maximum penalties that can be imposed are £250 million on the ABS, and £50 million on an individual manager or employee of the ABS (Legal Services Act 2007 (Licensing Authorities) (Maximum Penalty) Rules 2011, SI 2011/1659). Further, the SRA has the power of disqualification – it can disqualify an individual from acting as a HOLP or HOFA (COLP or COFA in

SUPERVISION AND ENFORCEMENT

SRA terminology) of any ABS, being a manager of any ABS, and even being an employee of any ABS (LSA 2007, s.99).

The disciplinary powers in relation to ABSs and managers and employees of ABSs are dealt with under the same rules and the same procedures as are applied to traditional firms, the SRA Disciplinary Procedure Rules 2011.

6.2 INVESTIGATORY POWERS

Whilst the SRA's investigatory powers in relation to traditional solicitors' practices and individual solicitors (including those working within ABSs) are provided for under ss.44B and 44BA of the Solicitors Act 1974, they do not otherwise apply to ABSs. The parallel provisions in relation to ABSs, non-lawyer managers, employees and owners of ABSs are in LSA 2007, ss.93 and 94.

Section 93 provides that the SRA may require information to be provided and documents to be produced by giving notice to the ABS, any manager or employee (or former manager or employee) of the ABS, or any non-authorised person who has an interest or an indirect interest, or holds a material interest, in the ABS. However, the powers are not backed by criminal sanctions and the remedy for non-compliance, provided by s.94, is an application by the licensing authority to the High Court for an order to comply with the notice.

The duty to co-operate fully with the SRA in relation to any investigation (Chapter 10 of the SRA Code of Conduct 2011, in particular outcomes 10.6 to 10.10) continues to apply to every person and body regulated by the SRA, as does rule 31 of the SRA Accounts Rules 2011, which imposes an obligation to produce at the SRA's request any information and documents related to the practice's accounts.

6.3 SUSPENSION OR REVOCATION OF A LICENCE

Under LSA 2007, s.101, the licence of an ABS may be suspended or revoked by the licensing authority in circumstances which are regulated by Sched.11, para.24. These are incorporated into the SRA Authorisation Rules 2011 as rule 22. Under rule 22.1, the SRA may revoke or suspend a body's authorisation, where:

- in the case of an authorised body (that is, any practice that the SRA has authorised, including ABSs):
  - authorisation was granted as a result of error, misleading or inaccurate information, or fraud;
  - the body is or becomes ineligible to be authorised in accordance with the criteria set out in rule 6 of the SRA Authorisation Rules 2011 (see **5.3**);
  - the SRA is satisfied that the body has no intention of carrying on the legal activities for which it has been authorised;

- the body has failed to provide any information required by the SRA under the SRA Authorisation Rules 2011;
- the body has failed to pay any fee payable to the SRA under the SRA Authorisation Rules 2011;
- a relevant insolvency event (e.g. voluntary winding up or entering administration) has occurred in relation to the body;
- the body makes an application to the SRA for its authorisation to be revoked or suspended;
- the SRA has decided to exercise its intervention powers;
- the body, or an owner, interest holder, manager or employee of the body fails to comply with the duties imposed by or under the SRA Authorisation Rules 2011 or under any statutory obligations in relation to the body's business of carrying on authorised activities including payment of any fine or other financial penalty imposed on the body by the SRA, the SDT, or the High Court;
- in the case of a licensed body (an ABS), the body fails to comply with the prohibition on appointing disqualified managers; or in the case of an authorised body, the body fails to comply with the prohibition on employing disqualified persons (struck-off solicitors and the like), if the manager or employee concerned was disqualified as a result of breach of the duties imposed upon the manager or employee by LSA 2007, ss.90 or 176 (the general duties imposed to comply with all regulatory arrangements of an approved regulator);
- the body does not comply with the requirements in relation to compliance officers;
- the body fails to comply with the management and control requirements (to ensure that those requiring approval are approved and that no disqualified person is employed without permission); or
- for any other reason it is in the public interest;

- in the case of a licensed body (i.e. an ABS), a non-authorised person holds an interest in the licensed body:
  - as a result of the person taking a step in circumstances where that constitutes an offence under LSA 2007, Sched.13, para.24(1), i.e. failing to give notice as to the proposed or actual acquisition of a material interest in an ABS (whether or not the person is charged with or convicted of an offence under that paragraph);
  - in breach of conditions imposed on the holders of material interests in the ABS under LSA 2007, Sched.13, paras.17, 28 or 33; or
  - the person's holding of which is subject to an objection by the SRA as the licensing authority.

Before the SRA can revoke or suspend an authorisation it must first give the authorised body an opportunity to make representations to it on the issues which have arisen which have led the SRA to consider this course of action, and it must also give at least 28 days' notice of its intention to make the decision to revoke or suspend (SRA Authorisation Rules 2011, rule 22.2).

The SRA's power to revoke or suspend authorisation is discretionary. Guidance note (iv) to rule 22 states that the SRA 'is unlikely to revoke or suspend authorisation if doing so at that time would present any risk to clients, the public, the protection of public money or to any SRA investigation'.

6.4 ENFORCEMENT OF LICENCE CONDITIONS

Where an interest holder holds a restricted interest in an ABS in breach of conditions imposed by a licensing authority, the authority may apply to the High Court for an order to secure compliance with the conditions (LSA 2007, Sched.13, para.46). The licensing authority may not make an application to the court unless it has given notice of its intention to do so if, at the end of the notice period, the interest holder is still in breach of the conditions. In other words, an opportunity must be given to the interest holder to regularise the position. The minimum notice period is 28 days (see the LSB's Ownership of Licensed Bodies: Schedule 13 – Prescribed Rules, available at **www.legalservicesboard.org.uk**). No order may be made by the court until the end of any period for appeal against the imposition of conditions and, if there is an appeal, until the appeal is disposed of (LSA 2007, Sched.13, para.46(5)).

6.5 DIVESTITURE

Paragraphs 41–45 of Sched.13 to LSA 2007 contain provisions enabling the licensing authority to apply to the High Court for an order divesting an interest holder of an interest in an ABS where the interest consists of a shareholding in a company with a share capital, if the non-authorised person holds a restricted interest in the licensed body either in circumstances where notice has not been given of the acquisition or intended acquisition of the interest so that an offence has been committed under Sched.13, para.24(1), or the interest is held in breach of conditions imposed by the licensing authority or in contravention of an objection by the authority.

The licensing authority may serve a 'restriction notice' which may provide that a transfer of shares or similar arrangement is void, that no voting rights may be exercised, that no further shares be issued to the holder and that no payment may be made by the company in relation to the shares (other than in a liquidation) (Sched.13, para.44).

On an application to the High Court the court may order the sale of the shares. The licensing authority may not make an application to the court for a divestiture order unless it has given notice of its intention to do so and if, at the end of the notice period, the conditions for divestiture still apply. In other words, an opportunity must be given to the interest holder to regularise the position. The notice period is to be prescribed by the LSB and at the time of writing has not been set (Sched.13, para.45).

No order may be made by the court until the end of any period for appeal against the imposition of conditions or the objection and, if there is an appeal, until the appeal is disposed of (Sched.13, para.45(5)).

6.6 INTERVENTION

Powers of intervention are available to a licensing authority which are broadly comparable to those applying to solicitors' practices under Sched.1 to the Solicitors Act 1974. They are set out in LSA 2007, Sched.14.

A intervention may be authorised where a licence granted to a body has expired, and has not been renewed or replaced by the relevant licensing authority, or where one or more of the intervention conditions is satisfied (LSA 2007, Sched.14, para.1(1)).

The intervention conditions are (Sched.14, para.1(2)):

(a) that the licensing authority is satisfied that one or more of the terms of the licensed body's licence have not been complied with;
(b) that a person has been appointed receiver or manager of property of the licensed body;
(c) that a relevant insolvency event has occurred in relation to the licensed body;
(d) that the licensing authority has reason to suspect dishonesty on the part of any manager or employee of the licensed body in connection with –

   (i) that body's business,
   (ii) any trust of which that body is or was a trustee,
   (iii) any trust of which the manager or employee of the body is or was a trustee in that person's capacity as such a manager or employee, or
   (iv) the business of another body in which the manager or employee is or was a manager or employee, or the practice (or former practice) of the manager or employee;

(e) that the licensing authority is satisfied that there has been undue delay –

   (i) on the part of the licensed body in connection with any matter in which it is or was acting for a client or with any trust of which it is or was a trustee, or
   (ii) on the part of a person who is or was a manager or employee of the licensed body in connection with any trust of which that person is or was a trustee in that person's capacity as such a manager or employee,

   and the notice conditions are satisfied [these are that the licensing authority has given the licensed body a notice requesting an explanation within a period of not less than eight days, and if the licensing authority does not regard the explanation as satisfactory, it gives notice of the failure to the licensed body and notice that its the powers of intervention will apply (Sched.14, para.1(4))];

(f) that the licensing authority is satisfied that it is necessary to exercise the powers conferred by this Schedule (or any of them) in relation to a licensed body to protect –

    (i) the interests of clients (or former or potential clients) of the licensed body,
    (ii) the interests of the beneficiaries of any trust of which the licensed body is or was a trustee, or
    (iii) the interests of the beneficiaries of any trust of which a person who is or was a manager or employee of the licensed body is or was a trustee in that person's capacity as such a manager or employee.

A challenge to a decision to intervene must be made to the High Court within eight days of the service of the notice of intervention (Sched.14, paras.3(7) and 10(5)). It is anticipated that such applications will be reserved to the Chancery Division as is the case with proceedings arising out of the SRA's intervention in solicitors' practices (Civil Procedure Rules, rule 67.4). It is also likely that the court will adopt an identical approach to this jurisdiction as it has in relation to solicitors. As such the court will first consider whether the grounds for intervention had arisen and if so whether in the light of all the evidence before it the intervention should continue. In addressing this question the court must carry out a balancing exercise between the public interest and the consequences for the solicitor (see *Dooley* v. *The Law Society* (unreported, HC, 15 September 2000), *Holder* v. *The Law Society* [2003] 3 All ER 183 and *Sheikh* v. *The Law Society* [2007] 3 All ER 183).

6.7 APPEALS TO THE SDT

Under the Legal Services Act 2007 (Appeals from Licensing Authority Decisions) (No.2) Order 2011, SI 2011/2863 and rule 31 of the SRA's Authorisation Rules 2011, a licensed body may appeal to the SDT against decisions of the SRA:

- to disqualify a person from acting as a HOLP or HOFA or from being a manager or employee of a licensed body;
- to refuse to bring a disqualification to an end following a review;
- to refuse an application for authorisation as a licensed body;
- to impose a condition on the authorisation of a licensed body;
- to revoke or suspend a licensed body's authorisation;
- to modify, or to refuse an application for modification of the terms and conditions of authorisation of a licensed body;
- not to approve a person to be a manager or compliance officer of a licensed body;
- to approve a person to be a manager or compliance officer of a licensed body subject to conditions on the body's authorisation;
- to withdraw approval of a manager or compliance officer of a licensed body;
- to impose fines on a licensed body or a manager or employee of a licensed body;
- not to approve a person being an owner of a licensed body;

- to impose conditions on the authorisation of a licensed body in connection with the approval of an owner;
- to withdraw approval of a person as an owner of a licensed body.

A licensed body can also appeal to the SDT against the SRA's failure to make a decision on an application for authorisation within the 'decision period', which is six months from the day on which the application was made to the SRA in accordance with the SRA Authorisation Rules 2011.

The SDT has not adapted its existing rules, the Solicitors (Disciplinary Proceedings) Rules 2007, SI 2007/3588, for its appellate jurisdiction but has made completely new rules specifically for this purpose. In fact, it has made two sets of rules. There was an immediate need to have rules in relation to appeals under the Solicitors Act 1974 and AJA 1985, as the SRA has had the power to rebuke and fine since 1 June 2010, although because the powers could only be exercised in respect of acts and failings occurring or continuing on or after that date, and the investigatory process takes a finite time, there has not been a pressing need until relatively recently.

In contrast, the first decisions in relation to the licensing of ABSs will not be made until early 2012, and it is not expected that there will be an early rash of appeals. Further, no rules could be made in relation to the SDT as an appellate body in respect of decisions made by the SRA until the Law Society had been designated as a licensing authority.

Accordingly the SDT has made, with the approval of the LSB, the Solicitors Disciplinary Tribunal (Appeals and Amendment) Rules 2011, SI 2011/2346 (the 'Appeal Rules') which deal with appeals under the Solicitors Act 1974 and AJA 1985 and are effective from 1 October 2011, and also the Solicitors Disciplinary Tribunal (Appeals) (Amendment) Rules 2011, SI 2011/3070, which amend the Appeal Rules to include provision for ABS appeals and came into force on 23 December 2011.

6.7.1 Constitution of appeal panels, delegation and general powers

The one certainty in relation to ABSs is that, however much informed opinion there may be, no one can predict reliably exactly how the market will develop, what forms the new businesses will take and what degree of complexity will be involved in licensing decisions, and therefore in appeals from licensing decisions. The SDT has therefore created for itself a degree of flexibility. The Solicitors (Disciplinary Proceedings) Rules 2007 dealing with the SDT's historical and original jurisdiction are rigid as to the constitution of an adjudicating panel (a 'division'); a division is defined under rule 2(1) as consisting of three and only three persons, and under rule 4 these are one lay member and two solicitor members. The Appeal Rules, however, state that for the hearing of any appeal a panel will be 'at least three members of the Tribunal', and that 'Unless the President otherwise directs, the majority of the Panel members shall be solicitor members' (rule 3).

Under rule 5(4) of the Appeal Rules, a single solicitor member may:

- make case management decisions and give directions under rule 9;
- waive a requirement of the Appeal Rules or require a procedural failure to be remedied under rule 11;
- make a direction adding, substituting or removing a party under rule 13;
- deal with the prohibition on disclosure of documents and information under rule 14;
- make orders about lead cases under rule 15;
- give consent to the withdrawal of an appeal under rule 16;
- give directions as to disclosure, evidence and submissions under rule 19(1).

The SDT clerks have delegated authority to give case management directions under rules 9, 13 and 19(1), subject to the right of a party to apply, within 14 days, for the decision to be considered afresh by a panel or single solicitor member (rule 5(1) and (3)).

The SDT (or a panel of SDT members consisting of not less than five members of whom no fewer than two shall be lay members) may make general practice directions, i.e. notices or directions concerning the SDT's practices or procedures, that are consistent with the Appeal Rules, which are to be promulgated under the authority of the SDT President (rule 10).

Subject to the Appeal Rules themselves, the SDT may regulate its own procedure, and may dispense with any requirements of the Appeal Rules in respect of notices, statements or other documents, witnesses, service or time in any case where it appears to the SDT to be just so to do (rule 18). This does not extend however to the time limit for appeals from decisions of the SRA as a licensing authority relating to the ownership of ABSs (see **6.7.2**).

The SDT may consent to a witness giving, or require any witness to give, evidence on oath, and may administer an oath for that purpose (rule 19(3)).

6.7.2 Preliminary steps

Time limit for appeal

The time limit for appeal is in all cases 28 days from notification of the decision. In relation to some appeals by ABSs, this is a statutory time limit fixed by the Rules on the Prescribed Period for the Making of Appeals Against Decisions of a Licensing Authority Regarding Ownership of Licensed Bodies (13 June 2011, available at **www.legalservicesboard.org.uk**), made by the LSB under its powers in LSA 2007, Sched.13, para.8, and may not be exceeded. Neither the SDT nor any other party has power to waive the limit or consent to its extension. This statutory time limit only applies to appeals concerning licensing decisions as to ownership of a licensed body, that is SRA decisions:

- on granting of a licence, to approve an investor's holding of a notified interest subject to conditions, made under LSA 2007, Sched.13, para.17(1);
- to object to an investor's holding of a notified interest, made under Sched.13, para.19(1);
- after a licence has been granted, to approve an investor's holding of a notifiable interest subject to conditions, made under Sched.13, para.28(1);
- to object to an investor's holding of a notifiable interest, made under Sched.13, para.31(1);
- to impose conditions or further conditions on a person's holding of an existing restricted interest, made under Sched.13, para.33(1);
- to object to a person's holding of an existing restricted interest, made under Sched.13, para.36(1);
- to notify the LSB that an owner has exceeded a share or voting limit, made under Sched.13, para.49(2).

Notice of appeal

The appellant must start the appeal proceedings by sending or delivering a notice of appeal to the SDT (Appeal Rules, rule 6(1)). There is no form for a notice of appeal, but under rule 6(4) the notice of appeal must set out:

(a) the name and address of the appellant;
(b) the name and address of the appellant's representative (if any);
(c) an address where documents for the appellant may be sent or delivered;
(d) the basis on which the appellant has standing to start proceedings before the Tribunal;
(e) the name and address of the respondent;
(f) details of the decision or act to which the proceedings relate;
(g) the result the appellant is seeking;
(h) the grounds on which the appellant relies;
(ha) any application for an order for a Stay, if the appellant is allowed to make such an application under the Society's licensing rules;
(i) whether the appellant would be content for the case to be dealt with without a hearing if the Tribunal considers it appropriate; and
(j) any further information or documents required by a practice direction.

A copy of any written record of the decision which is the subject of the appeal, and any statement of reasons for the decision that the appellant has or can reasonably obtain, must be supplied with the notice of appeal (rule 6(5)). At the same time as the appellant sends or delivers the notice of appeal to the SDT, he must send or deliver:

- three additional copies of the notice of appeal and any accompanying documents to the SDT (rule 6(6));
- a copy of the notice of appeal and any accompanying documents to the respondent (rule 6(7)).

SUPERVISION AND ENFORCEMENT

Response to notice of appeal

The respondent's response to the notice of appeal must be sent or delivered to the SDT within 28 days of the receipt of the notice of appeal by the respondent (rule 7(1)). There is no set form but the response must include (rule 7(2) and (3)):

- the name and address of the respondent;
- the name and address of the respondent's representative (if any);
- an address where documents for the respondent may be sent or delivered;
- any further information or documents required by a practice direction or direction given under the Appeal Rules;
- a statement as to whether the respondent would be content for the case to be dealt with without a hearing if the SDT considers it appropriate; and
- a statement as to whether the respondent opposes the appellant's case and, if so, any grounds for such opposition which are not contained in another document sent or delivered with the response.

Under rule 7(4), the respondent must send or deliver with the response:

(a) a copy of any written record of the decision, in respect of which the appeal is made, and any statement of reasons for that decision, that the appellant did not send or deliver with the notice of appeal and the respondent has or can reasonably obtain; and

(b) any documents relied upon by the respondent in making the decision in respect of which the appeal is made and which the respondent considers are relevant to the appeal.

At the same time as the respondent sends or delivers the response to the SDT, he must send or deliver:

- three additional copies of the response and accompanying documents to the SDT (rule 7(6));
- a copy of the response and accompanying documents to the appellant (rule 7(7)).

If the response is out of time, it must include a request for an extension of time and the reason why it was not sent or delivered in time (rule 7(5)).

Appellant's reply

An appellant may send or deliver to the SDT a reply to the respondent's response, and any additional documents he has relied upon in the reply, within 14 days from receipt of the respondent's response (rule 8(1) and (2)). At the same time the appellant may elect to supply a list of documents on which he is relying in support of the appeal that were not appended to the notice of appeal (rule 8(4)), and if requested by the respondent or the SDT must send or deliver copies of any of those documents to, or make any of those documents available for inspection or copying by, the respondent or SDT within seven days (rule 8(7)).

At the same time as the appellant sends or delivers the reply to the SDT, he must send or deliver:

- three additional copies of the reply and any accompanying documents to the SDT (rule 8(5));
- a copy of the reply and any accompanying documents to the respondent (rule 8(6)).

6.7.3 Case management

On the direction of the SDT, parties may be added, substituted or removed as an appellant or a respondent (Appeal Rules, rule 13).

The SDT may give a direction in relation to appeal proceedings at any time, including a direction amending, suspending or setting aside an earlier direction (rule 9(1)). In particular, the SDT may give directions to (rule 9(2)):

(a) extend or shorten the time for complying with any rule, practice direction or direction, unless such extension or shortening would conflict with a provision of another enactment (or of any rule made under another enactment) containing a time limit;
(b) consolidate or hear together two or more sets of proceedings or parts of proceedings raising common issues, or treat a case as a lead case (whether under rule 15 or otherwise);
(ba) hear any application for an Order for a Stay;
(c) permit or require a party to amend a document;
(d) permit or require a party or another person to provide documents, information or submissions which are relevant to the proceedings to the Tribunal or a party;
(e) deal with an issue in the proceedings as a preliminary issue;
(f) hold a hearing to consider any matter, including a case management issue;
(g) decide the form of any hearing;
(h) adjourn or postpone a hearing;
(i) require a party to produce a bundle for a hearing;
(j) require a party to provide a skeleton argument;
(k) decide the place and time of any hearing;
(l) make requirements about documentation and inspection;
(m) stay proceedings;
(n) suspend the effect of its own decision pending the determination by the High Court of an application for permission to appeal against, and any appeal of, that decision.

A clerk may appoint a time and place for the review of the progress of the matter and notify the parties (rule 9(3)).

The SDT may also give directions in relation to an appeal as to (rule 19(1)):

(a) the exchange between parties of lists of documents which are relevant to the appeal, or relevant to particular issues, and the inspection of such documents;
(b) the provision by parties of statements of agreed matters;
(c) issues on which it requires evidence or submissions;
(d) the nature of the evidence or submissions it requires;
(e) whether the parties are permitted or required to provide expert evidence, and if so whether the parties must jointly appoint a single expert to provide such evidence;

(f) any limit on the number of witnesses whose evidence a party may put forward, whether in relation to a particular issue or generally;
(g) the manner in which any evidence or submissions are to be provided, which may include a direction for them to be given –
  (i) orally at a hearing; or
  (ii) by written submissions or witness statement; and
(h) the time at which any evidence or submissions are to be sent or delivered.

The SDT may admit evidence whether or not the evidence would be admissible in a civil trial in the United Kingdom; or the evidence was available to a previous decision maker (rule 19(2)(a)). It may also exclude evidence that would otherwise be admissible where the evidence was not provided within the time allowed by a direction given under the Appeal Rules or a practice direction; or the evidence was otherwise provided in a manner that did not comply with such a direction; or it would otherwise be unfair, disproportionate or unnecessary in the interests of justice to admit it (rule 19(2)(b)).

The SDT may in its discretion proceed on the basis of a written statement, subject to provisions as to service, notice, and the entitlement of the other party to object (rule 20(1) and (2)). If a party is calling a witness to give oral evidence, at least 10 days before the hearing he must notify the clerk and the other party of his intention and send or deliver a witness statement with a statement of truth to the other party and lodge five copies with the clerk (rule 20(5)).

By rule 11(1) of the Appeal Rules a failure to comply with any provision of the rules, a practice direction or a direction does not render void either the appeal or any step taken in the appeal. The SDT may waive the requirement, require the failure to be remedied, exercise its power to strike out the whole or part of the appeal (see **6.7.5** below), or bar or restrict a party's participation in the appeal (rule 11(2)). An order barring or restricting a party's participation in the appeal may not be made without giving the party an opportunity to make representations in relation to the proposed action (rule 11(3)).

Where two or more appeals give rise to common or related issues of fact or law, the SDT may select one or more of the appeals as the lead case or lead cases, and direct that the other related appeals may be stayed (rule 15).

6.7.4 Private and public hearings

All hearings, including interlocutory hearings, are heard in public unless the SDT is satisfied that a public hearing would cause exceptional hardship or exceptional prejudice to a party, a witness or any other person affected by the appeal, or would prejudice the interests of justice, in which case the SDT shall conduct the hearing or part of it in private (rule 23(1) to (4)).

The SDT has the power to direct that someone be excluded from any hearing if his attendance will or is likely to prove disruptive, prevent another person from giving evidence or making submissions freely, undermine a decision by the SDT to prohibit the disclosure of a document or information, or defeat the purpose of the hearing (rule 23(5)). It may also, as it regularly does at present without an express power under the Solicitors (Disciplinary Proceedings) Rules 2007, exclude a witness until he has given evidence (rule 23(6)).

Under rule 14 of the Appeal Rules there is a power to prohibit the disclosure or publication of documents or other information likely to identify someone the SDT considers should not be identified (which is regularly if not invariably done to protect the identity of clients, by identifying them by initials alone).

Under the same rule there are more complex provisions enabling the SDT to direct that documents be withheld from a party altogether if there is a likelihood of serious harm to someone and in the interests of justice, with appropriate safeguards. The use of such powers is likely to be highly exceptional.

6.7.5 Hearings and other methods of disposal

Appeals may be disposed of without a hearing if both parties consent and the SDT considers it can properly determine the issues in this way (Appeal Rules, rule 21(1)). Otherwise, hearings are listed on the basis that at least 28 days' notice is given, unless all the parties agree and the SDT has ordered a shorter period (rule 22). Any party may appoint a representative, who need not be a legal representative (rule 28).

At the request of the parties and if it considers it appropriate, the SDT may dispose of an appeal by making a consent order, and in this event there need not be a hearing (rule 17).

Either party may withdraw the appeal or case against an appeal, but the withdrawal does not take effect until the SDT consents to it, which it may do on terms as to costs (rule 16(1) and (2)). A party may also apply to reinstate an appeal or case against an appeal, but it must do so by applying in writing to the SDT within 28 days of the notice of the withdrawal being given (whether that was by written notice or orally at a hearing) (rule 16(3) and (4)).

Under rule 12(2)(a) the SDT may strike out the whole or part of an appeal if the appellant has failed to comply with a direction which stated that a failure to comply with the direction could lead to that result (if the appeal or part of it is struck out on this basis, the appellant may apply to reinstate it, within 28 days – rule 12(4) and (5)). An appeal or part of it may also be struck out if the appellant has failed to co-operate to such an extent that the appeal cannot be dealt with fairly and justly (rule 12(2)(b)), or if the SDT considers that there is no reasonable prospect of the appellant's case, or that part of it, succeeding (rule 12(2)(c)). The same provisions apply in relation to striking out a respondent's opposition to an appeal *mutatis mutandis* (rule 12(6)).

If an appeal has been finally disposed of at a hearing at which a party neither attended in person nor was represented, that party may apply for a re-hearing under rule 25. The application must be made within 14 days of receipt of the SDT's order stating its decision. It can be expected that such applications will be dealt with in a similar way to applications made in the same circumstances under the Solicitors (Disciplinary Proceedings) Rules 2007.

6.7.6 Costs

By rule 29 of the Appeal Rules the SDT may make such order for costs as it thinks fit, at any stage of an appeal, including an order disallowing costs incurred unnecessarily, or that costs be paid by any party judged to be responsible for wasted or unnecessary costs. The SDT may order that any party bear the whole or a part or a proportion of the costs, and the amount of costs may either be fixed by the SDT or be subject to detailed assessment by a costs judge. The SDT may also make an order for costs where an appeal is withdrawn or amended.

6.7.7 Further appeals

All appeals from decisions of the SRA as a licensing authority for ABSs, whether made under Part 5 of LSA 2007 or the SRA's licensing rules, are governed by the Legal Services Act 2007 (Appeals from Licensing Authority Decisions) (No.2) Order 2011, SI 2011/2863. Article 5(3) of that Order provides that a party to such an appeal may appeal to the High Court only on a point of law arising from the decision of the SDT, and only with the permission of the High Court. The time limit for making such appeals to the High Court is a statutory limit set by the LSB under rule 6 of its Rules on the Prescribed Period for the Making of Appeals Against Decisions of a Licensing Authority Regarding Ownership of Licensed Bodies (13 June 2011) and is 28 days from the date the party is given notice of the SDT's decision. If the SDT follows its normal practice of making an immediate decision but providing full written reasons on a later date it may therefore be necessary to lodge an appeal before the reasons are available.

APPENDIX A

Legal Services Act 2007 (extracts)

Notes: Sections 20, 73, 83, 84, 86, 109 and Sched.12, para.2 are partially in force. Sections 103, 105–108 and Sched.12, paras.1, 3, 5–7 are yet to be appointed.

PART 3 RESERVED LEGAL ACTIVITIES

Reserved legal activities

12 Meaning of "reserved legal activity" and "legal activity"

(1) In this Act "reserved legal activity" means –

    (a) the exercise of a right of audience;
    (b) the conduct of litigation;
    (c) reserved instrument activities;
    (d) probate activities;
    (e) notarial activities;
    (f) the administration of oaths.

(2) Schedule 2 makes provision about what constitutes each of those activities.

(3) In this Act "legal activity" means –

    (a) an activity which is a reserved legal activity within the meaning of this Act as originally enacted, and
    (b) any other activity which consists of one or both of the following –

        (i) the provision of legal advice or assistance in connection with the application of the law or with any form of resolution of legal disputes;
        (ii) the provision of representation in connection with any matter concerning the application of the law or any form of resolution of legal disputes.

(4) But "legal activity" does not include any activity of a judicial or quasi-judicial nature (including acting as a mediator).

(5) For the purposes of subsection (3) "legal dispute" includes a dispute as to any matter of fact the resolution of which is relevant to determining the nature of any person's legal rights or liabilities.

(6) Section 24 makes provision for adding legal activities to the reserved legal activities.

Carrying on the activities

13 Entitlement to carry on a reserved legal activity

(1) The question whether a person is entitled to carry on an activity which is a reserved legal activity is to be determined solely in accordance with the provisions of this Act.

(2) A person is entitled to carry on an activity ("the relevant activity") which is a reserved legal activity where –

APPENDIX A

    (a) the person is an authorised person in relation to the relevant activity, or
    (b) the person is an exempt person in relation to that activity.

(3) Subsection (2) is subject to section 23 (transitional protection for non-commercial bodies).
(4) Nothing in this section or section 23 affects section 84 of the Immigration and Asylum Act 1999 (c. 33) (which prohibits the provision of immigration advice and immigration services except by certain persons).

Offences

14 Offence to carry on a reserved legal activity if not entitled

(1) It is an offence for a person to carry on an activity ("the relevant activity") which is a reserved legal activity unless that person is entitled to carry on the relevant activity.
(2) In proceedings for an offence under subsection (1), it is a defence for the accused to show that the accused did not know, and could not reasonably have been expected to know, that the offence was being committed.
(3) A person who is guilty of an offence under subsection (1) is liable –

    (a) on summary conviction, to imprisonment for a term not exceeding 12 months or a fine not exceeding the statutory maximum (or both), and
    (b) on conviction on indictment, to imprisonment for a term not exceeding 2 years or a fine (or both).

(4) A person who is guilty of an offence under subsection (1) by reason of an act done in the purported exercise of a right of audience, or a right to conduct litigation, in relation to any proceedings or contemplated proceedings is also guilty of contempt of the court concerned and may be punished accordingly.
(5) In relation to an offence under subsection (1) committed before the commencement of section 154(1) of the Criminal Justice Act 2003 (c. 44), the reference in subsection (3)(a) to 12 months is to be read as a reference to 6 months.

15 Carrying on of a reserved legal activity: employers and employees etc

(1) This section applies for the interpretation of references in this Act to a person carrying on an activity which is a reserved legal activity.
(2) References to a person carrying on an activity which is a reserved legal activity include a person ("E") who –

    (a) is an employee of a person ("P"), and
    (b) carries on the activity in E's capacity as such an employee.

(3) For the purposes of subsection (2), it is irrelevant whether P is entitled to carry on the activity.
(4) P does not carry on an activity ("the relevant activity") which is a reserved legal activity by virtue of E carrying it on in E's capacity as an employee of P, unless the provision of relevant services to the public or a section of the public (with or without a view to profit) is part of P's business.
(5) Relevant services are services which consist of or include the carrying on of the relevant activity by employees of P in their capacity as employees of P.
(6) Where P is an independent trade union, persons provided with relevant services do not constitute the public or a section of the public where –

(a) the persons are provided with the relevant services by virtue of their membership or former membership of P or of another person's membership or former membership of P, and
(b) the services are excepted membership services.

(7) Subject to subsection (8), "excepted membership services" means relevant services which relate to or have a connection with –

(a) relevant activities of a member, or former member, of the independent trade union;
(b) any other activities carried on for the purposes of or in connection with, or arising from, such relevant activities;
(c) any event which has occurred (or is alleged to have occurred) in the course of or in connection with such relevant activities or activities within paragraph (b);
(d) activities carried on by a person for the purposes of or in connection with, or arising from, the person's membership of the independent trade union;

and such other relevant services as the Lord Chancellor may by order specify.

(8) The Lord Chancellor may by order make provision about the circumstances in which relevant services do or do not relate to, or have a connection with, the matters mentioned in paragraphs (a) to (d) of subsection (7).
(9) Subject to that, the Lord Chancellor may by order make provision about –

(a) what does or does not constitute a section of the public;
(b) the circumstances in which the provision of relevant services to the public or a section of the public does or does not form part of P's business.

(10) The Lord Chancellor may make an order under subsection (7), (8) or (9) only on the recommendation of the Board.
(11) If P is a body, references to an employee of P include references to a manager of P.
(12) In subsection (7), "relevant activities", in relation to a person who is or was a member of an independent trade union, means any employment (including self-employment), trade, occupation or other activity to which the person's membership of the trade union relates or related.

16 Offence to carry on reserved legal activity through person not entitled

(1) Where subsection (2) applies it is an offence for a person ("P") to carry on an activity ("the relevant activity") which is a reserved legal activity, despite P being entitled to carry on the relevant activity.
(2) This subsection applies if –

(a) P carries on the relevant activity by virtue of an employee of P ("E") carrying it on in E's capacity as such an employee, and
(b) in carrying on the relevant activity, E commits an offence under section 14.

(3) If P is a body, references in subsection (2) to an employee of P include references to a manager of P.
(4) In proceedings for an offence under subsection (1), it is a defence for the accused to show that the accused took all reasonable precautions and exercised all due diligence to avoid committing the offence.
(5) A person who is guilty of an offence under subsection (1) is liable –

(a) on summary conviction, to imprisonment for a term not exceeding 12 months or a fine not exceeding the statutory maximum (or both), and
(b) on conviction on indictment, to imprisonment for a term not exceeding 2 years or a fine (or both).

APPENDIX A

(6) A person who is guilty of an offence under subsection (1) by reason of an act done in the purported exercise of a right of audience, or a right to conduct litigation, in relation to any proceedings or contemplated proceedings is also guilty of contempt of the court concerned and may be punished accordingly.

(7) In relation to an offence under subsection (1) committed before the commencement of section 154(1) of the Criminal Justice Act 2003 (c. 44), the reference in subsection (5)(a) to 12 months is to be read as a reference to 6 months.

17 Offence to pretend to be entitled

(1) It is an offence for a person –

    (a) wilfully to pretend to be entitled to carry on any activity which is a reserved legal activity when that person is not so entitled, or

    (b) with the intention of implying falsely that that person is so entitled, to take or use any name, title or description.

(2) A person who is guilty of an offence under subsection (1) is liable –

    (a) on summary conviction, to imprisonment for a term not exceeding 12 months or a fine not exceeding the statutory maximum (or both), and

    (b) on conviction on indictment, to imprisonment for a term not exceeding 2 years or a fine (or both).

(3) In relation to an offence under subsection (1) committed before the commencement of section 154(1) of the Criminal Justice Act 2003 (c. 44), the reference in subsection (2)(a) to 12 months is to be read as a reference to 6 months.

Interpretation

18 Authorised persons

(1) For the purposes of this Act "authorised person", in relation to an activity ("the relevant activity") which is a reserved legal activity, means –

    (a) a person who is authorised to carry on the relevant activity by a relevant approved regulator in relation to the relevant activity (other than by virtue of a licence under Part 5), or

    (b) a licensable body which, by virtue of such a licence, is authorised to carry on the relevant activity by a licensing authority in relation to the reserved legal activity.

(2) A licensable body may not be authorised to carry on the relevant activity as mentioned in subsection (1)(a).

(3) But where a body ("A") which is authorised as mentioned in subsection (1)(a) becomes a licensable body, the body is deemed by virtue of this subsection to continue to be so authorised from that time until the earliest of the following events –

    (a) the end of the period of 90 days beginning with the day on which that time falls;

    (b) the time from which the relevant approved regulator determines this subsection is to cease to apply to A;

    (c) the time when A ceases to be a licensable body.

(4) Subsection (2) is subject to Part 2 of Schedule 5 (by virtue of which licensable bodies may be deemed to be authorised as mentioned in subsection (1)(a) in relation to certain activities during a transitional period).

(5) A person other than a licensable body may not be authorised to carry on the relevant activity as mentioned in subsection (1)(b).
(6) But where a body ("L") which is authorised as mentioned in subsection (1)(b) ceases to be a licensable body, the body is deemed by virtue of this subsection to continue to be so authorised from that time until the earliest of the following events –

    (a) the end of the period of 90 days beginning with the day on which that time falls;
    (b) the time from which the relevant licensing authority determines this subsection is to cease to apply to L;
    (c) the time when L becomes a licensable body.

19 Exempt persons

In this Act, "exempt person", in relation to an activity ("the relevant activity") which is a reserved legal activity, means a person who, for the purposes of carrying on the relevant activity, is an exempt person by virtue of –

(a) Schedule 3 (exempt persons), or
(b) paragraph 13 or 18 of Schedule 5 (additional categories of exempt persons during transitional period).

20 Approved regulators and relevant approved regulators

(1) In this Act, the following expressions have the meaning given by this section –

"approved regulator";
"relevant approved regulator".

(2) "Approved regulator" means –

    (a) a body which is designated as an approved regulator by Part 1 of Schedule 4 or under Part 2 of that Schedule (or both) and whose regulatory arrangements are approved for the purposes of this Act, and
    (b) if an order under section 62(1)(a) has effect, the Board.

(3) An approved regulator is a "relevant approved regulator" in relation to an activity which is a reserved legal activity if –

    (a) the approved regulator is designated by Part 1, or under Part 2, of Schedule 4 in relation to that reserved legal activity, or
    (b) where the approved regulator is the Board, it is designated in relation to that reserved legal activity by an order under section 62(1)(a).

(4) An approved regulator is a "relevant approved regulator" in relation to a person if the person is authorised by the approved regulator to carry on an activity which is a reserved legal activity.
(5) Schedule 4 makes provision with respect to approved regulators other than the Board. In that Schedule –

    (a) Part 1 designates certain bodies as approved regulators in relation to certain reserved legal activities,
    (b) Part 2 makes provision for bodies to be designated by order as approved regulators in relation to one or more reserved legal activities, and
    (c) Part 3 makes provision relating to the approval of changes to an approved regulator's regulatory arrangements.

(6) An approved regulator may authorise persons to carry on any activity which is a reserved legal activity in respect of which it is a relevant approved regulator.

APPENDIX A

21 Regulatory arrangements

(1) In this Act references to the "regulatory arrangements" of a body are to –

    (a) its arrangements for authorising persons to carry on reserved legal activities,
    (b) its arrangements (if any) for authorising persons to provide immigration advice or immigration services,
    (c) its practice rules,
    (d) its conduct rules,
    (e) its disciplinary arrangements in relation to regulated persons (including its discipline rules),
    (f) its qualification regulations,
    (g) its indemnification arrangements,
    (h) its compensation arrangements,
    (i) any of its other rules or regulations (however they may be described), and any other arrangements, which apply to or in relation to regulated persons, other than those made for the purposes of any function the body has to represent or promote the interests of persons regulated by it, and
    (j) its licensing rules (if any), so far as not within paragraphs (a) to (i),

(whether or not those arrangements, rules or regulations are contained in, or made under, an enactment).

(2) In this Act –

"compensation arrangements", in relation to a body, means arrangements to provide for grants or other payments for the purposes of relieving or mitigating losses or hardship suffered by persons in consequence of –

    (a) negligence or fraud or other dishonesty on the part of any persons whom the body has authorised to carry on activities which constitute a reserved legal activity, or of employees of theirs, in connection with their activities as such authorised persons, and
    (b) failure, on the part of regulated persons, to account for money received by them in connection with their activities as such regulated persons;

"conduct rules", in relation to a body, means any rules or regulations (however they may be described) as to the conduct required of regulated persons;

"discipline rules", in relation to a body, means any rules or regulations (however they may be described) as to the disciplining of regulated persons;

"indemnification arrangements", in relation to a body, means arrangements for the purpose of ensuring the indemnification of those who are or were regulated persons against losses arising from claims in relation to any description of civil liability incurred by them, or by employees or former employees of theirs, in connection with their activities as such regulated persons;

"practice rules", in relation to a body, means any rules or regulations (however they may be described) which govern the practice of regulated persons;

"qualification regulations", in relation to a body, means –

    (a) any rules or regulations relating to –

        (i) the education and training which persons must receive, or
        (ii) any other requirements which must be met by or in respect of them,

in order for them to be authorised by the body to carry on an activity which is a reserved legal activity,

    (b) any rules or regulations relating to –

        (i) the education and training which persons must receive, or

(ii) any other requirements which must be met by or in respect of them,

in order for them to be authorised by the body to provide immigration advice or immigration services, and

(c) any other rules or regulations relating to the education and training which regulated persons must receive or any other requirements which must be met by or in respect of them,

(however they may be described).

(3) In this section "regulated persons", in relation to a body, means any class of persons which consists of or includes –

    (a) persons who are authorised by the body to carry on an activity which is a reserved legal activity;

    (b) persons who are not so authorised, but are employees of a person who is so authorised.

(4) In relation to an authorised person other than an individual, references in subsection (2) and (3) to employees of the person include managers of the person.

Continuity of existing rights and transitional protection

22 Continuity of existing rights to carry on reserved legal activities

Schedule 5 makes provision for the continuity of existing rights and for certain persons to be deemed, during a transitional period, to be authorised by approved regulators to carry on certain activities.

23 Transitional protection for non-commercial bodies

(1) During the transitional period, a body within subsection (2) is entitled to carry on any activity which is a reserved legal activity.

(2) The bodies are –

    (a) a not for profit body,

    (b) a community interest company, or

    (c) an independent trade union.

(3) The transitional period is the period which –

    (a) begins with the day appointed for the coming into force of section 13, and

    (b) ends with the day appointed by the Lord Chancellor by order for the purposes of this paragraph.

(4) Different days may be appointed under subsection (3)(b) for different purposes.

(5) An order may be made under subsection (3)(b) only on the recommendation of the Board.

Alteration of reserved legal activities

24 Extension of the reserved legal activities

(1) The Lord Chancellor may, by order, amend section 12 or Schedule 2 (reserved legal activities) so as to add any legal activity to the activities which are reserved legal activities for the purposes of this Act.

(2) An order under subsection (1) may be made only on the recommendation of the Board.

APPENDIX A

(3) Schedule 6 makes provision about the making of recommendations for the purposes of this section.
(4) Where a recommendation is made in relation to an activity, the Lord Chancellor must –
- (a) consider the report containing the recommendation given to the Lord Chancellor under paragraph 16(3)(a) of that Schedule,
- (b) decide whether or not to make an order under this section in respect of the activity, and
- (c) publish a notice of that decision,

within the period of 90 days beginning with the day on which the report was given to the Lord Chancellor.
(5) Where the Lord Chancellor decides not to make an order under this section in respect of an activity, the notice under subsection (4)(c) must state the reasons for that decision.

25 Provisional designation as approved regulators and licensing authorities

(1) The Lord Chancellor may, by order, make provision –
- (a) enabling applications to be made, considered and determined under Part 2 of Schedule 4 or Part 1 of Schedule 10 in relation to a provisional reserved activity, as if the activity were a reserved legal activity;
- (b) enabling provisional designation orders to be made by the Lord Chancellor in respect of a provisional reserved activity, as if the activity were a reserved legal activity.

(2) An order under subsection (1) may, in particular, provide that Part 2 of Schedule 4 or Part 1 of Schedule 10 is to apply, in relation to such cases as may be specified by the order, with such modifications as may be so specified.
(3) The Lord Chancellor may also, by order, make provision –
- (a) for the purpose of enabling applications for authorisation to carry on an activity which is a provisional reserved activity to be made to and considered and determined by –
  - (i) a body in respect of which a provisional designation order is made;
- (b) for the purpose of enabling persons to be deemed to be authorised to carry on an activity which is a new reserved legal activity by a relevant approved regulator in relation to the activity for a period specified in the order.

(4) For this purpose –

"provisional reserved activity" means an activity in respect of which a provisional report under paragraph 10 of Schedule 6 states that the Board is minded to make a recommendation for the purposes of section 24;

"provisional designation order" means an order made by the Lord Chancellor under Part 2 of Schedule 4 or Part 1 of Schedule 10 which is conditional upon the Lord Chancellor making an order under section 24 in respect of the provisional reserved activity, pursuant to a recommendation made by the Board following the provisional report;

"new reserved legal activity" means a legal activity which has become a reserved legal activity by virtue of an order under section 24.

26 Recommendations that activities should cease to be reserved legal activities

(1) The Board may recommend that an activity should cease to be a reserved legal activity.

LEGAL SERVICES ACT 2007 (EXTRACTS)

(2) Schedule 6 makes provision about the making of recommendations for the purposes of this section.
(3) The Lord Chancellor must consider any recommendation made by the Board for the purposes of this section (but nothing in section 208 (minor and consequential provision etc) authorises the Lord Chancellor to give effect to such a recommendation).
(4) Where the Lord Chancellor disagrees with a recommendation (or any part of it), the Lord Chancellor must publish a notice to that effect which must include the Lord Chancellor's reasons for disagreeing.

PART 5 ALTERNATIVE BUSINESS STRUCTURES

Introductory

71 Carrying on of activities by licensed bodies

(1) The provisions of this Part have effect for the purpose of regulating the carrying on of reserved legal activities and other activities by licensed bodies.
(2) In this Act "licensed body" means a body which holds a licence in force under this Part.

72 "Licensable body"

(1) A body ("B") is a licensable body if a non-authorised person –
  (a) is a manager of B, or
  (b) has an interest in B.
(2) A body ("B") is also a licensable body if –
  (a) another body ("A") is a manager of B, or has an interest in B, and
  (b) non-authorised persons are entitled to exercise, or control the exercise of, at least 10% of the voting rights in A.
(3) For the purposes of this Act, a person has an interest in a body if –
  (a) the person holds shares in the body, or
  (b) the person is entitled to exercise, or control the exercise of, voting rights in the body.
(4) A body may be licensable by virtue of both subsection (1) and subsection (2).
(5) For the purposes of this Act, a non-authorised person has an indirect interest in a licensable body if the body is licensable by virtue of subsection (2) and the non-authorised person is entitled to exercise, or control the exercise of, voting rights in A.
(6) In this Act "shares" means –
  (a) in relation to a body with a share capital, allotted shares (within the meaning of the Companies Acts);
  (b) in relation to a body with capital but no share capital, rights to share in the capital of the body;
  (c) in relation to a body without capital, interests –
    (i) conferring any right to share in the profits, or liability to contribute to the losses, of the body, or
    (ii) giving rise to an obligation to contribute to the debts or expenses of the body in the event of a winding up;

and references to the holding of shares, or to a shareholding, are to be construed accordingly.

APPENDIX A

Licensing authorities

73 Licensing authorities and relevant licensing authorities

(1) In this Act "licensing authority" means –

    (a) the Board, or

    (b) an approved regulator which is designated as a licensing authority under Part 1 of Schedule 10 and whose licensing rules are approved for the purposes of this Act.

(2) For the purposes of this Act –

    (a) the Board is a licensing authority in relation to all reserved legal activities, and

    (b) an approved regulator within subsection (1)(b) is a licensing authority in relation to any reserved legal activity in relation to which the designation is made.

(3) The Board –

    (a) may delegate any of its functions as a licensing authority to such persons as it considers appropriate;

    (b) must take such steps as are necessary to ensure an appropriate financial and organisational separation between the activities of the Board that relate to the carrying out of its functions as a licensing authority and the other activities of the Board.

(4) In this Part "relevant licensing authority" –

    (a) in relation to a licensed body, means the licensing authority by which the licensed body is authorised to carry on an activity which is a reserved legal activity;

    (b) in relation to an applicant for a licence, means the licensing authority to which the application is made.

74 Designation of approved regulator as licensing authority

Part 1 of Schedule 10 makes provision for approved regulators to be designated, by order, as licensing authorities in relation to one or more reserved legal activities.

75 Automatic cancellation of designation as licensing authority

(1) This section applies where a body is designated –

    (a) as an approved regulator in relation to a reserved legal activity ("the activity"), and

    (b) as a licensing authority in relation to the activity.

(2) If the Lord Chancellor makes an order under section 45 cancelling the body's designation as an approved regulator in relation to the activity, the body's designation as a licensing authority in relation to the activity is also cancelled.

(3) The cancellation takes effect at the same time as cancellation of the body's designation as an approved regulator.

76 Cancellation of designation as licensing authority by order

(1) The Lord Chancellor may by order cancel an approved regulator's designation as a licensing authority –

(a) in relation to all the reserved legal activities in relation to which it is designated, or
(b) in relation to one or more, but not all, of those reserved legal activities, with effect from a date specified in the order.

(2) But the Lord Chancellor may only make an order under subsection (1) in accordance with a recommendation made by the Board under subsection (3) or (5).
(3) The Board must recommend that an order is made cancelling an approved regulator's designation as a licensing authority in relation to one or more reserved legal activities, if –

(a) the approved regulator applies to the Board for such a recommendation to be made,
(b) the application is made in such form and manner as may be prescribed by rules made by the Board, and is accompanied by the prescribed fee, and
(c) the approved regulator publishes a notice giving details of the application in accordance with such requirements as may be specified in rules made by the Board.

(4) In this section "the prescribed fee", in relation to an application, means the fee specified in or determined in accordance with rules made by the Board, with the consent of the Lord Chancellor.
(5) The Board may recommend that an order is made cancelling an approved regulator's designation as a licensing authority in relation to one or more reserved legal activities if it is satisfied –

(a) that an act or omission of the licensing authority (or a series of such acts or omissions) has had, or is likely to have, an adverse impact on one or more of the regulatory objectives, and
(b) that it is appropriate to cancel the approved regulator's designation in relation to the activity or activities in question in all the circumstances of the case (including in particular the impact of cancelling the designation on the other regulatory objectives).

(6) The Board may not determine that it is appropriate to cancel an approved regulator's designation as a licensing authority in relation to an activity or activities unless it is satisfied that the matter cannot be adequately addressed by the Board exercising the powers available to it under sections 31 to 43.
(7) Part 2 of Schedule 10 makes further provision about the making of recommendations under subsection (5).
(8) If the Lord Chancellor decides not to make an order in response to a recommendation made under subsection (3) or (5), the Lord Chancellor must give the Board notice of the decision and the reasons for it.
(9) The Lord Chancellor must publish a notice given under subsection (8).

77 Cancellation of designation: further provision

(1) This section applies where an approved regulator ("the former authority") has its designation as a licensing authority in relation to one or more reserved legal activities cancelled –

(a) by virtue of section 75, or
(b) by an order under section 76.

(2) The Lord Chancellor may by order make –

(a) such modifications of provisions made by or under any enactment (including

APPENDIX A

   this Act or any enactment passed after this Act), prerogative instrument or other instrument or document, and
   (b) such transitional or consequential provision,

as the Lord Chancellor considers necessary or expedient in consequence of the cancellation.

(3) The Lord Chancellor may, by order, make transfer arrangements.

(4) "Transfer arrangements" are arrangements in accordance with which each consenting licensed body is, from the time the cancellation takes effect, treated as being authorised to carry on each protected activity by virtue of a licence issued under this Part by a licensing authority, in relation to the protected activity, which consents to the transfer arrangements.

(5) "Consenting licensed body" means a licensed body authorised by the former authority which consents to the transfer arrangements.

(6) The transfer arrangements –

   (a) must make such provision as is necessary to ensure that, where a licensed body is treated under those arrangements as being authorised to carry on a protected activity by the new authority, that licensed body is subject to the licensing rules of the new authority;
   (b) may make provision requiring amounts held by the former authority which represent amounts paid to it by way of licensing fees by the consenting licensed bodies (or a part of the amounts so held) to be paid to the new authority and treated as if they were amounts paid by those licensed bodies by way of licensing fees to the new authority.

(7) Subsection (6)(a) is subject to any transitional provision which may be made by the transfer arrangements, including provision modifying the licensing rules of the new authority as they apply to the bodies to whom the transfer arrangements apply.

(8) The Lord Chancellor may make an order under this section only if –

   (a) the Board has made a recommendation in accordance with section 78, and
   (b) the order is in the same form as, or in a form which is not materially different from, the draft order annexed to that recommendation.

(9) For the purposes of this section –

   (a) a licensed body is "authorised by the former authority" if immediately before the time the cancellation takes effect the body is, by virtue of a licence under this Part, authorised by the former authority to carry on an activity which is a reserved legal activity to which the cancellation relates, and
   (b) in relation to that body –
       (i) the activity which the body is authorised to carry on as mentioned in paragraph (a) is a "protected activity", and
       (ii) "the new authority" means the licensing authority by which (in accordance with transfer arrangements under subsection (4)) the body is treated as authorised to carry on a protected activity.

(10) In this section "licensing fee", in relation to a licensing authority, means a fee payable by a licensed body under the authority's licensing rules made in accordance with paragraph 21 of Schedule 11.

LEGAL SERVICES ACT 2007 (EXTRACTS)

78 The Board's power to recommend orders made under section 77

(1) The Board may recommend to the Lord Chancellor that the Lord Chancellor make an order under section 77 in the form of a draft order prepared by the Board and annexed to the recommendation.
(2) Before making a recommendation under this section, the Board must publish a draft of –
   (a) the proposed recommendation, and
   (b) the proposed draft order.
(3) The draft must be accompanied by a notice which states that representations about the proposals may be made to the Board within a specified period.
(4) Before making the recommendation, the Board must have regard to any representations duly made.
(5) If the draft order to be annexed to the recommendation differs from the draft published under subsection (2)(b) in a way which is, in the opinion of the Board, material, the Board must, before making the recommendation, publish the draft order along with a statement detailing the changes made and the reasons for those changes.

79 Cancellation of designation: powers of entry etc

(1) This section applies where an approved regulator ("the former authority") has its designation in relation to one or more reserved legal activities cancelled by by virtue of section 75 or an order under section 76.
(2) The Board may request the former authority to provide assistance to the new authority and the Board, for the purpose of continuing regulation.
(3) On an application by a person appointed by the Board to act on its behalf, a judge of the High Court, Circuit judge or justice of the peace may issue a warrant authorising that person to –
   (a) enter and search the premises of the former authority, and
   (b) take possession of any written or electronic records found on the premises.
(4) A person so authorised may, for the purpose of continuing regulation, take copies of written or electronic records found on a search carried out by virtue of the warrant.
(5) The judge or justice of the peace may not issue the warrant unless satisfied that its issue is necessary or desirable for the purpose of continuing regulation.
(6) The Lord Chancellor must make regulations –
   (a) specifying further matters which a judge or justice of the peace must be satisfied of, or matters which a judge or justice of the peace must have regard to, before issuing a warrant, and
   (b) regulating the exercise of a power conferred by a warrant issued under subsection (3) or by subsection (4) (whether by restricting the circumstances in which a power may be exercised, by specifying conditions to be complied with in the exercise of a power, or otherwise).
(7) Regulations under subsection (6)(b) must in particular make provision as to circumstances in which written or electronic records of which a person has taken possession by virtue of a warrant issued under subsection (3) may be copied or must be returned.
(8) But the Lord Chancellor may not make regulations under subsection (6) unless –
   (a) they are made in accordance with a recommendation made by the Board, or
   (b) the Lord Chancellor has consulted the Board about the making of the regulations.

APPENDIX A

(9) The Board must make rules as to the persons it may appoint for the purposes of subsection (3).
(10) For the purposes of this section –

"authorised by the former authority", "protected activity" and "new authority" have the same meaning as for the purposes of section 77;

"the purpose of continuing regulation" means the purpose of enabling bodies authorised by the former authority to continue to be authorised and regulated in relation to the protected activity.

Appeals

80 Functions of appellate bodies

(1) The Lord Chancellor may by order –

    (a) establish a body to hear and determine appeals from decisions, made by a person specified in the order in the person's capacity as a licensing authority, which are appealable under this Part or licensing rules made by the person;

    (b) modify, or make any other provision relating to, the functions of a body within subsection (2) or any other body, for the purpose of enabling the body to hear and determine appeals from such decisions.

(2) The bodies mentioned in subsection (1)(b) are –

    (a) the Solicitors Disciplinary Tribunal;

    (b) the Discipline and Appeals Committee established by the Council of Licensed Conveyancers under section 25 of the Administration of Justice Act 1985 (c. 61).

(3) The Lord Chancellor may make an order under subsection (1) only if –

    (a) the Board has made a recommendation in accordance with section 81,

    (b) a draft order was annexed to the recommendation, and

    (c) the order is in the same form as, or not materially different from, that draft order.

(4) An order under this section may –

    (a) make provision as to the payment of fees, and award of costs, in relation to such appeals;

    (b) modify provisions made by or under any enactment (including this Act or any Act passed after this Act), prerogative instrument or other instrument or document.

(5) Any provision made by an order under this section may be expressed to be conditional upon the person specified in the order being designated by an order under Part 1 of Schedule 10 as a licensing authority in relation to one or more reserved legal activities.

(6) The powers to make an order conferred by this section are without prejudice to any powers (statutory or non-statutory) which a body may have apart from this section.

81 Procedural requirements relating to recommendations under section 80

(1) A recommendation may be made under section 80 only with the consent of –

    (a) the person from whose decisions the appeals are to be made, and

    (b) where the recommendation is for an order under section 80(1)(b), the body to which appeals are to be made.

(2) Before making a recommendation under that section, the Board must publish a draft of –
- (a) the proposed recommendation, and
- (b) the proposed draft order.

(3) The draft must be accompanied by a notice which states that representations about the proposals may be made to the Board within a specified period.

(4) Before making any recommendation, the Board must have regard to any representations duly made.

(5) If the draft order to be annexed to the recommendation differs from the draft published under subsection (2)(b) in a way which is, in the opinion of the Board, material, the Board must, before making the recommendation, publish the draft order along with a statement detailing the changes made and the reasons for those changes.

Policy statement

82 Licensing authority policy statement

(1) Each licensing authority must prepare and issue a statement of policy as to how, in exercising its functions under this Part, it will comply with the requirements of section 28 (duties to promote regulatory objectives etc).

(2) A licensing authority may issue a statement under subsection (1) only with the approval of the Board (acting otherwise than in its capacity as an approved regulator).

(3) A licensing authority may, with the approval of the Board (acting otherwise than in its capacity as an approved regulator), alter or replace a statement issued under this section.

(4) If it does so, it must issue the altered or replacement statement.

(5) In exercising its functions under this Part, a licensing authority must have regard to the statement issued by it under this section.

(6) A licensing authority must publish a statement issued by it under this section.

Licensing rules

83 Licensing rules

(1) The Board (acting in its capacity as a licensing authority) –

- (a) must make suitable licensing rules before the end of the period of 12 months beginning with the day on which a licensable body first becomes entitled to make an application to it for a licence by virtue of a decision of the Board (acting otherwise than in its capacity as a licensing authority or as an approved regulator) under Schedule 12;
- (b) may make or modify its licensing rules only with the approval of the Board (acting otherwise than in its capacity as a licensing authority or as an approved regulator).

(2) In subsection (1)(a), "suitable licensing rules" means licensing rules which constitute suitable regulatory arrangements (within the meaning of Schedule 12) in respect of licensable bodies entitled by virtue of a decision under that Schedule to make an application to the Board for a licence.

(3) Licensing rules made by an approved regulator have effect only at a time when the approved regulator is a licensing authority (subject to any provision made by an order under section 25).

(4) Licensing rules of a licensing authority are rules as to –

APPENDIX A

      (a)   the licensing by the authority of licensable bodies, and
      (b)   the regulation by the licensing authority of licensable bodies licensed by it, and their managers and employees.

(5) Licensing rules of a licensing authority must contain –

      (a)   appropriate qualification regulations in respect of licensable bodies to which the licensing authority proposes to issue licences under this Part,
      (b)   provision as to how the licensing authority, when considering the regulatory objectives (in compliance with its duties under section 3(2) or 28(2)) in connection with an application for a licence, should take account of the objective of improving access to justice,
      (c)   appropriate arrangements (including conduct rules, discipline rules and practice rules) under which the licensing authority will be able to regulate the conduct of bodies licensed by it, and their managers and employees,
      (d)   appropriate indemnification arrangements,
      (e)   appropriate compensation arrangements,
      (f)   the provision required by sections 52 and 54 (resolution of regulatory conflict) (including those provisions as applied by section 103),
      (g)   the provision required by sections 112 and 145 (requirements imposed in relation to the handling of complaints), and
      (h)   any other provision required to be contained in licensing rules by this Act.

(6) Without prejudice to the generality of subsection (4), licensing rules of a licensing authority may contain any provision authorised by this Act.
(7) Schedule 11 makes further provision as to the contents of licensing rules.
(8) Subsections (5) to (7) are subject to –

      (a)   section 105 (which exempts trade unions from certain provisions), and
      (b)   section 106 (which provides for the modification of licensing rules in their application to bodies to which that section applies).

(9) Licensing rules may not apply to bodies to which section 106 applies in a way which is different from the way they apply to other bodies, except by virtue of an order under that section.

Licensing

84   Application for licence

(1) A licensing authority must determine any application for a licence which is made to it.
(2) The Board (acting in its capacity as a licensing authority) may determine an application for a licence which is made to it only if the applicant is entitled to make the application by virtue of a decision of the Board (acting otherwise than in its capacity as a licensing authority) under Schedule 12.
(3) A licensing authority may not grant an application for a licence unless it is satisfied that if the licence is granted the applicant will comply with its licensing rules.
(4) If the licensing authority grants an application for a licence, it must issue the licence as soon as reasonably practicable.
(5) The licence has effect from the date on which it is issued.
(6) References in this section to an application for a licence are to an application for a licence which is –

      (a)   made to a licensing authority by a licensable body, in accordance with the authority's licensing rules, and
      (b)   accompanied by the required application fee (if any).

85 Terms of licence

(1) A licence issued under section 84 must specify –

    (a) the activities which are reserved legal activities and which the licensed body is authorised to carry on by virtue of the licence, and

    (b) any conditions subject to which the licence is granted.

(2) If an order under section 106 has been made in relation to the licensed body, the licence must also specify the terms of the order.

(3) The licence may authorise the licensed body to carry on activities which are reserved legal activities only if the licensing authority is designated in relation to the reserved legal activities in question.

(4) A licence must be granted subject to the condition that –

    (a) any obligation which may from time to time be imposed on the licensed body or a person within subsection (5) by or under the licensing authority's licensing rules is complied with, and

    (b) any other obligations imposed on the licensed body or a person within that subsection by or under this or any other enactment (whether passed before or after this Act) are complied with.

(5) The persons mentioned in subsection (4) are the managers and employees of a licensed body, and non-authorised persons having an interest or an indirect interest, or holding a material interest, in the licensed body (in their capacity as such).

(6) A licence may be granted subject to such other conditions as the licensing authority considers appropriate.

(7) Those conditions may include conditions as to the non-reserved activities which the licensed body may or may not carry on.

(8) In this Part references to the terms of the licence are to the matters listed in subsections (1) and (2).

86 Modification of licence

(1) A licensing authority may modify the terms of a licence granted by it –

    (a) if the licensed body applies to the licensing authority, in accordance with its licensing rules, for it to do so;

    (b) in such other circumstances as may be specified in its licensing rules.

(2) If a licensed body is a body to which section 106 applies, the licensing authority may modify the terms of its licence in accordance with sections 106 and 107.

(3) A licensing authority modifies the terms of a licensed body's licence by giving the licensed body notice in writing of the modifications; and the modifications have effect from the time the licensing authority gives the licensed body the notice or such later time as may be specified in the notice.

(4) The licensing authority's power under this section is subject to –

    (a) section 85(3) and (4), and

    (b) licensing rules made under paragraph 6 of Schedule 11.

87 Registers of licensed bodies

(1) Each licensing authority must keep a register containing the names and places of business of all bodies which hold or have held licences granted by the licensing authority.

APPENDIX A

(2) Where any licence held by a body is for the time being suspended, the licensing authority shall cause that fact to be noted in the register in the entry for that body.
(3) A licensing authority must provide facilities for making the information contained in the entries in its register available for inspection by any person during office hours and without payment.
(4) The Board may make rules about –
   (a) the register to be kept by the Board under this section, and
   (b) the register to be kept under this section by each licensing authority designated under Part 1 of Schedule 10.
(5) Rules under subsection (4) may in particular prescribe any further information which must be contained in an entry in the register in relation to a licensed body or former licensed body.

88 Evidence of status

(1) A certificate signed by an officer of a licensing authority appointed for the purpose and stating one of the matters within subsection (2) is, unless the contrary is proved, evidence of the facts stated in the certificate.
(2) The matters are that any person does or does not, or did or did not at any time, hold a licence granted by the licensing authority under this Part.
(3) A certificate purporting to be so signed is to be taken to have been so signed unless the contrary is proved.

Ownership of licensed bodies

89 Ownership of licensed bodies

Schedule 13 makes provision about the holding of certain interests in licensed bodies by non-authorised persons.

Regulation of licensed bodies

90 Duties of non-authorised persons

A non-authorised person who is an employee or manager of a licensed body, or has an interest or an indirect interest, or holds a material interest, in a licensed body, must not do anything which causes or substantially contributes to a breach by –

(a) the licensed body, or
(b) an employee or manager of the licensed body who is an authorised person in relation to an activity which is a reserved legal activity,

of the duties imposed on them by section 176.

91 Duties of Head of Legal Practice

(1) The Head of Legal Practice of a licensed body must –
   (a) take all reasonable steps to ensure compliance with the terms of the licensed body's licence, and
   (b) as soon as reasonably practicable, report to the licensing authority any failure to comply with the terms of the licence.
(2) Subsection (1) does not apply to the terms of the licence so far as they require

compliance with licensing rules made under paragraph 20 of Schedule 11 (accounts) (as to which see section 92).

(3) The Head of Legal Practice of a licensed body must –

   (a) take all reasonable steps to ensure that the licensed body, and any of its employees or managers who are authorised persons in relation to an activity which is a reserved legal activity, comply with the duties imposed by section 176, and

   (b) as soon as reasonably practicable, report to the licensing authority such failures by those persons to comply with those duties as may be specified in licensing rules.

(4) The Head of Legal Practice of a licensed body must –

   (a) take all reasonable steps to ensure that non-authorised persons subject to the duty imposed by section 90 in relation to the licensed body comply with that duty, and

   (b) as soon as reasonably practicable, report to the licensing authority any failure by a non-authorised person to comply with that duty.

92 Duties of Head of Finance and Administration

(1) The Head of Finance and Administration of a licensed body must take all reasonable steps to ensure compliance with licensing rules made under paragraph 20 of Schedule 11 (accounts).

(2) The Head of Finance and Administration must report any breach of those rules to the licensing authority as soon as reasonably practicable.

93 Information

(1) The relevant licensing authority in relation to a licensed body may by notice require a person within subsection (2) –

   (a) to provide information, or information of a description, specified in the notice, or

   (b) produce documents, or documents of a description, specified in the notice,

   for the purpose of enabling the licensing authority to ascertain whether the terms of the licensed body's licence are being, or have been, complied with.

(2) The persons are –

   (a) the licensed body;
   (b) any manager or employee (or former manager or employee) of the licensed body;
   (c) any non-authorised person who has an interest or an indirect interest, or holds a material interest, in the licensed body.

(3) A notice under subsection (1) –

   (a) may specify the manner and form in which any information is to be provided;
   (b) must specify the period within which the information is to be provided or the document produced;
   (c) may require the information to be provided, or the document to be produced, to the licensing authority or to a person specified in the notice.

(4) The licensing authority may, by notice, require a person within subsection (2) (or a

APPENDIX A

representative of such a person) to attend at a time and place specified in the notice to provide an explanation of any information provided or document produced under this section.
(5) The licensing authority may pay to any person such reasonable costs as may be incurred by that person in connection with –

    (a) the provision of any information, or production of any document, by that person pursuant to a notice under subsection (1), or

    (b) that person's compliance with a requirement imposed under subsection (4).

(6) The licensing authority, or a person specified under subsection (3)(c) in a notice, may take copies of or extracts from a document produced pursuant to a notice under subsection (1).
(7) For the purposes of this section and section 94, references to a licensed body include a body which was, but is no longer, a licensed body.

94 Enforcement of notices under section 93

(1) Where a person is unable to comply with a notice given to the person under section 93, the person must give the licensing authority a notice to that effect stating the reasons why the person cannot comply.
(2) If a person refuses or otherwise fails to comply with a notice under section 93, the licensing authority may apply to the High Court for an order requiring the person to comply with the notice or with such directions for the like purpose as may be contained in the order.

95 Financial penalties

(1) A licensing authority may, in accordance with its licensing rules, impose on a licensed body, or a manager or employee of a licensed body, a penalty of such amount as it considers appropriate.
(2) The amount must not exceed the maximum amount prescribed under subsection (3).
(3) The Board must make rules prescribing the maximum amount of a penalty which may be imposed under this section.
(4) Rules may be made under subsection (3) only with the consent of the Lord Chancellor.
(5) A penalty under this section is payable to the licensing authority.
(6) For the purposes of this section –

    (a) references to a licensed body are to a body which was a licensed body at the time the act or omission in respect of which the penalty is imposed occurred, and

    (b) references to a manager or employee of a licensed body are to a person who was a manager or employee of a licensed body at that time,

(whether or not the body subsequently ceased to be a licensed body or the person subsequently ceased to be a manager or employee).
(7) In sections 96 and 97 references to a "penalty" are to a penalty under this section.

96 Appeals against financial penalties

(1) A person on whom a penalty is imposed under section 95 may, before the end of such period as may be prescribed by rules made by the Board, appeal to the relevant appellate body on one or more of the appeal grounds.
(2) The appeal grounds are –

(a) that the imposition of the penalty is unreasonable in all the circumstances of the case;
(b) that the amount of the penalty is unreasonable;
(c) that it is unreasonable of the licensing authority to require the penalty imposed or any portion of it to be paid by the time or times by which it was required to be paid.

(3) On any such appeal, where the relevant appellate body considers it appropriate to do so in all the circumstances of the case and is satisfied of one or more of the appeal grounds, that body may –
    (a) quash the penalty,
    (b) substitute a penalty of such lesser amount as it considers appropriate, or
    (c) in the case of the appeal ground in subsection (2)(c), substitute for any time imposed by the licensing authority a different time or times.

(4) Where the relevant appellate body substitutes a penalty of a lesser amount it may require the payment of interest on the substituted penalty at such rate, and from such time, as it considers just and equitable.

(5) Where the relevant appellate body specifies as a time by which the penalty, or a portion of the penalty, is to be paid a time before the determination of the appeal under this section it may require the payment of interest on the penalty, or portion, from that time at such rate as it considers just and equitable.

(6) A party to the appeal may appeal to the High Court on a point of law arising from the decision of the relevant appellate body, but only with the permission of the High Court.

(7) The High Court may make such order as it thinks fit.

(8) Except as provided by this section, the validity of a penalty is not to be questioned by any legal proceedings whatever.

97 Recovery of financial penalties

(1) If the whole or any part of a penalty is not paid by the time by which, in accordance with licensing rules, it is required to be paid, the unpaid balance from time to time carries interest at the rate for the time being specified in section 17 of the Judgments Act 1838 (c. 110).

(2) Where a penalty, or any portion of it, has not been paid by the time by which, in accordance with licensing rules, it is required to be paid and –
    (a) no appeal relating to the penalty has been made under section 96 during the period within which such an appeal can be made, or
    (b) an appeal has been made under that section and determined or withdrawn,

the licensing authority may recover from the person on whom the penalty was imposed, as a debt due to the licensing authority, any of the penalty and any interest which has not been paid.

(3) A licensing authority must pay into the Consolidated Fund any sum received by it as a penalty (or as interest on a penalty).

98 Referral of employees etc to appropriate regulator

(1) The relevant licensing authority may refer to an appropriate regulator any matter relating to the conduct of –
    (a) an employee or manager of a licensed body;
    (b) a person designated as a licensed body's Head of Legal Practice or Head of Finance and Administration.

APPENDIX A

(2) The licensing authority may also refer any matter relating to the conduct of such a person to the Board.
(3) Appropriate regulators are –
    (a) if the person is an authorised person in relation to a reserved legal activity, any relevant approved regulator in relation to that person, and
    (b) if the person carries on non-reserved activities, any person who exercises regulatory functions in relation to the carrying on of such activities by the person.

99 Disqualification

(1) A licensing authority may in accordance with its licensing rules disqualify a person from one or more of the activities mentioned in subsection (2) if –
    (a) the disqualification condition is satisfied in relation to the person, and
    (b) the licensing authority is satisfied that it is undesirable for the person to engage in that activity or those activities.
(2) The activities are –
    (a) acting as Head of Legal Practice of any licensed body,
    (b) acting as Head of Finance and Administration of any licensed body,
    (c) being a manager of any licensed body, or
    (d) being employed by any licensed body.
(3) The disqualification condition is satisfied in relation to a person if, in relation to a licensed body licensed by the licensing authority, the person (intentionally or through neglect) –
    (a) breaches a relevant duty to which the person is subject, or
    (b) causes, or substantially contributes to, a significant breach of the terms of the licensed body's licence.
(4) The relevant duties are –
    (a) the duties imposed on a Head of Legal Practice by section 91,
    (b) the duties imposed on a Head of Finance and Administration by section 92,
    (c) the duties imposed by section 176 on regulated persons (within the meaning of that section), and
    (d) the duty imposed on non-authorised persons by section 90.

100 Lists of disqualified persons

(1) The Board must keep lists of persons who are disqualified from –
    (a) acting as Head of Legal Practice of any licensed body,
    (b) acting as Head of Finance and Administration of any licensed body,
    (c) being a manager of any licensed body, or
    (d) being employed by any licensed body.
(2) A person is disqualified from acting in a way mentioned in subsection (1) if –
    (a) the person has been disqualified from so acting by a licensing authority under section 99, and
    (b) the disqualification continues in force.
(3) The disqualification ceases to be in force if the appropriate licensing authority so

determines, on a review or otherwise, in accordance with licensing rules made under paragraph 23 of Schedule 11.
(4) The appropriate licensing authority is –
  (a) the licensing authority which disqualified the person, or
  (b) if the person was disqualified by an approved regulator which is no longer designated as a licensing authority, the successor licensing authority.
(5) The successor licensing authority is –
  (a) the licensing authority which licenses the body in relation to which the disqualification condition (within the meaning of section 99) was satisfied in respect of the person, or
  (b) if there is no such licensing authority, the licensing authority designated by the Board on an application by the disqualified person.
(6) The Board must publish the lists kept by it under subsection (1).

101 Suspension and revocation of licence

(1) A licensing authority may, in accordance with its licensing rules, suspend or revoke any licence granted by it under this Part.
(2) A licence is to be treated as not being in force at any time while it is suspended under this section.

102 Intervention

Schedule 14 confers powers of intervention on licensing authorities.

103 Regulatory conflict and the Board as licensing authority

(1) Sections 52 and 54 (regulatory conflict between approved regulators and between approved regulators and other regulators) apply in relation to the Board in its capacity as a licensing authority and its licensing rules as they apply in relation to an approved regulator (including the Board in its capacity as approved regulator) and its regulatory arrangements.
(2) Section 68 (regulatory conflict and the Board as approved regulator) applies in relation to the Board in its capacity as a licensing authority and its licensing rules as it applies in relation to the Board in its capacity as an approved regulator and its regulatory arrangements.

104 Prevention of regulatory conflict: accounts rules

(1) Where a licensed body carries on an activity through a solicitor, the rules made under paragraph 20 of Schedule 11 apply instead of those made under sections 32 to 34 of the Solicitors Act 1974 (c. 47).
(2) Where a licensed body carries on an activity through a licensed conveyancer, the rules made under paragraph 20 of Schedule 11 apply instead of those made under sections 22 and 23 of the Administration of Justice Act 1985 (c. 61).

APPENDIX A

Special kinds of body

105 Trade union exemptions

(1) Paragraphs 11 to 14 of Schedule 11 (Head of Legal Practice and Head of Finance and Administration) do not apply in relation to a licensed body which is an independent trade union.
(2) Schedule 13 (ownership) does not apply in relation to an applicant for a licence, or a licensed body, which is an independent trade union.

106 Power to modify application of licensing rules etc to special bodies

(1) This section applies to a licensed body (or an applicant for a licence) which is –

    (a) an independent trade union,
    (b) a not for profit body,
    (c) a community interest company,
    (d) a low-risk body (see section 108), or
    (e) a body of such other description as may be prescribed by order made by the Lord Chancellor on the recommendation of the Board.

(2) A body to which this section applies may apply to the relevant licensing authority, in accordance with its licensing rules, for the authority to make an order under this section.
(3) The licensing authority may make one or both of the following orders –

    (a) that the authority's licensing rules apply in relation to the body with such modifications as may be specified in the order;
    (b) that Schedule 13 does not apply in relation to the body, or applies in relation to the body with such modifications as may be specified in the order.

(4) On an application under subsection (2), the licensing authority may make any order which the authority –

    (a) has power to make under subsection (3), and
    (b) considers appropriate in all the circumstances of the case,

whether or not it is the order for which the applicant applied.

(5) In deciding what order (if any) is appropriate in all the circumstances of the case, the licensing authority must in particular have regard to –

    (a) the reserved legal activities and non-reserved activities which the body carries on (or proposes to carry on),
    (b) the nature of the persons to whom the body provides (or proposes to provide) services,
    (c) any non-authorised persons who have an interest or an indirect interest in the licensed body or hold a material interest in the licensed body, or are managers of the body, and
    (d) any other matter specified in the authority's licensing rules.

(6) If the licensing authority makes an order under subsection (3), the authority's licensing rules or Schedule 13 or both (as the case may be) have effect in relation to that body in accordance with that order.
(7) The licensing authority may not make an order under subsection (3)(a) in relation to provisions of its licensing rules made in accordance with the following paragraphs of Schedule 11 –

    (a) paragraphs 2 and 3 (determination and review of applications for a licence);
    (b) paragraphs 7 and 8 (applications under this section);

(c) paragraphs 9(3), 18 and 23 (disqualifications);
(d) paragraph 10(2) (management);
(e) paragraph 16 (carrying on of licensed activities);
(f) paragraph 24(1), (2), (3) and (8) (grounds for suspending and revoking licences);
(g) paragraph 24(10) and (11) (procedure for suspending or revoking licence);
(h) paragraph 26(2) (review of decision to suspend or revoke licence).

(8) The licensing authority may not make an order under subsection (3)(a) which results in its licensing rules, as they apply in relation to the body to which the order relates, not making the provision required by –

(a) section 83(5)(a) to (g);
(b) paragraph 1 of Schedule 11 (applications for licences);
(c) paragraph 4(3) of that Schedule (renewal of licences);
(d) paragraph 6 of that Schedule (modification of licence);
(e) paragraph 20 of that Schedule (accounts).

(9) If the licensing authority's licensing rules, as they apply in relation to a body to which an order under subsection (3)(a) relates, make provision requiring the body to have –

(a) a Head of Legal Practice approved by the licensing authority, or
(b) a Head of Finance and Administration approved by the licensing authority,

they must also provide for a review by the licensing authority of any decision by it to refuse or withdraw that approval.

107 Modifications under section 106: supplementary

(1) This section applies where a licensing authority has made an order under section 106 in relation to a body to which that section applies.
(2) The licensing authority must revoke the order under section 106 if it becomes aware that the body in respect of which the order was made is no longer a body to which that section applies.
(3) The licensing authority may revoke or otherwise modify an order under section 106 –

(a) on the application of the body in relation to which the order was made, or
(b) of its own motion.

(4) It may do so only if it considers it appropriate to do so in all the circumstances of the case, having regard to the matters mentioned in section 106(5).

108 "Low risk body"

(1) A body ("B") is a low risk body if the management condition and the ownership condition are satisfied in relation to it.
(2) The management condition is that the number of managers of the body who are within subsection (4) is less than 10% of the total number of managers.
(3) The ownership condition is that –

(a) the proportion of shares in B held by persons within subsection (4) is less than 10%, and
(b) the proportion of the voting rights in B which such persons are entitled to exercise, or control the exercise of, is less than 10%, and
(c) if B has a parent undertaking ("P") –

(i) the proportion of shares in P held by such persons is less than 10%, and

APPENDIX A

    (ii) the proportion of the voting rights in P which such persons are entitled to exercise, or control the exercise of, is less than 10%.

(4) The persons within this subsection are –
  (a) non-authorised persons;
  (b) licensed bodies.

(5) For the purposes of this section "parent undertaking" has the same meaning as in the Financial Services and Markets Act 2000 (c. 8) (see section 420 of that Act).

109 Foreign bodies

The Lord Chancellor may by order make provision for the modification of any provision of this Part in its application to a body of persons formed under, or in so far as the body is recognised by, law having effect outside England and Wales.

Supplementary provision

110 Reporting requirements relating to Part 5

(1) The Board's annual report must deal with how, in the Board's opinion, the activities of licensing authorities and licensed bodies have affected the regulatory objectives.

(2) This section does not apply to an annual report for a financial year before the first financial year in which a licence is issued under this Part.

(3) In this section "annual report" and "financial year" have the same meaning as in section 6.

111 Interpretation of Part 5

(1) In this Part –

  "licensed activity", in relation to a licensed body, means an activity –
    (a) which is a reserved legal activity, and
    (b) which the licensed body is authorised to carry on by virtue of its licence;

  "non-authorised person" means a person who is not within subsection (2);
  "non-reserved activity" means an activity which is not a reserved legal activity;
  "relevant appellate body", in relation to decisions made by a licensing authority under this Part, means the body having power to hear appeals from those decisions (whether by virtue of an order under section 80 or otherwise).

(2) The following persons are within this subsection –
  (a) an authorised person in relation to an activity which constitutes a reserved legal activity,
  (b) a registered foreign lawyer (within the meaning of section 89 of the Courts and Legal Services Act 1990 (c. 41)),
  (c) a person entitled to pursue professional activities under a professional title to which the Directive applies in a state to which the Directive applies (other than the title of barrister or solicitor in England and Wales),
  (d) a body which provides professional services such as are provided by persons within paragraph (a) or lawyers of other jurisdictions, and all the managers of which and all the persons with an interest in which –
    (i) are within paragraphs (a) to (c), or

(ii) are bodies in which persons within paragraphs (a) to (c) are entitled to exercise, or control the exercise of, more than 90% of the voting rights.

(3) In subsection (2)(c) "the Directive" means Directive 98/5/EC of the European Parliament and the Council, to facilitate practice of the profession of lawyer on a permanent basis in a Member State other than that in which the qualification was obtained.

SCHEDULE 2 THE RESERVED LEGAL ACTIVITIES

Section 12

Introduction

1   This Schedule makes provision about the reserved legal activities.
2   In this Schedule "the appointed day" means the day appointed for the coming into force of section 13 (entitlement to carry on reserved legal activities).

Rights of audience

3   (1) A "right of audience" means the right to appear before and address a court, including the right to call and examine witnesses.

    (2) But a "right of audience" does not include a right to appear before or address a court, or to call or examine witnesses, in relation to any particular court or in relation to particular proceedings, if immediately before the appointed day no restriction was placed on the persons entitled to exercise that right.

Conduct of litigation

4   (1) The "conduct of litigation" means –

      (a) the issuing of proceedings before any court in England and Wales,
      (b) the commencement, prosecution and defence of such proceedings, and
      (c) the performance of any ancillary functions in relation to such proceedings (such as entering appearances to actions).

    (2) But the "conduct of litigation" does not include any activity within paragraphs (a) to (c) of sub-paragraph (1), in relation to any particular court or in relation to any particular proceedings, if immediately before the appointed day no restriction was placed on the persons entitled to carry on that activity.

Reserved instrument activities

5   (1) "Reserved instrument activities" means –

      (a) preparing any instrument of transfer or charge for the purposes of the Land Registration Act 2002 (c. 9);
      (b) making an application or lodging a document for registration under that Act;
      (c) preparing any other instrument relating to real or personal estate for the purposes of the law of England and Wales or instrument relating to court proceedings in England and Wales.

    (2) But "reserved instrument activities" does not include the preparation of an

APPENDIX A

          instrument relating to any particular court proceedings if, immediately before the appointed day, no restriction was placed on the persons entitled to carry on that activity.

    (3)   In this paragraph "instrument" includes a contract for the sale or other disposition of land (except a contract to grant a short lease), but does not include –

        (a)   a will or other testamentary instrument,
        (b)   an agreement not intended to be executed as a deed, other than a contract that is included by virtue of the preceding provisions of this sub-paragraph,
        (c)   a letter or power of attorney, or
        (d)   a transfer of stock containing no trust or limitation of the transfer.

    (4)   In this paragraph a "short lease" means a lease such as is referred to in section 54(2) of the Law of Property Act 1925 (c. 20) (short leases).

Probate activities

6   (1)   "Probate activities" means preparing any probate papers for the purposes of the law of England and Wales or in relation to any proceedings in England and Wales.

    (2)   In this paragraph "probate papers" means papers on which to found or oppose –

        (a)   a grant of probate, or
        (b)   a grant of letters of administration.

Notarial activities

7   (1)   "Notarial activities" means activities which, immediately before the appointed day, were customarily carried on by virtue of enrolment as a notary in accordance with section 1 of the Public Notaries Act 1801 (c. 79).

    (2)   Sub-paragraph (1) does not include activities carried on –

        (a)   by virtue of section 22 or 23 of the Solicitors Act 1974 (c. 47) (reserved instrument activities and probate activities), or
        (b)   by virtue of section 113 of the Courts and Legal Services Act 1990 (c. 41) (administration of oaths).

Administration of oaths

8   The "administration of oaths" means the exercise of the powers conferred on a commissioner for oaths by –

        (a)   the Commissioners for Oaths Act 1889 (c. 10);
        (b)   the Commissioners for Oaths Act 1891 (c. 50);
        (c)   section 24 of the Stamp Duties Management Act 1891 (c. 38).

LEGAL SERVICES ACT 2007 (EXTRACTS)

SCHEDULE 3   EXEMPT PERSONS

Section 19

Rights of audience

1   (1) This paragraph applies to determine whether a person is an exempt person for the purpose of exercising a right of audience before a court in relation to any proceedings (subject to paragraph 7).

(2) The person is exempt if the person –

(a) is not an authorised person in relation to that activity, but
(b) has a right of audience granted by that court in relation to those proceedings.

(3) The person is exempt if the person –

(a) is not an authorised person in relation to that activity, but
(b) has a right of audience before that court in relation to those proceedings granted by or under any enactment.

(4) The person is exempt if the person is the Attorney General or the Solicitor General and –

(a) the name of the person is on the roll kept by the Law Society under section 6 of the Solicitors Act 1974 (c. 47), or
(b) the person has been called to the Bar by an Inn of Court.

(5) The person is exempt if the person is the Advocate General for Scotland and is admitted –

(a) as a solicitor in Scotland under section 6 of the Solicitors (Scotland) Act 1980 (c. 46), or
(b) to practise as an advocate before the courts of Scotland.

(6) The person is exempt if the person –

(a) is a party to those proceedings, and
(b) would have a right of audience, in the person's capacity as such a party, if this Act had not been passed.

(7) The person is exempt if –

(a) the person is an individual whose work includes assisting in the conduct of litigation,
(b) the person is assisting in the conduct of litigation –

  (i) under instructions given (either generally or in relation to the proceedings) by an individual to whom sub-paragraph (8) applies, and
  (ii) under the supervision of that individual, and

(c) the proceedings are being heard in chambers in the High Court or a county court and are not reserved family proceedings.

(8) This sub-paragraph applies to –

(a) any authorised person in relation to an activity which constitutes the conduct of litigation;
(b) any person who by virtue of section 193 is not required to be entitled to carry on such an activity.

APPENDIX A

(9) The person is an exempt person in relation to the exercise of a right of audience in proceedings on an appeal from the Comptroller-General of Patents, Designs and Trade Marks to the Patents Court under the Patents Act 1977 (c. 37), if the person is a solicitor of the Court of Judicature of Northern Ireland.

(10) For the purposes of this paragraph –

"family proceedings" has the same meaning as in the Matrimonial and Family Proceedings Act 1984 (c. 42) and also includes any other proceedings which are family proceedings for the purposes of the Children Act 1989 (c. 41);

"reserved family proceedings" means such category of family proceedings as the Lord Chancellor may, after consulting the President of the Law Society and with the concurrence of the President of the Family Division, by order prescribe;

and any order made under section 27(9) of the Courts and Legal Services Act 1990 (c. 41) before the day appointed for the coming into force of this paragraph is to have effect on and after that day as if it were an order made under this sub-paragraph.

Conduct of litigation

2   (1) This paragraph applies to determine whether a person is an exempt person for the purpose of carrying on any activity which constitutes the conduct of litigation in relation to any proceedings (subject to paragraph 7).

(2) The person is exempt if the person –

(a) is not an authorised person in relation to that activity, but
(b) has a right to conduct litigation granted by a court in relation to those proceedings.

(3) The person is exempt if the person –

(a) is not an authorised person in relation to that activity, but
(b) has a right to conduct litigation in relation to those proceedings granted by or under any enactment.

(4) The person is exempt if the person –

(a) is a party to those proceedings, and
(b) would have a right to conduct the litigation, in the person's capacity as such a party, if this Act had not been passed.

(5) The person is an exempt person in relation to any activity which is carried on in or in connection with proceedings on an appeal from the Comptroller-General of Patents, Designs and Trade Marks to the Patents Court under the Patents Act 1977 (c. 37), if the person is a solicitor of the Court of Judicature of Northern Ireland.

Reserved instrument activities

3   (1) This paragraph applies to determine whether a person is an exempt person for the purpose of carrying on any activity which constitutes reserved instrument activities (subject to paragraph 7).

(2) The person is exempt if the person prepares the instruments or applications in the course of the person's duty as a public officer.

(3) The person ("E") is exempt if –

LEGAL SERVICES ACT 2007 (EXTRACTS)

    (a)   E is an individual,
    (b)   E carries on the activity at the direction and under the supervision of another individual ("P"),
    (c)   when E does so, P and E are connected, and
    (d)   P is entitled to carry on the activity, otherwise than by virtue of sub-paragraph (10).

(4) For the purposes of sub-paragraph (3), P and E are connected if –

    (a)   P is E's employer,
    (b)   P is a fellow employee of E,
    (c)   P is a manager or employee of a body which is an authorised person in relation to the activity, and E is also a manager or employee of that body.

(5) If the person is an accredited person, the person is exempt to the extent that the activity consists of the preparation of any instrument –

    (a)   which creates, or which the person believes on reasonable grounds will create, a farm business tenancy (within the meaning of the Agricultural Tenancies Act 1995 (c. 8)), or
    (b)   which relates to an existing tenancy which is, or which the person believes on reasonable grounds to be, such a tenancy.

(6) In sub-paragraph (5) "accredited person" means a person who is –

    (a)   a Fellow of the Central Association of Agricultural Valuers, or
    (b)   a Member or Fellow of the Royal Institution of Chartered Surveyors.

(7) The person is exempt to the extent that the activity carried on by the person is also a reserved legal activity within sub-paragraph (8) and the person is –

    (a)   authorised to carry on that activity (other than under Part 5) by a relevant approved regulator in relation to the activity,
    (b)   authorised to carry on that activity by a licence under Part 5, or
    (c)   an exempt person in relation to that activity by virtue of paragraph 1 or 2 of this Schedule.

(8) The activities are –

    (a)   the exercise of a right of audience;
    (b)   the conduct of litigation.

(9) The person is exempt if the person is employed merely to engross the instrument or application.

(10) The person is exempt if the person is an individual who carries on the activity otherwise than for, or in expectation of, any fee, gain or reward.

(11) The person is exempt if –

    (a)   the person is a person qualified to practise as a solicitor in Scotland in accordance with section 4 of the Solicitors (Scotland) Act 1980 (c. 46), and
    (b)   the reserved instrument activities fall within paragraph 5(1)(c) of Schedule 2 (preparation of certain instruments relating to real or personal property or legal proceedings).

Probate activities

4   (1)   This paragraph applies to determine whether a person is an exempt person for

APPENDIX A

            the purpose of carrying on any activity which constitutes probate activities (subject to paragraph 7).

    (2)   The person ("E") is an exempt person if –

         (a)   E is an individual,

         (b)   E provides the probate activities at the direction and under the supervision of another individual ("P"),

         (c)   when E does so, P and E are connected, and

         (d)   P is entitled to carry on the activity, otherwise than by virtue of sub-paragraph (4).

    (3)   For the purposes of sub-paragraph (2), P and E are connected if –

         (a)   P is E's employer,

         (b)   P is a fellow employee of E,

         (c)   P is a manager or employee of a body which is an authorised person in relation to the activity, and E is also a manager or employee of that body.

    (4)   The person is exempt if the person is an individual who carries on the activity otherwise than for, or in expectation of, any fee, gain or reward.

Notarial activities

5   (1)   This paragraph applies to determine whether a person is an exempt person for the purpose of carrying on any activity which constitutes notarial activities (subject to paragraph 7).

    (2)   The person is exempt if the person is not an authorised person in relation to that activity under this Act, but is authorised to carry on that activity by or by virtue of any other enactment.

    (3)   The person is exempt if section 14 of the Public Notaries Act 1801 (c. 79) applies to the person, and

         (a)   where that section applies by virtue of the person holding or exercising an office or appointment, the person carries on the activity for ecclesiastical purposes;

         (b)   where that section applies by virtue of the person performing a public duty or service under government, the person carries on the activity in the course of performing that duty or service.

    (4)   The person is exempt if the person is an individual who carries on the notarial activities otherwise than for or in expectation of a fee, gain or reward.

Administration of oaths

6   (1)   This paragraph applies to determine whether a person is an exempt person for the purpose of carrying on any activity which constitutes the administration of oaths (subject to paragraph 7).

    (2)   The person is exempt if the person is not an authorised person in relation to that activity under this Act, but is authorised to carry on that activity by or by virtue of any other enactment.

    (3)   The person is exempt if the person has a commission under section 1(1) of the Commissioners for Oaths Act 1889 (c. 10).

European lawyers

7   A European lawyer (within the meaning of the European Communities (Services of

Lawyers) Order 1978 (S.I. 1978/1910)) is an exempt person for the purposes of carrying on an activity which is a reserved legal activity and which the European lawyer is entitled to carry on by virtue of that order.

Employers etc acting through exempt person

8 (1) This paragraph applies where –

    (a) a person ("P") carries on an activity ("the relevant activity") which is a reserved legal activity,

    (b) P carries on the relevant activity by virtue of an employee of P ("E") carrying it on in E's capacity as such an employee, and

    (c) E is an exempt person in relation to the relevant activity.

(2) P is an exempt person in relation to the relevant activity to the extent that P carries on that activity by virtue of E so carrying it on.

(3) This paragraph does not apply where E –

    (a) carries on the relevant activity at the direction and under the supervision of an authorised person in relation to that activity, and

    (b) is exempt in relation to that activity by virtue of paragraph 1(7), 3(3) or 4(2).

(4) If P is a body, in this paragraph references to an employee of P include references to a manager of P.

Further exempt persons

9 (1) The Lord Chancellor may, by order, amend this Schedule so as to provide –

    (a) for persons to be exempt persons in relation to any activity which is a reserved legal activity (including any activity which is a reserved legal activity by virtue of an order under section 24 (extension of reserved legal activities)),

    (b) for persons to cease to be such persons, or

    (c) for the amendment of any provision made in respect of an exempt person.

(2) The Lord Chancellor may make an order under sub-paragraph (1) only on the recommendation of the Board.

SCHEDULE 4   APPROVED REGULATORS

Section 20

PART 1   EXISTING REGULATORS

1 (1) Each body listed in the first column of the Table in this paragraph is an approved regulator.

(2) Each body so listed is an approved regulator in relation to the reserved legal activities listed in relation to it in the second column of the Table.

APPENDIX A

Table

Approved regulator	Reserved legal activities
The Law Society	The exercise of a right of audience. The conduct of litigation. Reserved instrument activities. Probate activities. The administration of oaths.
The General Council of the Bar	The exercise of a right of audience. The conduct of litigation. Reserved instrument activities. Probate activities. The administration of oaths.
The Master of the Faculties	Reserved instrument activities. Probate activities. Notarial activities. The administration of oaths.
The Institute of Legal Executives	The exercise of a right of audience. The administration of oaths.
The Council for Licensed Conveyancers	Reserved instrument activities. The administration of oaths. Probate activities.
The Chartered Institute of Patent Attorneys	The exercise of a right of audience. The conduct of litigation. Reserved instrument activities. The administration of oaths.
The Institute of Trade Mark Attorneys	The exercise of a right of audience. The conduct of litigation. Reserved instrument activities. The administration of oaths.
The Association of Law Costs Draftsmen	The exercise of a right of audience. The conduct of litigation. The administration of oaths.
The Institute of Chartered Accountants of Scotland	Probate activities.
The Association of Chartered Certified Accountants	Probate activities.

2   (1) The regulatory arrangements of a listed body, as they have effect immediately before paragraph 1 comes into force, are to be treated as having been approved by the Board for the purposes of this Act at the time that paragraph comes into force.

    (2) "Listed body" means a body listed in the first column of the Table in paragraph 1 as that Table has effect at the time that paragraph comes into force.

    (3) Sub-paragraph (1) is without prejudice to the Board's power to give directions under section 32 (powers to direct an approved regulator to take steps in certain circumstances, including steps to amend its regulatory arrangements).

LEGAL SERVICES ACT 2007 (EXTRACTS)

SCHEDULE 11 LICENSING RULES

Section 83

PART 1 LICENSING PROCEDURE

Applications for licences

1 (1) Licensing rules must make provision about the form and manner in which applications for licences are to be made, and the fee (if any) which is to accompany an application
   (2) They may make provision about –

   (a) the information which applications must contain, and
   (b) the documents which must accompany applications.

Determination of applications

2 (1) Licensing rules must make the following provision about the determination of applications for licences.
   (2) Before the end of the decision period the licensing authority must –

   (a) decide the application,
   (b) notify the applicant of its decision, and
   (c) if it decides to refuse the application, set out in the notice the reasons for the refusal.

   (3) The decision period is the period of 6 months beginning with the day on which the application is made to the licensing authority in accordance with its licensing rules.
   (4) The licensing authority may, on one or more occasions, give the applicant a notice (an "extension notice") extending the decision period by a period specified in the notice.
   (5) But –

   (a) an extension notice may only be given before the time when the decision period would end, but for the extension notice, and
   (b) the total decision period must not exceed 9 months.

   (6) An extension notice must set out the reasons for the extension.

Review of determination

3 Licensing rules must make provision for review by the licensing authority of –

   (a) a decision to refuse an application for a licence;
   (b) if a licence is granted, the terms of the licence.

Period of licence and renewal

4 (1) The licensing rules may make provision –

   (a) limiting the period for which any licence is (subject to the provision of this Part of this Schedule and of the licensing rules) to remain in force;
   (b) about the renewal of licences, including provision about the form and

APPENDIX A

   manner in which an application for the renewal is to be made, and the fee (if any) which is to accompany an application.

(2) The licensing rules may make provision about –

   (a) the information which applications for renewal must contain, and
   (b) the documents which must accompany applications.

(3) Licensing rules must provide that a licence issued to a licensed body by the licensing authority ceases to have effect if the licensed body is issued with a licence by another licensing authority.

Continuity of licences

5 (1) Licensing rules may make provision about the effect, on a licence issued to a partnership or other unincorporated body ("the existing body"), of any change in the membership of the existing body.
   (2) The provision which may be made includes provision for the existing body's licence to be transferred where the existing body ceases to exist and another body succeeds to the whole or substantially the whole of its business.

Modification of licences

6 (1) Licensing rules must make provision about the form and manner in which applications are to be made for modification of the terms of a licence under section 86, and the fee (if any) which is to accompany the application.
   (2) They may make provision as to the circumstances in which the licensing authority may modify the terms of a licence under section 86 without an application being made.
   (3) They must make provision for review by the licensing authority of –

   (a) a decision to refuse an application for modification of the terms of a licence;
   (b) if the licensing authority makes licensing rules under sub-paragraph (2), a decision under those rules to modify the terms of a licence.

Modifications under section 106 or 107

7 (1) Licensing rules must make provision about the form and manner in which applications are to be made under section 106 or 107, and the fee (if any) which is to accompany the application.
   (2) They may make provision as to the matters to which the licensing authority must have regard in determining whether to make an order under section 106, or to revoke or modify such an order.
   (3) They must make provision for review by the licensing authority of –

   (a) a decision to refuse an application under those sections;
   (b) the terms of any order made under section 106 or any decision under section 107.

8 (1) Licensing rules must make the following provision in relation to licensed bodies to which section 106 applies ("special bodies"), and in relation to which an order under section 106 has been made.
   (2) If a special body becomes a special body of a different kind, it must notify the licensing authority of that fact before the end of the relevant period.

(3) If a special body ceases to be a special body, it must notify the licensing authority of that fact before the end of the relevant period.
(4) The relevant period is the period of 30 days (or such longer period as may be specified in licensing rules) beginning with the day on which the body first became a special body of a different kind, or ceased to be a special body.
(5) Licensing rules may make provision requiring a special body to provide the licensing authority with such information relevant to the matters mentioned in section 106(5) as may be specified in the licensing rules.

PART 2   STRUCTURAL REQUIREMENTS

Management

9 (1) Licensing rules must require a licensed body to comply with the following requirement at all times.
   (2) At least one of the licensed body's managers must be a person (other than a licensed body) who is an authorised person in relation to a licensed activity.
   (3) No manager of the licensed body may be a person who under this Part of this Act is disqualified from acting as a manager of a licensed body.

10 (1) Licensing rules may make further provision as to –
   (a) the managers of licensed bodies, and
   (b) the arrangements for the management by them of the licensed body and its activities.
   (2) They must not require all the managers of a licensed body to be authorised persons in relation to a reserved legal activity.

Head of Legal Practice

11 (1) Licensing rules must include the following requirements.
   (2) A licensed body must at all times have an individual –
   (a) who is designated as Head of Legal Practice, and
   (b) whose designation is approved by the licensing authority.
   (3) A designation of an individual as Head of Legal Practice has effect only while the individual –
   (a) consents to the designation,
   (b) is an authorised person in relation to one or more of the licensed activities, and
   (c) is not under this Part of this Act disqualified from acting as Head of Legal Practice of a licensed body.
   (4) The licensing authority may approve a person's designation only if it is satisfied that the person is a fit and proper person to carry out the duties imposed by section 91 in relation to that body.
   (5) The licensing authority may approve a person's designation in the course of determining an application for a licence under section 84.
   (6) If the licensing authority is satisfied that the person designated as a licensed body's Head of Legal Practice has breached a duty imposed by section 91, it may withdraw its approval of that person's designation.

12 (1) Licensing rules must make provision –

APPENDIX A

        (a)   about the procedures and criteria that will be applied by the licensing authority when determining under paragraph 11(4) whether an individual is a fit and proper person;
        (b)   for a review by the licensing authority of a determination under that paragraph that an individual is not a fit and proper person;
        (c)   about the procedures and criteria that will be applied by the licensing authority in determining under paragraph 11(6) whether to withdraw its approval;
        (d)   for a review by the licensing authority of a determination under that paragraph to withdraw its approval;
        (e)   about the procedure which is to apply where a licensed body ceases to comply with the requirement imposed by virtue of paragraph 11(2).

(2)   Rules made in accordance with sub-paragraph (1)(e) may in particular provide that the requirement imposed by virtue of paragraph 11(2) is suspended until such time as may be specified by the licensing authority if the licensed body complies with such other requirements as may be specified in the rules.

Head of Finance and Administration

13   (1)   Licensing rules must include the following requirements.
     (2)   A licensed body must at all times have an individual –

        (a)   who is designated as Head of Finance and Administration, and
        (b)   whose designation is approved by the licensing authority.

     (3)   A designation of an individual as Head of Finance and Administration has effect only while the individual –

        (a)   consents to the designation, and
        (b)   is not under this Part of this Act disqualified from acting as Head of Finance and Administration of a licensed body.

     (4)   The licensing authority may approve a person's designation only if it is satisfied that the person is a fit and proper person to carry out the duties imposed by section 92 in relation to that body.
     (5)   The licensing authority may approve a person's designation in the course of determining an application for a licence under section 84.
     (6)   If the licensing authority is satisfied that the person designated as a licensed body's Head of Finance and Administration has breached a duty imposed by section 92, it may withdraw its approval of that person's designation.

14   (1)   Licensing rules must make provision –

        (a)   about the procedures and criteria that will be applied by the licensing authority when determining under paragraph 13(4) whether an individual is a fit and proper person;
        (b)   for a review by the licensing authority of a determination under that paragraph that an individual is not a fit and proper person;
        (c)   about the procedures and criteria that will be applied by the licensing authority in determining under paragraph 13(6) whether to withdraw its approval;
        (d)   for a review by the licensing authority of a determination under that paragraph to withdraw its approval;
        (e)   about the procedure which is to apply where a licensed body ceases to comply with the requirement imposed by virtue of paragraph 13(2).

(2) The rules made in accordance with sub-paragraph (1)(e) may in particular provide that the requirement imposed by virtue of sub-paragraph 13(2) is suspended until such time as may be specified by the licensing authority if the licensed body complies with such other requirements as may be specified in the rules.

PART 3   PRACTICE REQUIREMENTS

Practising address

15   (1)   Licensing rules must require a licensed body, other than one to which sub-paragraph (3) applies, at all times to have a practising address in England and Wales.
(2) For this purpose "practising address", in relation to a licensed body, means an address from which the body provides services which consist of or include the carrying on of reserved legal activities.
(3) This sub-paragraph applies to a licensed body –
   (a) which is a company or limited liability partnership, and
   (b) the registered office of which is situated in England and Wales (or in Wales).

Licensed activities

16   Licensing rules must provide that a licensed body may carry on a licensed activity only through a person who is entitled to carry on the activity.

Compliance with regulatory arrangements etc

17   (1)   Licensing rules must include the following provision.
(2) A licensed body must at all times have suitable arrangements in place to ensure that –
   (a) it, and its managers and employees, comply with the duties imposed by section 176, and
   (b) it, and any person to whom sub-paragraph (3) applies, maintain the professional principles set out in section 1(3).
(3) This sub-paragraph applies to any manager or employee of the licensed body who is an authorised person in relation to an activity which is a reserved legal activity.
(4) A licensed body must at all times have suitable arrangements in place to ensure that non-authorised persons subject to the duty imposed by section 90 in relation to the licensed body comply with that duty.
(5) Licensing rules may make provision as to the arrangements which are suitable for the purposes of rules made under sub-paragraphs (2) and (4).

Disqualified employees

18   (1)   Licensing rules must include the following requirement.
(2) A licensed body may not employ a person who under this Part of this Act is disqualified from being an employee of a licensed body.

APPENDIX A

Indemnification arrangements and compensation arrangements

19   (1)   For the purpose of giving effect to indemnification arrangements and compensation arrangements, licensing rules may –

        (a)   authorise or require the licensing authority to establish and maintain a fund or funds;

        (b)   authorise or require the licensing authority to take out and maintain insurance with authorised insurers;

        (c)   require licensed bodies or licensed bodies of any specific description to take out and maintain insurance with authorised insurers.

   (2)   In this paragraph "authorised insurer" has the same meaning as in section 64.

Accounts

20   (1)   The licensing rules must make provision as to the treatment of money within sub-paragraph (2), and the keeping of accounts in respect of such money.

   (2)   The money referred to in sub-paragraph (1) is money (including money held on trust) which is received, held or dealt with by the licensed body, its managers and employees for clients or other persons.

PART 4   REGULATION

Fees

21   (1)   The licensing rules must require licensed bodies to pay periodical fees to the licensing authority.

   (2)   The rules may provide for the payment of different fees by different descriptions of licensed body.

Financial penalties

22   The licensing rules must make provision as to –

        (a)   the acts and omissions in respect of which the licensing authority may impose a penalty under section 95, and

        (b)   the criteria and procedure to be applied by the licensing authority in determining whether to impose a penalty under that section, and the amount of any penalty.

Disqualifications

23   (1)   Licensing rules must make provision as to the criteria and procedure to be applied by the licensing authority in determining whether a person should be disqualified under section 99.

   (2)   Licensing rules must make provision –

        (a)   for a review by the licensing authority of a determination by the licensing authority that a person should be disqualified;

        (b)   as to the criteria and procedure to be applied by the licensing authority in determining whether a person's disqualification should cease to be in force;

LEGAL SERVICES ACT 2007 (EXTRACTS)

    (c)   requiring the licensing authority to notify the Board of any determination by the licensing authority that a person should be disqualified, of the results of any review of that determination, and of any decision by the licensing authority that a person's disqualification should cease to be in force.

Suspension or revocation of licence under section 101

24   (1)   Licensing rules must make the following provision.
      (2)   The licensing authority may suspend or revoke a licensed body's licence under section 101 in the following cases.
      (3)   The first case is that the licensed body becomes a body which is not a licensable body.
      (4)   The second case is that the licensed body fails to comply with licensing rules made under paragraph 16 (carrying on of licensed activities).
      (5)   The third case is that –

          (a)   a non-authorised person holds a restricted interest in the licensed body –

              (i)   as a result of the person taking a step in circumstances where that constitutes an offence under paragraph 24(1) of Schedule 13 (whether or not the person is charged with or convicted of an offence under that paragraph),
              (ii)   in breach of conditions imposed under paragraph 17, 28, or 33 of that Schedule, or
              (iii)   the person's holding of which is subject to an objection by the licensing authority under paragraph 31 or 36 of that Schedule,

          (b)   if the relevant licensing rules make the provision mentioned in paragraph 38(1)(a) of that Schedule, a non-authorised person has under those rules a shareholding in the licensed body, or a parent undertaking of the licensed body, which exceeds the share limit,
          (c)   if the relevant licensing rules make the provision mentioned in paragraph 38(1)(b) of that Schedule, a non-authorised person has under those rules an entitlement to exercise, or control the exercise of, voting rights in the licensed body or a parent undertaking of the licensed body which exceeds the voting limit,
          (d)   if the relevant licensing rules make the provision mentioned in paragraph 38(1)(c) of that Schedule, the total proportion of shares in the licensed body or a parent undertaking of the licensed body held by non-authorised persons exceeds the limit specified in the rules, or
          (e)   if the relevant licensing rules make the provision mentioned in paragraph 38(1)(d) of that Schedule, the total proportion of voting rights in the licensed body or a parent undertaking of the licensed body which non-authorised persons are entitled to exercise, or control the exercise of, exceeds the limit specified in the rules.

      (6)   The fourth case is that a non-authorised person subject to the duty in section 90 in relation to the licensed body fails to comply with that duty.
      (7)   The fifth case is that the licensed body, or a manager or employee of the licensed body, fails to comply with the duties imposed by section 176.
      (8)   The sixth case is that –

APPENDIX A

        (a)   the licensed body fails to comply with licensing rules made under paragraph 9(3) or 18 (prohibition on disqualified managers and employees), and

        (b)   the manager or employee concerned was disqualified as a result of breach of a duty within section 99(4)(c) or (d).

  (9)   The seventh case is that the licensed body is unable to comply with licensing rules made under –

        (a)   paragraph 11 (requirement for Head of Legal Practice), or

        (b)   paragraph 13 (requirement for Head of Finance and Administration).

  (10)   Before suspending or revoking a licence in accordance with sub-paragraph (2), the licensing authority must give the licensed body notice of its intention.

  (11)   The licensing authority may not suspend or revoke the licence before the end of the period of 28 days beginning with the day on which the notice is given to the licensed body (or any longer period specified in the notice).

25   Licensing rules may make provision about other circumstances in which the licensing authority may exercise its power under section 101 to suspend or revoke a licence.

26   (1)   Licensing rules must make provision about the criteria and procedure the licensing authority will apply in deciding whether to suspend or revoke a licence, or to end the suspension of a licence, under section 101.

     (2)   They must make provision for a review by the licensing authority of a decision by the licensing authority to suspend or revoke a licence.

SCHEDULE 12   ENTITLEMENT TO MAKE AN APPLICATION FOR A LICENCE TO THE BOARD

Section 84

Application to Board

1   (1)   A licensable body may apply to the Board for a decision that the body is entitled to make an application for a licence to the Board acting in its capacity as a licensing authority.

     (2)   An application under sub-paragraph (1) may be made only on one of the grounds specified in this paragraph.

     (3)   The first ground is that –

        (a)   there is no competent licensing authority, and

        (b)   there is no potentially competent licensing authority.

     (4)   The second ground is that –

        (a)   each competent licensing authority has determined that it does not have suitable regulatory arrangements,

        (b)   if one or more competent licensing authorities have made an application to the Board under Part 3 of Schedule 4 for the approval of alterations of their regulatory arrangements, each of those authorities has determined that it will not have suitable regulatory arrangements if the application is granted, and

        (c)   each potentially competent licensing authority has determined that it will not have suitable regulatory arrangements if it becomes a competent licensing authority.

(5) The third ground applies only in relation to a licensable body within sub-paragraph (6), and is that –

    (a) the body has made an application for a licence to each competent licensing authority which has suitable regulatory arrangements, and

    (b) no such licensing authority is prepared to grant the body a licence on terms which are appropriate to that body, having regard to the matters in section 106(5)(a) to (c) and any other matter specified in rules made by the Board for the purposes of this sub-paragraph.

(6) The licensable bodies within this sub-paragraph are –

    (a) a not for profit body;

    (b) a community interest company;

    (c) an independent trade union;

    (d) if an order under section 106(1)(e) so provides in relation to a description of body prescribed under that section, a body of that description.

Board's decision on an application under paragraph 1

2 (1) On an application under paragraph 1 the Board must, before the end of the decision period, decide whether the licensable body is entitled to make an application for a licence to the Board acting in its capacity as a licensing authority.

(2) The decision period is –

    (a) in relation to an application on the first ground, the period of 14 days beginning with the day on which the application is made,

    (b) in relation to an application on the second ground, the period of 28 days beginning with the day on which the application is made, and

    (c) in relation to an application on the third ground, the period of 60 days beginning with the day on which the application is made.

(3) The Board must give a notice to the licensable body –

    (a) stating its decision, and

    (b) giving reasons for its decision.

(4) The Board must make rules providing for a review of any decision made by it under this paragraph.

(5) The rules may in particular provide that if the Board decides to grant the application, the Board may review that decision if the ground on which the application was granted ceases to be made out before the Board (in its capacity as a licensing authority) determines any application for a licence made by the licensable body.

Licensing authority's duty to make relevant determinations

3 (1) A licensable body may apply to each competent licensing authority for –

    (a) a determination as to whether the authority has suitable regulatory arrangements;

    (b) a statement as to whether the authority has made an application as mentioned in paragraph 1(4)(b) and if it has, a determination as to whether, if the application is granted, the authority will have suitable regulatory arrangements.

APPENDIX A

(2) A licensable body may apply to each potentially competent licensing authority for a determination as to whether it will have suitable regulatory arrangements in place if it becomes a competent licensing authority.

(3) A competent (or potentially competent) licensing authority to which a licensable body makes an application under sub-paragraph (1) or (2) may require the licensable body to provide it with such information in relation to the licensable body as it may specify.

(4) The authority may specify only information which it reasonably requires for the purpose of making the determination applied for.

(5) A competent (or potentially competent) licensing authority to which an application is made under sub-paragraph (1) or (2) must make the determination before the end of –

(a) the decision period, or
(b) if it requires the licensable body to provide it with information under sub-paragraph (3), the period of 28 days beginning with the day on which the information is provided.

(6) The decision period, in relation to an application under sub-paragraph (1) or (2), is the period of 28 days beginning with the day on which the application is made.

"The Board"

4   In this Schedule references to the Board, unless otherwise stated, are to the Board acting otherwise than in its capacity as a licensing authority or an approved regulator.

"Competent licensing authority"

5   "Competent licensing authority", in relation to a licensable body, means an approved regulator designated as a licensing authority in relation to each reserved legal activity which the licensable body proposes to carry on.

"Potentially competent licensing authority"

6   (1)   "Potentially competent licensing authority", in relation to a licensable body, means an approved regulator –

(a) which has made an application to the Board under Part 1 of Schedule 10 for a recommendation that the Lord Chancellor make a relevant designation order, and whose application has not been determined, or
(b) in respect of which the Board has made such a recommendation, but in respect of which no relevant designation order (or decision not to make such an order) has been made by the Lord Chancellor.

(2) A relevant designation order is an order –

(a) designating the approved regulator as a licensing authority in respect of one or more reserved legal activities, and
(b) the effect of which will be that the approved regulator becomes a competent licensing authority in relation to the licensable body.

"Suitable regulatory arrangements"

7   (1)   "Suitable regulatory arrangements", in relation to a licensable body and a

LEGAL SERVICES ACT 2007 (EXTRACTS)

competent licensing authority, means regulatory arrangements which are suitable in relation to the licensable body, having regard to –

(a) the composition of the licensable body, including in particular the matters in sub-paragraph (2);
(b) the services the licensable body proposes to provide;
(c) if the licensable body proposes to carry on non-reserved activities, any regulation to which the carrying on of such activities is subject;
(d) the persons to whom the licensable body proposes to provide services.

(2) The matters are –

(a) the kinds of authorised persons who are managers of, or have an interest in, the licensable body,
(b) the proportion of persons who are managers of, or have an interest in, the licensable body who are authorised persons or authorised persons of a particular kind,
(c) the kinds of non-authorised persons who are managers of, or have an interest in, the licensable body,
(d) the proportion of persons who are managers of, or have an interest in, the licensable body who are non-authorised persons or non-authorised persons of a particular kind, and
(e) the kinds of non-authorised persons who have an indirect interest in the licensable body.

(3) In sub-paragraph (2) –

(a) "authorised person" means a person who is an authorised person in relation to any activity which is a reserved legal activity, and
(b) authorised persons are of different kinds if they are authorised to carry on such activities by different approved regulators.

SCHEDULE 13   OWNERSHIP OF LICENSED BODIES

Section 89

PART 1   INTRODUCTORY

Restricted interests subject to approval

1   (1) The holding by a non-authorised person of a restricted interest in a licensed body is subject to the approval of the relevant licensing authority in accordance with the provisions of this Schedule.

(2) In relation to a licensed body which is a partnership, for the purposes of section 34 of the Partnership Act 1890 (c. 39) (dissolution by illegality) the holding by a non-authorised person of a restricted interest in the body without the approval of the relevant licensing authority does not make it unlawful for the business of the partnership to be carried on, or for the partners to carry it on in partnership.

Restricted interest

2   (1) "Restricted interest" means each of the following –

APPENDIX A

        (a)   a material interest;
        (b)   if licensing rules are made by the relevant licensing authority under sub-paragraph (2), a controlled interest.

    (2)   Licensing rules may specify that a controlled interest is a restricted interest for the purposes of this Schedule.

Material interest

3   (1)   For the purposes of this Part of this Act, a person holds a material interest in a body ("B") if the person –

        (a)   holds at least 10% of the shares in B,
        (b)   is able to exercise significant influence over the management of B by virtue of the person's shareholding in B,
        (c)   holds at least 10% of the shares in a parent undertaking ("P") of B,
        (d)   is able to exercise significant influence over the management of P by virtue of the person's shareholding in P,
        (e)   is entitled to exercise, or control the exercise of, voting power in B which, if it consists of voting rights, constitutes at least 10% of the voting rights in B,
        (f)   is able to exercise significant influence over the management of B by virtue of the person's entitlement to exercise, or control the exercise of, voting rights in B,
        (g)   is entitled to exercise, or control the exercise of, voting power in P which, if it consists of voting rights, constitutes at least 10% of the voting rights in P,
        (h)   is able to exercise significant influence over the management of P by virtue of the person's entitlement to exercise, or control the exercise of, voting rights in P.

    (2)   Licensing rules made by the relevant licensing authority may provide –

        (a)   that the references in sub-paragraph (1) to 10% are to have effect as references to such lesser percentage as may be specified in the rules;
        (b)   that in relation to a partnership, for the purposes of this Part a person has a material interest in the partnership if he is a partner (whether or not the person has a material interest by virtue of sub-paragraph (1)).

    (3)   For the purposes of sub-paragraph (1) "the person" means –

        (a)   the person,
        (b)   any of the person's associates, or
        (c)   the person and any of the person's associates taken together.

    (4)   For the purposes of this Schedule, material interests held by virtue of different paragraphs of sub-paragraph (1) are restricted interests of different kinds.

Controlled interest

4   (1)   For the purposes of this Schedule, a person holds a controlled interest in a body ("B") if the person –

        (a)   holds at least x% of the shares in B,
        (b)   holds at least x% of the shares in a parent undertaking ("P") of B,
        (c)   is entitled to exercise, or control the exercise of, at least x% of the voting rights in B, or

(d) is entitled to exercise, or control the exercise of, at least x% of the voting rights in P.

(2) For the purposes of sub-paragraph (1) "the person" means –

    (a) the person,
    (b) any of the person's associates, or
    (c) the person and any of the person's associates taken together.

(3) In sub-paragraph (1), "x" means such percentage as may be specified in licensing rules made by the relevant licensing authority under paragraph 2(2).

(4) Licensing rules made under paragraph 2(2) may specify more than one percentage.

(5) Any percentage specified by licensing rules made under paragraph 2(2) must be greater than –

    (a) 10%, or
    (b) if the relevant licensing authority makes licensing rules under paragraph 3(2)(a), the percentage specified in those rules.

(6) For the purposes of this Schedule –

    (a) controlled interests held by virtue of different paragraphs of sub-paragraph (1) are restricted interests of different kinds;
    (b) if licensing rules made under paragraph 2(2) specify more than one percentage, controlled interests held by virtue of each of those percentages are restricted interests of different kinds.

Associates, parent undertakings and voting power

5 (1) For the purposes of this Schedule "associate", in relation to a person ("A") and –

    (a) a shareholding in a body ("S"), or
    (b) an entitlement to exercise or control the exercise of voting power in a body ("V"),

means a person listed in sub-paragraph (2).

(2) The persons are –

    (a) the spouse or civil partner of A,
    (b) a child or stepchild of A (if under 18),
    (c) the trustee of any settlement under which A has a life interest in possession (in Scotland a life interest),
    (d) an undertaking of which A is a director,
    (e) an employee of A,
    (f) a partner of A (except, where S or V is a partnership in which A is a partner, another partner in S or V),
    (g) if A is an undertaking –

        (i) a director of A,
        (ii) a subsidiary undertaking of A, or
        (iii) a director or employee of such a subsidiary undertaking,

    (h) if A has with any other person an agreement or arrangement with respect to the acquisition, holding or disposal of shares or other interests in S or V (whether or not they are interests within the meaning of section 72(3)), that other person, or

APPENDIX A

        (i)   if A has with any other person an agreement or arrangement under which they undertake to act together in exercising their voting power in relation to S or V, that person.

(3) In sub-paragraph (2)(c), "settlement" means any disposition or arrangement under which property is held on trust (or subject to a comparable obligation).

(4) For the purposes of this Schedule –

"parent undertaking" and "subsidiary undertaking" have the same meaning as in the Financial Services and Markets Act 2000 (c. 8) (see section 420 of that Act);

"voting power", in relation to a body which does not have general meetings at which matters are decided by the exercise of voting rights, means the right under the constitution of the body to direct the overall policy of the body or alter the terms of its constitution.

The approval requirements

6   (1) For the purposes of this Schedule, the approval requirements are met in relation to a person's holding of a restricted interest if –

        (a) the person's holding of that interest does not compromise the regulatory objectives,

        (b) the person's holding of that interest does not compromise compliance with the duties imposed by section 176 by the licensed body or persons to whom sub-paragraph (2) applies, and

        (c) the person is otherwise a fit and proper person to hold that interest.

(2) This sub-paragraph applies to any employee or manager of the licensed body who is an authorised person in relation to an activity which is a reserved legal activity.

(3) In determining whether it is satisfied of the matters mentioned in sub-paragraph (1)(a) to (c), the licensing authority must in particular have regard to –

        (a) the person's probity and financial position,

        (b) whether the person is disqualified as mentioned in section 100(1), or included in the list kept by the Board under paragraph 51,

        (c) the person's associates, and

        (d) any other matter which may be specified in licensing rules.

(4) Licensing rules must make provision about the procedures that will be applied by the licensing authority when determining whether it is satisfied of the matters mentioned in sub-paragraph (1)(a) to (c).

Approval of multiple restricted interests

7   (1) This paragraph applies if a person ("P") holds a kind of restricted interest in a body ("B") by virtue of –

        (a) holding a particular percentage of the shares in B or a parent undertaking of B, or

        (b) an entitlement to exercise, or control the exercise of, a particular percentage of the voting rights in B or a parent undertaking of B.

(2) If the relevant licensing authority approves P's holding of that interest, it is to be treated as also approving P's holding of any lesser restricted interest in B held by P.

(3) A lesser restricted interest is a kind of restricted interest held by P by virtue of –

    (a) holding a smaller percentage of the shares mentioned in sub-paragraph (1)(a), or

    (b) an entitlement to exercise, or control the exercise of, a smaller percentage of the voting rights mentioned in sub-paragraph (1)(b).

Board's power to prescribe rules

8   In this Schedule "prescribed" means prescribed by rules made by the Board for the purposes of this Schedule.

Lord Chancellor's power to modify

9   The Lord Chancellor may, on the recommendation of the Board, by order modify –

    (a) paragraph 3 (material interest);

    (b) paragraphs 4(2), 5, 6(3)(c), 38(3), 41(3) and 42(3) (associates).

PART 2   APPROVAL OF RESTRICTED INTERESTS ON APPLICATION FOR LICENCE

Requirement to identify non-authorised persons

10   (1) Where a body applies to a licensing authority for a licence, it must identify in its application –

    (a) any non-authorised person who holds a restricted interest in the body, or whom the body expects to hold such an interest when the licence is issued, and

    (b) the kind of restricted interest held, or expected to be held, by that person.

    (2) If, before the licence is issued, there is any change in –

    (a) the identity of the non-authorised persons within sub-paragraph (1)(a), or

    (b) the kind of restricted interest held, or expected to be held, by a person identified to the licensing authority under that sub-paragraph,

the applicant must inform the relevant licensing authority within such period as may be specified by order made by the Lord Chancellor on the recommendation of the Board.

11   (1) It is an offence for a person to fail to comply with a requirement imposed on the person by paragraph 10.

    (2) A person who is guilty of an offence under sub-paragraph (1) is liable on summary conviction to a fine not exceeding level 5 on the standard scale.

    (3) It is a defence for a person charged with an offence under sub-paragraph (1) to show that at the time of the alleged offence the person had no knowledge of the facts by virtue of which the duty to notify arose.

12   (1) This paragraph applies if a person under a duty to notify imposed by paragraph 10 –

APPENDIX A

(a) had no knowledge of the facts by virtue of which that duty arose, but
(b) subsequently becomes aware of those facts.

(2) The person must give the licensing authority the required notification within such period, after the person becomes so aware, as may be specified by order made by the Lord Chancellor on the recommendation of the Board.
(3) A person who fails to comply with the duty to notify imposed by sub-paragraph (2) is guilty of an offence.
(4) A person who is guilty of an offence under sub-paragraph (3) is liable on summary conviction to a fine not exceeding level 5 on the standard scale.

Requirement to notify non-authorised persons

13 (1) Where an applicant for a licence identifies a non-authorised person to a licensing authority in accordance with paragraph 10 or 12, it must give that person a notice –

(a) stating that it has applied for a licence and identified the person to the licensing authority in accordance with paragraph 10 or 12, and
(b) explaining the effect of paragraph 14.

(2) It is an offence for a person to fail to comply with a requirement imposed on it by sub-paragraph (1).
(3) A person who is guilty of an offence under sub-paragraph (2) is liable on summary conviction to a fine not exceeding level 5 on the standard scale.

Licensing authority's power to require information

14 (1) A licensing authority may require a non-authorised person identified to it in accordance with paragraph 10 or 12 to provide it with such documents and information as it may require.
(2) It is an offence for a person who is required to provide information or documents under sub-paragraph (1) knowingly to provide false or misleading information or documents.
(3) A person who is guilty of an offence under sub-paragraph (2) is liable –

(a) on summary conviction, to a fine not exceeding the statutory maximum, and
(b) on conviction on indictment, to a term of imprisonment not exceeding 2 years or a fine (or both).

Licence may not be granted unless non-authorised persons approved

15 (1) This paragraph applies where an applicant for a licence ("the applicant") gives the licensing authority notification under paragraph 10 or 12 in relation to one or more non-authorised persons.
(2) The licensing authority may not grant the application for a licence unless, in relation to each non-authorised person in respect of which notification is given ("the investor"), it approves the investor's holding of the restricted interest to which the notification relates ("the notified interest").
(3) Sub-paragraph (2) does not apply in relation to a non-authorised person who does not hold the notified interest when the licence is issued.
(4) In this Part of this Schedule, "the applicant", "the investor" and "the notified interest" are to be construed in accordance with this paragraph.

LEGAL SERVICES ACT 2007 (EXTRACTS)

Unconditional approval of notified interest

16 (1) If the licensing authority is satisfied that the approval requirements are met in relation to the investor's holding of the notified interest, it must approve the investor's holding of that interest without conditions.

    (2) If the licensing authority approves the investor's holding of the notified interest without conditions, it must notify the investor and the applicant of its approval as soon as reasonably practicable.

Conditional approval of notified interest

17 (1) If the licensing authority is not satisfied that the approval requirements are met in relation to the investor's holding of the notified interest, it may approve the investor's holding of the notified interest subject to conditions.

    (2) It may do so only if it considers that, if the conditions are complied with, it will be appropriate for the investor to hold the notified interest without the approval requirements being met.

    (3) If the licensing authority proposes to approve the investor's holding of the notified interest subject to conditions it must give the investor and the applicant a warning notice.

    (4) The warning notice must –

        (a) specify the nature of the conditions proposed and the reasons for their imposition, and

        (b) state that representations may be made to the licensing authority within the prescribed period.

    (5) The licensing authority must consider any representations made within the prescribed period.

    (6) If the licensing authority approves the investor's holding of the notified interest subject to conditions, it must notify the investor and the applicant of its approval as soon as reasonably practicable.

    (7) The notice must –

        (a) specify the reasons for the imposition of the conditions, and

        (b) explain the effect of Part 5 of this Schedule.

18 (1) The investor and the applicant may before the end of the prescribed period appeal to the relevant appellate body against the imposition of any or all of the conditions.

    (2) The relevant appellate body may dismiss the appeal, or allow the appeal and –

        (a) order the licensing authority to approve the investor's holding of the notified interest without conditions, or subject to such conditions as may be specified in the order, or

        (b) remit the matter to the licensing authority.

    (3) A party to the appeal may before the end of the prescribed period appeal to the High Court on a point of law arising from the decision of the relevant appellant body, but only with the permission of the High Court.

    (4) The High Court may make such order as it thinks fit.

    (5) If the investor's holding of the notified interest is subject to conditions as a result of an order made on an appeal under this paragraph, for the purposes of this Schedule the conditions are to be treated as having been imposed under paragraph 17.

APPENDIX A

Objection to notified interest

19 (1) If the licensing authority is not satisfied that the approval requirements are met in relation to the investor's holding of the notified interest, it may object to the investor's holding of that interest.

(2) If the licensing authority proposes to object to the investor's holding of the notified interest, it must give the investor and the applicant a warning notice.

(3) The warning notice must –

   (a) specify the reasons for the proposed objection, and
   (b) state that representations may be made to the licensing authority within the prescribed period.

(4) The licensing authority must consider any representations made within the prescribed period.

(5) If the licensing authority objects to the investor's holding of the notified interest, it must notify the investor and the applicant of its objection as soon as reasonably practicable.

(6) The notice must –

   (a) specify the reasons for the objection, and
   (b) explain the effect of Part 5 of this Schedule.

20 (1) The investor and the applicant may before the end of the prescribed period appeal to the relevant appellate body against the objection.

(2) The relevant appellate body may dismiss the appeal, or allow the appeal and –

   (a) order the licensing authority to approve the investor's holding of the notified interest without conditions, or subject to such conditions as may be specified in the order, or
   (b) remit the matter to the licensing authority.

(3) A party to the appeal may before the end of the prescribed period appeal to the High Court on a point of law arising from the decision of the relevant appellate body, but only with the permission of the High Court.

(4) The High Court may make such order as it thinks fit.

(5) If the investor's holding of the notified interest is subject to conditions as a result of an order made on an appeal under this paragraph, for the purposes of this Schedule the conditions are to be treated as having been imposed under paragraph 17.

PART 3 APPROVAL OF RESTRICTED INTERESTS AFTER LICENCE IS ISSUED

Powers of licensing authority in relation to change of interests

Continuing notification requirements

21 (1) This paragraph applies where a non-authorised person ("the investor") –

   (a) proposes to take a step which would result in the investor acquiring a restricted interest in a licensed body (or, if the investor already has one or more kinds of restricted interest, acquiring an additional kind of restricted interest), or
   (b) acquires such an interest in a licensed body without taking such a step.

(2) In a case within sub-paragraph (1)(a) the investor must notify the licensed body and the relevant licensing authority of the proposal.

(3) In a case within sub-paragraph (1)(b) the investor must notify the licensed body and the relevant licensing authority of the acquisition within such period, after the investor becomes aware of it, as may be specified by order made by the Lord Chancellor on the recommendation of the Board.

(4) In this Part of this Schedule –

    (a) references to "the investor" are to be construed in accordance with this paragraph, and

    (b) references to a notifiable interest are to the restricted interest which the investor will have as a result of the step the investor proposes to take (or has as a result of the acquisition which has taken place).

Offences in connection with paragraph 21

22 (1) It is an offence for a person to fail to comply with a requirement imposed by –

    (a) paragraph 21(2), or

    (b) paragraph 21(3).

(2) A person who is guilty of an offence under sub-paragraph (1) is liable on summary conviction to a fine not exceeding level 5 on the standard scale.

(3) It is a defence for a person charged with an offence under sub-paragraph (1)(a) to show that at the time of the alleged offence the person had no knowledge of the facts by virtue of which the duty to notify arose.

23 (1) This paragraph applies if a person under the duty to notify imposed by paragraph 21(2) –

    (a) had no knowledge of the facts by virtue of which that duty arose, but

    (b) subsequently becomes aware of those facts.

(2) The person must give the licensed body and the licensing authority the required notification within such period, after the person becomes so aware, as may be specified by order made by the Lord Chancellor on the recommendation of the Board.

(3) A person who fails to comply with the duty to notify imposed by sub-paragraph (2) is guilty of an offence.

(4) A person who is guilty of an offence under sub-paragraph (3) is liable on summary conviction to a fine not exceeding level 5 on the standard scale.

24 (1) It is an offence for a non-authorised person, who under paragraph 21(2) is required to notify the licensed body and the relevant licensing authority of a proposal to take a step, to take the step, unless the relevant licensing authority has approved the investor's holding of the notifiable interest under paragraph 27 or 28.

(2) If paragraph 22(3) applies, the reference in sub-paragraph (1) to paragraph 21(2) is to be read as a reference to paragraph 23(2).

(3) A person who is guilty of an offence under sub-paragraph (1) is liable –

    (a) on summary conviction, to a fine not exceeding the statutory maximum, and

    (b) on conviction on indictment, to a term of imprisonment not exceeding 2 years or a fine (or both).

APPENDIX A

Duty of licensing authority following notification etc

25   (1)   The relevant licensing authority must –

           (a)   following receipt of a notification under paragraph 21(2) or (3) or 23(2), or

           (b)   if the licensing authority becomes aware that an investor has failed to comply with a notification requirement imposed by paragraph 21(2) or (3) or 23(2),

determine which of the steps in sub-paragraph (3) to take.

       (2)   The licensing authority must make the determination within such period as may be prescribed.

       (3)   The steps are –

           (a)   to approve the investor's holding of the notifiable interest unconditionally under paragraph 27,

           (b)   to warn the investor under paragraph 28(3) that it proposes to approve the investor's holding of the notifiable interest subject to conditions,

           (c)   to approve under paragraph 28(4) the investor's holding of the notifiable interest subject to conditions,

           (d)   to warn the investor under paragraph 31(2) that it proposes to object to the investor's holding of the notifiable interest, or

           (e)   to object under paragraph 31(3) to the investor's holding of the notifiable interest.

Licensing authority's power to require information

26   (1)   A licensing authority may require the investor to provide it with such documents and information as it may require.

       (2)   It is an offence for a person who is required to provide information or documents under sub-paragraph (1) knowingly to provide false or misleading information or documents.

       (3)   A person who is guilty of an offence under sub-paragraph (2) is liable –

           (a)   on summary conviction, to a fine not exceeding the statutory maximum, and

           (b)   on conviction on indictment, to a term of imprisonment not exceeding 2 years or a fine (or both).

Unconditional approval of notifiable interest

27   (1)   If the licensing authority is satisfied that the approval requirements are met in relation to the investor's holding of the notifiable interest, it must approve the investor's holding of that interest without conditions.

       (2)   If the licensing authority approves the investor's holding of the notifiable interest without conditions, it must notify the investor and the licensed body of its approval as soon as reasonably practicable.

Conditional approval of notifiable interest

28   (1)   If the licensing authority is not satisfied that the approval requirements are met in relation to the investor's holding of the notifiable interest, it may approve the investor's holding of that interest subject to conditions.

       (2)   It may do so only if it considers that, if the conditions are complied with, it will

be appropriate for the investor to hold the notifiable interest without the approval requirements being met.

(3) If the licensing authority proposes to approve the investor's holding of the notifiable interest subject to conditions it must give the investor and the licensed body a warning notice.

(4) But the licensing authority may approve the investor's holding of the notifiable interest subject to conditions without giving a warning notice if it considers it necessary or desirable to do so for the purpose of protecting any of the regulatory objectives.

(5) The warning notice must –

    (a) specify the nature of the conditions proposed and the reasons for their imposition, and

    (b) state that representations may be made to the licensing authority within the prescribed period.

(6) The licensing authority must consider any representations made within the prescribed period.

(7) If the licensing authority approves the investor's holding of the notifiable interest subject to conditions, it must notify the investor and the licensed body of its approval as soon as reasonably practicable.

(8) The notice must –

    (a) specify the reasons for the imposition of the conditions and (if the investor already holds the notifiable interest) the time from which they have effect, and

    (b) explain the effect of Part 5 of this Schedule.

29 (1) The investor and the licensed body may before the end of the prescribed period appeal to the relevant appellate body against the imposition of any or all the conditions.

(2) The relevant appellate body may dismiss the appeal, or allow the appeal and –

    (a) order the licensing authority to approve the investor's holding of the notifiable interest without conditions, or subject to such conditions as may be specified in the order, or

    (b) remit the matter to the licensing authority.

(3) A party to the appeal may before the end of the prescribed period appeal to the High Court on a point of law arising from the decision of the relevant appellate body, but only with the permission of the High Court.

(4) The High Court may make such order as it thinks fit.

(5) If the investor's holding of the notifiable interest is subject to conditions as a result of an order made on an appeal under this paragraph, for the purposes of this Schedule the conditions are to be treated as having been imposed under paragraph 28.

Duration of unconditional or conditional approval

30 In a case within paragraph 21(1)(a), the licensing authority's approval under paragraph 27 or 28 remains effective only if the investor acquires the notifiable interest –

    (a) before the end of such period as may be specified in the notice under paragraph 27(2) or 28(7), or

    (b) if no such period is specified, before the end of the period of one year beginning with the date of that notice.

APPENDIX A

Objection to acquisition of notifiable interest

31 (1) If the licensing authority is not satisfied that the approval requirements are met in relation to the investor's holding of the notifiable interest, it may object to the investor's holding of that interest.
 (2) If the licensing authority proposes to object to the investor's holding of the notifiable interest, it must give the investor and the licensed body a warning notice.
 (3) But the licensing authority may object to the investor's holding of the notifiable interest without giving a warning notice if it considers it necessary or desirable to do so for the purpose of protecting any of the regulatory objectives.
 (4) The warning notice must –

 (a) specify the reasons for the proposed objection, and
 (b) state that representations may be made to the licensing authority within the prescribed period.

 (5) The licensing authority must consider any representations made within the prescribed period.
 (6) If the licensing authority objects to the investor's holding of the notifiable interest, it must notify the investor and the licensed body of its objection as soon as reasonably practicable.
 (7) The notice must –

 (a) specify the reasons for the objection, and
 (b) explain the effect of Part 5 of this Schedule.

32 (1) The investor and the licensed body may before the end of the prescribed period appeal to the relevant appellate body against the objection.
 (2) The relevant appellate body may dismiss the appeal, or allow the appeal and –

 (a) order the licensing authority to approve the investor's holding of the notifiable interest without conditions, or subject to such conditions as may be specified in the order, or
 (b) remit the matter to the licensing authority.

 (3) A party to the appeal may before the end of the prescribed period appeal to the High Court on a point of law arising from the decision of the relevant appellant body, but only with the permission of the High Court.
 (4) The High Court may make such order as it thinks fit.
 (5) If the investor's holding of the notifiable interest is subject to conditions as a result of an order made on an appeal under this paragraph, for the purposes of this Schedule the conditions are to be treated as having been imposed under paragraph 28.

Powers of licensing authority where no change of interests

Imposition of conditions (or further conditions) on existing restricted interest

33 (1) The relevant licensing authority may impose conditions (or further conditions) on a person's holding of a restricted interest in a licensed body (or a restricted interest of a particular kind) if –

 (a) it is not satisfied that the approval requirements are met in relation to the person's holding of that interest, or

(b) it is satisfied that a condition imposed under paragraph 17 or 28 or this paragraph on the person's holding of that interest has not been, or is not being, complied with.

(2) The licensing authority may act under sub-paragraph (1) only –

(a) if it considers that, if the conditions are complied with, it will be appropriate for the investor to hold the restricted interest without the approval requirements being met, and

(b) before the end of such period (beginning with the time when the licensing authority becomes aware of the matters in question) as may be prescribed.

(3) If the licensing authority proposes to impose conditions (or further conditions) on the person's holding of the restricted interest, it must give the person and the licensed body a warning notice.

(4) But the licensing authority may impose conditions (or further conditions) on the person's holding of the restricted interest without giving a warning notice if it considers it necessary or desirable to do so for the purpose of protecting any of the regulatory objectives.

(5) The warning notice must –

(a) specify the nature of the conditions proposed and the reasons for their imposition, and

(b) state that representations may be made to the licensing authority within the prescribed period.

(6) The licensing authority must consider any representations made within the prescribed period.

(7) If the licensing authority imposes conditions (or further conditions) on the person's holding of the restricted interest, it must notify the person and the licensed body as soon as reasonably practicable.

(8) The notice must –

(a) specify the reasons for the imposition of the conditions, and the time from which they are to take effect, and

(b) explain the effect of Part 5 of this Schedule.

34 (1) The person and the licensed body may before the end of the prescribed period appeal to the relevant appellate body against any or all of the conditions (or further conditions).

(2) The relevant appellate body may dismiss the appeal, or allow the appeal and –

(a) modify or quash the conditions imposed by the licensing authority under paragraph 33, or

(b) remit the matter to the licensing authority.

(3) A party to the appeal may before the end of the prescribed period appeal to the High Court on a point of law arising from the decision of the relevant appellate body, but only with the permission of the High Court.

(4) The High Court may make such order as it thinks fit.

(5) If the person's holding of the restricted interest is subject to any conditions as a result of an order made on an appeal under this paragraph, for the purposes of this Schedule those conditions are to be treated as having been imposed under paragraph 33.

APPENDIX A

Variation and cancellation of conditions

35 (1) A person whose holding of a restricted interest in a licensed body is subject to a condition imposed under paragraph 17, 28 or 33 may apply to the relevant licensing authority –

   (a) for the condition to be varied, or
   (b) for the condition to be cancelled.

   (2) The licensing authority may, on its own initiative, cancel a condition imposed under one of those paragraphs.
   (3) If the licensing authority varies or cancels a condition under this paragraph, it must notify the person and the licensed body as soon as reasonably practicable.

Objection to existing restricted interest

36 (1) The relevant licensing authority may object to a person's holding of a restricted interest in a licensed body (or a restricted interest of a particular kind) if –

   (a) it is not satisfied that the approval requirements are met in relation to the person's holding of that interest, or
   (b) it is satisfied that a condition imposed under paragraph 17, 28 or 33 on the person's holding of the interest has not been, or is not being, complied with.

   (2) The licensing authority may act under sub-paragraph (1) only before the end of such period (beginning with the time when the licensing authority becomes aware of the matters in question) as may be prescribed.
   (3) If the licensing authority proposes to object to a person's holding of the restricted interest, it must give the person and the licensed body a warning notice.
   (4) But the licensing authority may object to the person's holding of the restricted interest without giving a warning notice if it considers it necessary or desirable to do so for the purpose of protecting any of the regulatory objectives.
   (5) The warning notice must –

   (a) specify the reasons for the proposed objection, and
   (b) state that representations may be made to the licensing authority within the prescribed period.

   (6) The licensing authority must consider any representations made within the prescribed period.
   (7) If the licensing authority objects to the person's holding of the restricted interest, it must notify the person and the licensed body of its objection as soon as reasonably practicable.
   (8) The notice must –

   (a) specify the reasons for the objection, and
   (b) explain the effect of Part 5 of this Schedule.

37 (1) The person and the licensed body may before the end of the prescribed period appeal to the relevant appellate body against the objection.
   (2) The relevant appellate body may dismiss or allow the appeal.
   (3) If the relevant appellate body allows the appeal it may also –

  (a) order the licensing authority to impose under paragraph 33 such conditions on the person's holding of the restricted interest as may be specified in the order, or
  (b) remit the matter to the licensing authority.
(4) A party to the appeal may before the end of the prescribed period appeal to the High Court on a point of law arising from the decision of the relevant appellant body, but only with the permission of the High Court.
(5) The High Court may make such order as it thinks fit.
(6) If the person's holding of the restricted interest is subject to conditions as a result of an order made on an appeal under this paragraph, for the purposes of this Schedule the conditions are to be treated as having been imposed under paragraph 33.

PART 4 ADDITIONAL RESTRICTIONS

Power to impose share limit, voting limit etc

38 (1) Licensing rules may provide that –
  (a) a non-authorised person may not have a shareholding in a licensed body, or in a parent undertaking of a licensed body, which exceeds a limit specified in the rules ("the share limit");
  (b) a non-authorised person may not have an entitlement to exercise, or control the exercise of, voting rights in a licensable body, or a parent undertaking of a licensable body, which exceeds a limit specified in the rules ("the voting limit");
  (c) the total proportion of shares in a licensed body, or a parent undertaking of a licensed body, held by non-authorised persons may not exceed a limit specified in the rules;
  (d) the total proportion of voting rights in a licensed body, or a parent undertaking of a licensed body, which non-authorised persons are entitled to exercise or control the exercise of, may not exceed a limit specified in the rules.
(2) Rules made under any paragraph of sub-paragraph (1) in relation to a licensed body and a parent undertaking may specify different limits in relation to the licensed body and the parent undertaking.
(3) Licensing rules made under sub-paragraph (1)(a) or (b) may provide that references in those rules to a person, in relation to a person's shareholding or entitlement to exercise or control the exercise of voting rights, are to –
  (a) the person,
  (b) any of the person's associates, or
  (c) the person and any of the person's associates taken together.
(4) In relation to a licensed body which is a partnership, for the purposes of section 34 of the Partnership Act 1890 (c. 39) (dissolution by illegality) a breach of licensing rules made under sub-paragraph (1) does not make it unlawful for the business of the partnership to be carried on, or for the partners to carry it on in partnership.

APPENDIX A

Obligation to notify where share limit or voting limit exceeded

39 (1) This paragraph applies in relation to a licensed body, or a parent undertaking of a licensed body, if licensing rules made by the relevant licensing authority make the provision mentioned in paragraph 38(1)(a) or (b) in relation to the body.

(2) Any non-authorised person who acquires –

(a) a shareholding in the body which exceeds the share limit, or
(b) an entitlement to exercise, or control the exercise of, voting rights in the body which exceeds the voting limit,

must notify the body (and, if the body is a parent undertaking of a licensed body, the licensed body) and the licensing authority of the acquisition within such period, after the person becomes aware of it, as may be specified by order made by the Lord Chancellor on the recommendation of the Board.

(3) It is an offence for a person to fail to comply with a requirement imposed by sub-paragraph (2).

(4) A person who is guilty of an offence under sub-paragraph (3) is liable on summary conviction to a fine not exceeding level 5 on the standard scale.

(5) It is a defence for a person charged with an offence under sub-paragraph (3) to show that at the time of the alleged offence the person had no knowledge of the facts by virtue of which the duty to notify arose.

40 (1) This paragraph applies if a person under the duty to notify imposed by paragraph 39(2) –

(a) had no knowledge of the facts by virtue of which that duty arose, but
(b) subsequently becomes aware of those facts.

(2) The person must give the body (and, if the body is a parent undertaking of a licensed body, the licensed body) and the licensing authority the required notification within such period, after the person becomes so aware, as may be specified by order made by the Lord Chancellor on the recommendation of the Board.

(3) A person who fails to comply with the duty to notify imposed by sub-paragraph (2) is guilty of an offence.

(4) A person who is guilty of an offence under sub-paragraph (3) is liable on summary conviction to a fine not exceeding level 5 on the standard scale.

PART 5   ENFORCEMENT

Divestiture

The divestiture condition

41 (1) The divestiture condition is satisfied in relation to a non-authorised person and a licensed body if –

(a) the person holds a restricted interest in the licensed body in the circumstances mentioned in sub-paragraph (2), and
(b) the person holds that interest, in whole or in part, by virtue of the person's shareholding in a body corporate with a share capital (in this Part of this Schedule referred to as "the relevant shares").

(2) The circumstances are that the person holds the restricted interest –

    (a) as a result of the person taking a step in circumstances in which that constitutes an offence under paragraph 24(1) (whether or not the person is charged with or convicted of an offence under that paragraph),

    (b) in breach of conditions imposed under paragraph 17, 28, or 33, or

    (c) in contravention of an objection by the licensing authority under paragraph 31 or 36.

(3) In sub-paragraph (1)(b), references to a person's shareholding are to be read in accordance with paragraph 3(3) or 4(2) (as the case may be).

42 (1) If the relevant licensing rules make the provision mentioned in paragraph 38(1)(a) or (b), the divestiture condition is also satisfied in relation to a non-authorised person and a licensed body if –

    (a) the person's shareholding in the body, or a parent undertaking of the body, exceeds the share limit, and the body or parent undertaking (as the case may be) is a body corporate with a share capital, or

    (b) the person's entitlement to exercise or control the exercise of voting rights in the body, or a parent undertaking of the body, exceeds the voting limit by virtue of the person holding shares in a body corporate with a share capital.

(2) In this Part of this Schedule, "excess shares" means

    (a) in a case within sub-paragraph (1)(a), the number of shares by which the person's shareholding exceeds the share limit, and

    (b) in a case within sub-paragraph (1)(b), the number of shares held by the person in excess of the number of shares the person could hold without the person's entitlement to exercise, or control the exercise of, voting rights exceeding the voting limit.

(3) References in this paragraph to a person's shareholding (or holding of shares) or entitlement are to be read in accordance with any applicable licensing rules made under paragraph 38(3).

Application for divestiture

43 (1) If the divestiture condition is satisfied in relation to a non-authorised person and a licensed body, the licensing authority may give the person a restriction notice under paragraph 44 and apply to the High Court for an order under paragraph 45.

(2) The licensing authority may not make an application to the High Court for an order under paragraph 45 unless –

    (a) it has notified the person that it intends to do so if the divestiture condition is satisfied in relation to the person and the body at the end of the relevant period, and

    (b) the relevant period has expired.

(3) The relevant period is such period (not less than the prescribed period) as may be specified in the notice.

Restriction notice

44 (1) A restriction notice is a notice directing that such of the relevant shares or

APPENDIX A

excess shares (as the case may be) as are specified in the notice are, until further notice, subject to one or more of the following restrictions.

(2) The restrictions are –

(a) a transfer of (or agreement to transfer) those shares, or in the case of unissued shares a transfer of (or agreement to transfer) the right to be issued with them, is void;
(b) no voting rights are to be exercisable in respect of the shares;
(c) no further shares are to be issued in right of them or in pursuance of any offer made to their holder;
(d) except in a liquidation, no payment is to be made of any sums due from the company on the shares, whether in respect of capital or otherwise.

(3) A copy of the restriction notice must be given to the body to whose shares it relates.

(4) A restriction notice ceases to have effect –

(a) in accordance with an order of the High Court under paragraph 45(4);
(b) if no application has been made to the High Court for an order under paragraph 45 before the end of such period as may be prescribed, at the end of that period;
(c) if the licensed body ceases to be licensed by the licensing authority.

Divestiture by High Court

45 (1) If the divestiture condition is satisfied by virtue of paragraph 41 the High Court may, on the application of the licensing authority, order the sale of the appropriate number of the relevant shares.

(2) The appropriate number of the relevant shares is the number of those shares, the sale of which will result in the non-authorised person no longer holding –

(a) a restricted interest in the licensed body, or
(b) if the non-authorised person holds more than one kind of restricted interest, a restricted interest the person's holding of which is within paragraph 41(2).

(3) If the divestiture condition is satisfied by virtue of paragraph 42 the High Court may, on the application of the licensing authority, order the sale of the excess shares.

(4) If shares are for the time being subject to any restriction under paragraph 44, the court may order that they are to cease to be subject to that restriction.

(5) If the divestiture condition is satisfied by virtue of paragraph 41(2)(b) or (c), no order may be made under sub-paragraph (1) or (4) –

(a) until the end of the period within which an appeal may be made against the imposition of the conditions or the objection, or
(b) if an appeal is made, until the appeal has been determined or withdrawn.

(6) If an order has been made under sub-paragraph (1) or (3) the court may, on the application of the licensing authority, make such further order relating to the sale or transfer of the shares as it thinks fit.

(7) If shares are sold in pursuance of an order under this paragraph, the proceeds of sale, less the costs of sale, must be paid into court for the benefit of the persons beneficially interested in them.

(8) Any such person may apply to the court for the whole or part of the proceeds to be paid to the person.

LEGAL SERVICES ACT 2007 (EXTRACTS)

Conditions

Enforcement of conditions

46   (1)   If a person holds a restricted interest in a licensed body in breach of conditions imposed under paragraph 17, 28 or 33, the licensing authority may make an application to the High Court for an order under this paragraph.

       (2)   The licensing authority may not make such an application unless –

           (a)   it has notified the person that it intends to do so if the conditions are not complied with before the end of the relevant period, and
           (b)   the relevant period has expired.

       (3)   The relevant period is such period (not less than the prescribed period) as may be specified in the notice.

       (4)   The High Court may, on the application of the licensing authority, make such order as the court thinks fit to secure compliance with the conditions to which the person's holding of the restricted interest is subject.

       (5)   No order may be made under this paragraph –

           (a)   until the end of the period within which an appeal may be made against the imposition of the conditions, or
           (b)   if an appeal is made, until the appeal has been determined or withdrawn.

Records of decisions

Duty to notify Board of decisions under this Schedule

47   (1)   The relevant licensing authority must notify the Board where –

           (a)   it has objected under paragraph 19, 31, or 36 to a person's holding of a restricted interest, or
           (b)   it has imposed conditions under paragraph 17, 28, or 33 on a person's holding of a restricted interest.

       (2)   The notification must state –

           (a)   the reasons for the objection or imposition of conditions, and
           (b)   the kind of restricted interest to which the objection or conditions related.

       (3)   If the licensing authority takes any action under paragraph 43 in relation to a person notified to the Board under sub-paragraph (1), it must notify the Board of that fact.

       (4)   If there is an appeal to the relevant appellate body against the objection or imposition of conditions, the licensing authority must notify the Board of the outcome of that appeal (and any subsequent appeal to the High Court).

       (5)   If the licensing authority has imposed conditions on a person's holding of a restricted interest, it must notify the Board of any decision taken by it under paragraph 35 (variation and cancellation of conditions).

       (6)   The licensing authority must give the person and the licensed body concerned a copy of any notification it gives the Board under this paragraph.

48   (1)   A licensing authority must notify the Board where under paragraph 16, 17, 27 or 28 it approves the holding of a restricted interest in a licensed body by a person included in the list kept by the Board under paragraph 51.

       (2)   The notification must state –

APPENDIX A

   (a) if the approval was under paragraph 17 or 28, the conditions to which the approval was subject, and
   (b) the reasons for the licensing authority's decision to approve the person's holding of the interest.

 (3) If the approval was under paragraph 17 or 28 and there is an appeal to the relevant appellate body against the imposition of conditions, the licensing authority must notify the Board of the outcome of that appeal (and any subsequent appeal to the High Court).

 (4) If the approval was under paragraph 17 or 28, the licensing authority must notify the Board of any decision taken by it under paragraph 35 (variation and cancellation of conditions).

 (5) The licensing authority must give the person and the licensed body concerned a copy of any notification it gives the Board under this paragraph.

Power to notify Board where share limit or voting limit breached

49 (1) This paragraph applies if the relevant licensing rules make the provision mentioned in paragraph 38(1)(a) or (b).

 (2) The licensing authority may, if it considers it appropriate to do so in all the circumstances of the case, notify the Board where a non-authorised person acquires –

   (a) a shareholding in a licensed body or parent undertaking of a licensed body which exceeds the share limit, or
   (b) an entitlement to exercise, or control the exercise of, voting rights in a licensed body or parent undertaking of a licensed body which exceeds the voting limit.

 (3) If the licensing authority proposes to make a notification under sub-paragraph (2), it must give the person and the licensed body a warning notice.

 (4) The warning notice must –

   (a) specify the reasons for the proposed notification, and
   (b) state that representations may be made to the licensing authority within the prescribed period.

 (5) The licensing authority must consider any representations made within the prescribed period.

 (6) If the licensing authority notifies the Board under sub-paragraph (2), it must give the person concerned and the licensed body a copy of the notification and a notice stating the reasons for the notification.

 (7) If the share limit or voting limit is breached in relation to a parent undertaking of a licensed body, references in sub-paragraphs (3) and (6) to the licensed body include the parent undertaking.

50 (1) The person concerned and the licensed body may before the end of the prescribed period appeal to the relevant appellate body against the notification.

 (2) The relevant appellate body may –

   (a) dismiss the appeal, or
   (b) allow the appeal and order the person's name to be removed from the list kept by the Board under paragraph 51.

 (3) A party to the appeal may before the end of the prescribed period appeal to the

High Court on a point of law arising from the decision of the relevant appellant body, but only with the permission of the High Court.

(4) The High Court may make such order as it thinks fit.

(5) The licensing authority must notify the Board of the outcome of any appeal under this paragraph, and give the person concerned and the licensed body a copy of the notification.

(6) If the share limit or voting limit is breached in relation to a parent undertaking of a licensed body, references in sub-paragraphs (1) and (5) to the licensed body include the parent undertaking.

Board's list of persons subject to objections and conditions

51 (1) The Board must keep a list of the persons in respect of which it receives a notification under paragraph 47(1) or 49(2).

(2) The list must record –

(a) in relation to a person notified to the Board under paragraph 47(1), the information included in the notification by virtue of paragraph 47(2) and any notification under paragraph 47(3), and

(b) in relation to any person included in the list, the information included in any notification relating to that person under paragraph 48.

(3) If the Board receives a notification under paragraph 47(4) or (5), 48(3) or (4) or 50(5) it must make such alterations to the list as it considers appropriate having regard to the decision of the licensing authority or the outcome of the appeal (which may include removing a person from the list).

(4) The Board must make the list kept by it under this paragraph available to every licensing authority.

SCHEDULE 14 LICENSING AUTHORITY'S POWERS OF INTERVENTION

Section 102

Introductory

1 (1) This Schedule applies –

(a) where, in relation to a licensed body and the relevant licensing authority, one or more of the intervention conditions is satisfied;

(b) where a licence granted to a body has expired (and has not been renewed or replaced by the relevant licensing authority).

(2) The intervention conditions are –

(a) that the licensing authority is satisfied that one or more of the terms of the licensed body's licence have not been complied with;

(b) that a person has been appointed receiver or manager of property of the licensed body;

(c) that a relevant insolvency event has occurred in relation to the licensed body;

(d) that the licensing authority has reason to suspect dishonesty on the part of any manager or employee of the licensed body in connection with –

(i) that body's business,

(ii) any trust of which that body is or was a trustee,

APPENDIX A

        (iii)   any trust of which the manager or employee of the body is or was a trustee in that person's capacity as such a manager or employee, or

        (iv)   the business of another body in which the manager or employee is or was a manager or employee, or the practice (or former practice) of the manager or employee;

(e) that the licensing authority is satisfied that there has been undue delay –

        (i)   on the part of the licensed body in connection with any matter in which it is or was acting for a client or with any trust of which it is or was a trustee, or

        (ii)   on the part of a person who is or was a manager or employee of the licensed body in connection with any trust of which that person is or was a trustee in that person's capacity as such a manager or employee,

and the notice conditions are satisfied;

(f) that the licensing authority is satisfied that it is necessary to exercise the powers conferred by this Schedule (or any of them) in relation to a licensed body to protect –

        (i)   the interests of clients (or former or potential clients) of the licensed body,

        (ii)   the interests of the beneficiaries of any trust of which the licensed body is or was a trustee, or

        (iii)   the interests of the beneficiaries of any trust of which a person who is or was a manager or employee of the licensed body is or was a trustee in that person's capacity as such a manager or employee.

(3) For the purposes of sub-paragraph (2) a relevant insolvency event occurs in relation to a licensed body if –

(a) a resolution for a voluntary winding-up of the body is passed without a declaration of solvency under section 89 of the Insolvency Act 1986 (c. 45);

(b) the body enters administration within the meaning of paragraph 1(2)(b) of Schedule B1 to that Act;

(c) an administrative receiver within the meaning of section 251 of that Act is appointed;

(d) a meeting of creditors is held in relation to the body under section 95 of that Act (creditors' meeting which has the effect of converting a members' voluntary winding up into a creditors' voluntary winding up);

(e) an order for the winding up of the body is made.

(4) The notice conditions referred to in sub-paragraph (2)(e) are –

(a) that the licensing authority has given the licensed body a notice inviting it to give an explanation within such period (of not less than 8 days) following the giving of the notice as may be specified in it;

(b) that the licensed body has failed within that period to give an explanation which the licensing authority regards as satisfactory; and

(c) that the licensing authority gives notice of the failure to the licensed body and (at the same time or later) notice that this Schedule applies in its case by virtue of sub-paragraph (2)(e).

(5) Where this Schedule applies in relation to a licensed body by virtue of sub-paragraph (1)(a) it continues to apply after the body's licence has been revoked or has otherwise ceased to have effect.

(6) For the purposes of this Schedule "licensed body" includes –

    (a) a body whose licence is suspended;
    (b) a body to whom this Schedule continues to apply by virtue of sub-paragraph (5);
    (c) except in this paragraph, a body whose licence has ceased to have effect as mentioned in sub-paragraph (1)(b).

Money: prohibition on payment

2 (1) The licensing authority may apply to the High Court for an order under sub-paragraph (2), and the High Court may make the order if it thinks fit.

(2) The order is that a person holding money on behalf of the licensed body may not make any payment of the money, except with the leave of the court.

(3) An order under sub-paragraph (2) may take effect in relation to a person –

    (a) whether or not the person is named in the order;
    (b) however the money is held;
    (c) whether the money was received before or after the order was made.

(4) But an order under sub-paragraph (2) does not take effect in relation to a person until the licensing authority –

    (a) has given the person a copy of the order, and
    (b) (in the case of a bank or other financial institution) has indicated the branches at which it believes money to which the order relates is held.

(5) A person is not to be treated as having disobeyed an order under sub-paragraph (2) by making a payment of money if the court is satisfied that the person –

    (a) exercised due diligence to ascertain whether it was money to which the order related, and
    (b) failed to ascertain that the order related to it.

Money etc: vesting in licensing authority

3 (1) The sums of money to which this paragraph applies, and the right to recover or receive them, vest in the licensing authority if the licensing authority decides that they should do so.

(2) This paragraph applies to all sums of money held by or on behalf of the licensed body in connection with –

    (a) its activities as a licensed body,
    (b) any trust of which it is or was a trustee, or
    (c) any trust of which a person who is or was a manager or employee of the licensed body is or was a trustee in that person's capacity as such a manager or employee.

(3) Sub-paragraph (1) applies whether the sums were received by the person holding them before or after the licensing authority's decision.

(4) Those sums and that right are held by the licensing authority –

    (a) on trust to exercise the powers conferred by this Schedule in relation to them, and

APPENDIX A

        (b)   subject to that and to rules under paragraph 6, on trust for the persons beneficially entitled.

  (5)   The licensing authority must give the licensed body, and any other person in possession of sums of money to which this paragraph applies –

        (a)   a copy of the licensing authority's decision, and
        (b)   a notice prohibiting the payment out of those sums.

  (6)   A person to whom a notice under sub-paragraph (5) is given may apply to the High Court for an order directing the licensing authority to withdraw the notice.

  (7)   An application under sub-paragraph (6) must be made within 8 days of the licensing authority giving the person notice under sub-paragraph (5).

  (8)   The person must give not less than 48 hours notice of any application under sub-paragraph (6) –

        (a)   to the licensing authority, and
        (b)   if the notice under sub-paragraph (5) gives the name of a solicitor instructed by the licensing authority, to that solicitor.

  (9)   If the court makes the order, it may make any other order it thinks fit with respect to the matter.

  (10)   It is an offence for a person to whom a notice has been given under sub-paragraph (5) to pay out sums of money at a time when such payment is prohibited by the notice.

  (11)   A person who is guilty of an offence under sub-paragraph (10) is liable on summary conviction to a fine not exceeding level 3 on the standard scale.

4 (1)   Any rights to which this paragraph applies shall vest in the licensing authority if the licensing authority decides that they should do so.

  (2)   This paragraph applies to any right to recover or receive debts due to the licensed body in connection with its business.

  (3)   Any sums recovered by the licensing authority by virtue of the exercise of rights vested under sub-paragraph (1) vest in the licensing authority and are held by it –

        (a)   on trust to exercise the powers conferred by this Schedule in relation to them, and
        (b)   subject to that and to rules under paragraph 6, on trust for the persons beneficially entitled.

  (4)   The licensing authority must give the licensed body, and any other person who owes a debt to which the order applies a copy of the licensing authority's decision.

5 (1)   If the licensing authority takes possession of any sum of money to which paragraph 3 applies or by virtue of paragraph 4, it must pay it into a special account in the name of the licensing authority or a person nominated on its behalf.

  (2)   A person nominated under sub-paragraph (1) holds that sum –

        (a)   on trust to permit the licensing authority to exercise the powers conferred by this Schedule in relation to it, and
        (b)   subject to that and rules under paragraph 6, on trust for the persons beneficially entitled.

  (3)   A bank or other financial institution at which a special account is kept is under no obligation to ascertain whether it is being dealt with properly.

6 (1) The licensing authority may make rules governing its treatment of sums vested in it under paragraph 3 or 4(3).

(2) The rules may, in particular, make provision in respect of cases where the licensing authority, having taken such steps to do so as are reasonable in all the circumstances of the case, is unable to trace the person or persons beneficially entitled to any sum vested in the licensing authority under paragraph 3 or 4(3) (including provision which requires amounts to be paid into or out of any fund maintained by the licensing authority in connection with its compensation arrangements).

Money: information

7 (1) The licensing authority may apply to the High Court for an order requiring a person to give the licensing authority –

(a) information about any money held by the person on behalf of the licensed body, and the accounts in which it is held, or
(b) information relevant to identifying any money held by the licensed body or by another person on its behalf.

(2) The High Court may make the order if it is satisfied that there is reason to suspect –

(a) in a case within sub-paragraph (1)(a), that the person holds money on behalf of the licensed body, and
(b) in a case within sub-paragraph (1)(b), that the person has the information in question.

(3) This paragraph is without prejudice to paragraphs 2 to 6.

Notice to produce or deliver documents

8 (1) The licensing authority may give notice to the licensed body requiring it to produce or deliver all documents in its possession or under its control in connection with –

(a) its activities as a licensed body,
(b) any trust of which it is or was a trustee, or
(c) any trust of which a person who is or was a manager or employee of the licensed body is or was a trustee in that person's capacity as such a manager or employee.

(2) The notice may require the documents to be produced –

(a) to any person appointed by the licensing authority;
(b) at a time and place to be fixed by the licensing authority.

(3) The person appointed by the licensing authority may take possession of any such documents on behalf of the licensing authority.

(4) It is an offence for a person having possession of such documents to refuse, neglect or otherwise fail to comply with a notice under sub-paragraph (1).

(5) Sub-paragraph (4) does not apply where an application has been made to the High Court under paragraph 9(1)(a).

(6) A person who is guilty of an offence under sub-paragraph (4) is liable on summary conviction to a fine not exceeding level 3 on the standard scale.

APPENDIX A

Order to produce or deliver documents

9 (1) The High Court may, on the application of the licensing authority, make an order for production or delivery –

    (a) in relation to a person required to produce documents under paragraph 8 and the documents the person was required to produce;

    (b) if it is satisfied that there is reason to suspect that documents in relation to which the powers in paragraph 8 are exercisable have come into the possession or under the control of some person other than the licensed body, in relation to that person and those documents.

(2) An order for production or delivery is an order –

    (a) requiring a person to produce or deliver documents to any person appointed by the licensing authority, at a time and place specified in the order, and

    (b) authorising the appointed person to take possession of the documents on behalf of the licensing authority.

(3) The court may, on the application of the licensing authority, authorise a person appointed by the licensing authority to enter any premises (using such force as is reasonably necessary) to search for and take possession of –

    (a) any documents to which an order for production or delivery relates;

    (b) any property –

        (i) in the possession of or under the control of the licensed body, or

        (ii) in the case of an order under sub-paragraph (1)(b), which was in the possession or under the control of that body and has come into the possession or under the control of the person in respect of whom the order is made,

which the licensing authority reasonably requires for the purpose of accessing information contained in any such documents,

and to use property obtained under paragraph (b) for that purpose.

(4) It may do so on making the order for production or delivery, or at any later time.

Taking possession of documents etc under notice or order

10 (1) This paragraph applies where the licensing authority takes possession of documents or any other property under paragraph 8 or 9.

(2) On taking possession, it must give a notice to –

    (a) the licensed body, and

    (b) any other person from whom the documents or property were received or from whose possession they were taken.

(3) The notice must state that possession has been taken and specify the date on which possession was taken.

(4) A person to whom a notice under sub-paragraph (2) is given may apply to the High Court for an order directing the licensing authority to deliver the documents or other property to such person as the applicant requires.

(5) An application under sub-paragraph (4) must be made within 8 days of the licensing authority giving the person notice under sub-paragraph (2).

(6) The person must give not less than 48 hours notice of the application –

(a) to the licensing authority, and
(b) if the notice under sub-paragraph (2) gives the name of a solicitor instructed by the licensing authority, to that solicitor.

(7) The court may make any order it thinks fit.

Mail and other forms of communication

11 (1) The High Court, on the application of the licensing authority, may from time to time make a communications redirection order.
(2) A communications redirection order is an order that specified communications to the licensed body are to be directed, in accordance with the order, to the licensing authority or any person appointed by the licensing authority.
(3) For the purposes of this paragraph –
   (a) "specified communications" means communications of such description as are specified in the order;
   (b) the descriptions of communications which may be so specified include –
      (i) communications in the form of a postal packet;
      (ii) electronic communications;
      (iii) communications by telephone.
(4) A communications redirection order has effect for such time not exceeding 18 months as is specified in the order.
(5) Where a communications redirection order has effect, the licensing authority or the person appointed by the licensing authority may take possession or receipt of the communications redirected in accordance with the order.
(6) Where a communications redirection order is made the licensing authority must pay to the designated payee the like charges (if any) as would have been payable for the redirection of the communications to which the order relates if the addressee –
   (a) had permanently ceased to occupy or use the premises or other destination of the communications, and
   (b) had applied to the designated payee to redirect the communications as mentioned in the order.
(7) For this purpose "the designated payee" means –
   (a) in the case of an order relating to postal packets, the postal operator concerned, and
   (b) in any other case, the person specified in the order as the designated payee.
(8) The High Court may, on the application of the licensing authority, authorise the licensing authority, or a person appointed by it, to take such steps as may be specified in the order in relation to any website purporting to be or have been maintained by or on behalf of the licensed body, if the High Court is satisfied that the taking of those steps is necessary to protect the public interest or the interests of clients (or potential or former clients) of the licensed body.
(9) In this paragraph "postal operator" and "postal packet" have the meaning given by section 27 of the Postal Services Act 2011 (c. 5).
(10) This paragraph does not apply where the powers conferred by this Part of this Schedule are exercisable by virtue of paragraph 1(2)(e).

APPENDIX A

Use of documents in licensing authority's possession

12   (1)   The licensing authority may apply to the High Court for an order as to the disposal or destruction of any document or other property in its possession by virtue of paragraph 8, 9 or 11.

       (2)   The court may make any order it thinks fit.

13   (1)   The licensing authority may take copies of or extracts from any documents in its possession by virtue of paragraph 8, 9 or 11.

       (2)   If the licensing authority proposes to deliver such documents to any person, it may make the delivery conditional on the person giving a reasonable undertaking to supply copies or extracts to the licensing authority.

       (3)   Sub-paragraphs (1) and (2) are subject to any order made by the court under paragraph 10 or 12.

Trusts

14   (1)   If the licensed body is a trustee of any trust, the licensing authority may apply to the High Court for an order for the appointment of a new trustee in substitution for it.

       (2)   If a person who is a manager or employee of the licensed body is a trustee of any trust in that person's capacity as such a manager or employee, the licensing authority may apply to the High Court for an order for the appointment of a new trustee in substitution for that person.

       (3)   The Trustee Act 1925 (c. 19) has effect in relation to an appointment of a new trustee under this paragraph as it has effect in relation to an appointment under section 41 of that Act.

General powers of licensing authority

15   The powers conferred by this Schedule in relation to sums of money, documents or other property may be exercised despite any lien on them or right to their possession.

16   The licensing authority may do all things which are reasonably necessary to facilitate the exercise of its powers under this Schedule.

Licensing authority's costs

17   (1)   Any costs incurred by the licensing authority for the purposes of this Schedule (including the costs of any person exercising powers under this Schedule on behalf of the licensing authority) –

            (a)   are to be paid by the licensed body, and

            (b)   may be recovered from the licensed body as a debt owing to the licensing authority.

       (2)   Sub-paragraph (1) is subject to any order for payment of costs that may be made on an application to the court under this Schedule.

18   (1)   The High Court, on the application of the licensing authority, may order a liable party to pay a specified proportion of the costs mentioned in paragraph 17.

       (2)   For this purpose a "liable party" means –

            (a)   if the licensed body is a partnership, any former partner in the licensed body,

            (b)   in any other case, any manager or former manager of the licensed body.

(3) The High Court may make an order under this paragraph in respect of a liable party only if it is satisfied that the conduct (or any part of the conduct) by reason of which this Schedule applies was conduct carried on with the consent or connivance of, or was attributable to any neglect on the part of, the liable party.
(4) In this paragraph "specified" means specified in the order made by the High Court.

APPENDIX B

SRA Authorisation Rules for Legal Services Bodies and Licensable Bodies 2011

Rules dated 17 June 2011

commencing in respect of licensable bodies, on the designation of the Law Society as a licensing authority under Part 1 of Schedule 10 to the Legal Services Act 2007; and in respect of legal services bodies, on 31 March 2012

made by the Solicitors Regulation Authority Board, under sections 79 and 80 of the Solicitors Act 1974, sections 9 and 9A of the Administration of Justice Act 1985 and section 83 and Schedule 11 to the Legal Services Act 2007, with the approval of the Legal Services Board under paragraph 19 of Schedule 4 to the Legal Services Act 2007.

PART 1: INTERPRETATION AND APPLICATIONS

RULE 1: INTERPRETATION

1.1 All italicised terms in these rules are to be interpreted in accordance with Chapter 14 (Interpretation) of the *SRA Code of Conduct*, unless they are defined in Rule 1.2.

1.2 In these rules:

appellate body means the body with the power, by virtue of an order under section 80(1) of the *LSA*, to hear and determine appeals against decisions made by the *SRA* acting as a *licensing authority*.

applicant body means a *licensable body* or a *legal services body* which makes an application to the *SRA* for *authorisation* in accordance with these rules.

associate has the meaning given in paragraph 5 to Schedule 13 of the *LSA*, namely:

    (i) "associate", in relation to a *person* ("A") and –

        (A) a shareholding in a body ("S"), or

        (B) an entitlement to exercise or control the exercise of voting power in a body ("V"),

    means a *person* listed in sub-paragraph (ii).

    (ii) The *persons* are –

        (A) the spouse or civil partner of A,

        (B) a child or stepchild of A (if under 18),

        (C) the *trustee* of any settlement under which A has a life interest in possession (in Scotland a life interest),

        (D) an undertaking of which A is a *director*,

        (E) an *employee* of A,

        (F) a *partner* of A (except, where S or V is a *partnership* in which A is a *partner*, another *partner* in S or V),

(G) if A is an undertaking

    (I) a *director* of A,
    (II) a subsidiary undertaking of A, or
    (III) a *director* or *employee* of such a subsidiary undertaking,

(H) if A has with any other *person* an agreement or arrangement with respect to the acquisition, holding or disposal of shares or other interests in S or V (whether or not they are interests within the meaning of section 72(3) of the *LSA*), that other *person*, or

(I) if A has with any other *person* an agreement or arrangement under which they undertake to act together in exercising their voting power in relation to S or V, that *person*.

authorisation granted to a body under Rule 6 means:

(i) recognition under section 9 of the *AJA*, if it is granted to a *legal services body*; and
(ii) a licence under Part 5 of the *LSA*, if it is granted to a *licensable body*;

and the term "certificate of authorisation" shall be construed accordingly.

authorised activities means:

(i) any *reserved legal activity* in respect of which the body is authorised;
(ii) any other *legal activity*;
(iii) any other activity in respect of which a *licensed body* is regulated pursuant to Part 5 of the *LSA*; and
(iv) any other activity a *recognised body* carries out in connection with its *practice*.

authorised person(s) means a *person* who is authorised by the *SRA* or another *approved regulator* to carry on a legal activity and for the purpose of these rules includes a *solicitor*, a *sole practitioner*, an *REL*, an *EEL*, an *RFL*, an *authorised body*, an *authorised non-SRA firm*, and a *European corporate practice* and the terms "authorised individual" and "non-authorised person" shall be construed accordingly.

body where the context permits includes a *sole practitioner* and a special body within the meaning of section 106 of the *LSA*.

BSB means the Bar Standards Board.

candidate means a *person* who is assessed by the *SRA* for approval as an *owner*, *manager* or *compliance officer* under Part 4.

compliance officer is a reference to a body's *COLP* or its *COFA*.

Court of Protection deputy includes a deputy who was appointed by the Court of Protection as a receiver under the Mental Health Act 1983 before the commencement date of the Mental Capacity Act 2005, and also includes equivalents in other *Establishment Directive states*.

date of notification the date of any notification or notice given under these rules is deemed to be:

(i) the date on which the communication is delivered to or left at the recipient's address or is sent electronically to the recipient's e-mail or fax address;
(ii) if the recipient is *practising*, seven days after the communication has been sent by post or document exchange to the recipient's last notified *practising address*; or
(iii) if the recipient is not *practising*, seven days after the communication has been sent by post or document exchange to the recipient's last notified contact address.

decision period is the period specified in Rule 5.

disqualified refers to a *person* who has been disqualified under section 99 of the *LSA* by the *SRA* or by any other *approved regulator*.

EEL means exempt European *lawyer*, namely a member of an *Establishment Directive profession*:

(i) registered with the *BSB*; or
(ii) based entirely at an office or offices outside England and Wales,

who is not a *lawyer of England and Wales* (whether entitled to *practise* as such or not).

European corporate practice means a *lawyers'* practice which is a body incorporated in an *Establishment Directive state*, or a partnership with separate legal identity formed under the law of an *Establishment Directive state*:

(i) which has an office in an *Establishment Directive state* but does not have an office in England and Wales;
(ii) whose ultimate beneficial owners include at least one individual who is not a *lawyer of England and Wales* but is, and is entitled to practise as, a *lawyer* of an *Establishment Directive profession*; and
(iii) whose *managers* include at least one such individual, or at least one *body corporate* whose *managers* include at least one such individual.

HOFA means a Head of Finance and Administration within the meaning of paragraph 13(2) of Schedule 11 to the *LSA*.

HOLP means a Head of Legal Practice within the meaning of paragraph 11(2) of Schedule 11 to the *LSA*.

interest holder means a *person* who has an interest or an indirect interest, or holds a *material interest*, in a body (and "indirect interest" and "interest" have the same meaning as in the *LSA*), and references to "holds an interest" shall be construed accordingly;

legally qualified means any of the following:

(i) a *lawyer*;
(ii) a *recognised body*;
(iii) an *authorised non-SRA firm* of which all the *managers* and *interest holders* are *lawyers* save that where another body ("A") is a *manager* of or has an interest in the firm, *non-authorised persons* are entitled to exercise, or control the exercise of, less than 10% of the *voting rights* in A;
(iv) a *European corporate practice* of which all the *managers* and *interest holders* are *lawyers*.

and references to a "legally qualified body" shall be construed accordingly.

legal services body means a body which meets the criteria in Rule 13 (Eligibility criteria and fundamental requirements for recognised bodies) of the *SRA Practice Framework Rules*.

licensing authority means an *approved regulator* which is designated as a licensing authority under Part 1 of Schedule 10 to the *LSA*, and whose licensing rules have been approved for the purposes of the *LSA*.

material interest has the meaning given to it in Schedule 13 to the *LSA*; and a person holds a "material interest" in a body ("B"), if the person:

(i) holds at least 10% of the shares in B;
(ii) is able to exercise significant influence over the management of B by virtue of the person's shareholding in B;
(iii) holds at least 10% of the shares in a parent undertaking ("P") of B;
(iv) is able to exercise significant influence over the management of P by virtue of the person's shareholding in P;

(v) is entitled to exercise, or control the exercise of, voting power in B which, if it consists of *voting rights*, constitutes at least 10% of the *voting rights* in B;
(vi) is able to exercise significant influence over the management of B by virtue of the person's entitlement to exercise, or control the exercise of, *voting rights* in B;
(vii) is entitled to exercise, or control the exercise of, voting power in P which, if it consists of *voting rights*, constitutes at least 10% of the *voting rights* in P; or
(viii) is able to exercise significant influence over the management of P by virtue of the person's entitlement to exercise, or control the exercise of, *voting rights* in P;

and for the purpose of this definition, "person" means (a) the person, (b) any of the person's *associates*, or (c) the person and any of the person's *associates* taken together, and "parent undertaking" and "voting power" are to be construed in accordance with paragraphs 3 and 5 of Schedule 13 to the *LSA*.

owner means any *person* who holds a *material interest* in an *authorised body*, and in the case of a *partnership*, any *partner* regardless of whether they hold a *material interest* in the *partnership*.

person who lacks capacity under Part 1 of the Mental Capacity Act 2005 references to a person who lacks capacity under Part 1 of the Mental Capacity Act 2005 include a "patient" as defined by section 94 of the Mental Health Act 1983 and a person made the subject of emergency powers under that Act, and equivalents in other *Establishment Directive states*.

practising address in relation to an *authorised body* means an address from which the body provides services consisting of or including the carrying on of activities which it is authorised to carry on.

prescribed means prescribed by the *SRA* from time to time.

principal means a *sole practitioner* or a *partner* in a *partnership*.

professional principles the professional principles are as set out in section 1(3) of the *LSA*:

(i) that authorised persons should act with independence and integrity,
(ii) that authorised persons should maintain proper standards of work,
(iii) that authorised persons should act in the best interests of their *clients*,
(iv) that persons who exercise before any *court* a right of audience, or conduct litigation in relation to proceedings in any *court*, by virtue of being authorised persons should comply with their duty to the *court* to act with independence in the interests of justice, and
(v) that the affairs of *clients* should be kept confidential

and in this definition "authorised persons" has the meaning set out in section 18 of the *LSA*.

regulatory arrangements has the meaning given to it by section 21 of the *LSA*, and includes all rules and regulations of the *SRA* in relation to the authorisation, practice, conduct, discipline and qualification of *persons* carrying on *legal activities* and the accounts rules and indemnification and compensation arrangements in relation to their *practice*.

regulatory objectives has the meaning given to it by section 1 of the *LSA* and includes the objectives of protecting and promoting the public interest, supporting the constitutional principle of the rule of law, improving access to justice, protecting and promoting the interests of consumers, promoting competition in the provision of *legal activities* by *authorised persons*, encouraging an independent, strong, diverse and effective legal profession, increasing public understanding of the

APPENDIX B

citizen's legal rights and duties, and promoting and maintaining adherence to the *professional principles*.

relevant insolvency event a relevant insolvency event occurs in relation to a body if:

(i) a resolution for a voluntary winding-up of the body is passed without a declaration of solvency under section 89 of the Insolvency Act 1986;

(ii) the body enters administration within the meaning of paragraph 1(2)(b) of Schedule B1 to that Act;

(iii) an administrative receiver within the meaning of section 251 of that Act is appointed;

(iv) a meeting of creditors is held in relation to the body under section 95 of that Act (creditors' meeting which has the effect of converting a *members'* voluntary winding up into a creditors' voluntary winding up);

(v) an order for the winding up of the body is made;

(vi) all of the *managers* in a body which is unincorporated have been adjudicated bankrupt; or

(vii) the body is an overseas company or a *societas Europaea* registered outside England, Wales, Scotland and Northern Ireland and the body is subject to an event in its country of incorporation analogous to an event as set out in paragraphs (i) to (vi) above.

SA means the Solicitors Act 1974.

shareowner means:

(i) a *member* of a *company* with a share capital, who owns a share in the body; or

(ii) a *person* who is not a *member* of a *company* with a share capital, but owns a share in the body, which is held by a *member* as nominee.

SRA Accounts Rules means the SRA Accounts Rules 2011.

SRA Code of Conduct means the SRA Code of Conduct 2011.

SRA Practice Framework Rules means the SRA Practice Framework Rules 2011.

SRA Practising Regulations means the SRA Practising Regulations 2011.

the Tribunal means the Solicitors Disciplinary Tribunal which is an independent statutory tribunal constituted under section 46 of the *SA* but references to the Tribunal do not include the Tribunal when it is performing any function as an *appellate body*.

trustee includes a personal representative (i.e. an executor or an administrator), and "trust" includes the duties of a personal representative.

Guidance notes

(i) "Owner". Although Rule 1.2 limits the definition of "owner" to anyone holding a material interest, any person who is a partner in a partnership (including salaried partners) is within the definition regardless of the extent of their interest. This reflects paragraph 3(1) of Schedule 13 to the LSA as well as the principles of partnership law.

(ii) When assessing whether a person is an owner with a "material interest", the calculation of the person's interest takes into account not only that person's interest, but also the interests of any associates. "Associates" is defined for these purposes in accordance with paragraph 5 to Schedule 13 of the LSA and includes relationships where the Act assumes a likelihood of influence such as employer over employee.

RULE 2: FORM, TIMING AND FEES FOR APPLICATIONS MADE UNDER THESE RULES

2.1 All applications under these rules must comprise:

(a) the *prescribed* form, correctly completed;

(b) the fee or fees for the application, as determined from time to time by the *SRA* Board;

(c) such additional information, documents and references considered by the *SRA* to be necessary to enable it to discharge its functions under these rules, as may be specified by the *SRA*; and

(d) any additional information and documentation which the *SRA* may reasonably require.

2.2 It is not necessary to submit all documents, information and payments simultaneously, but an application will only have been made once the *SRA* has received all of the documentation, information and payments comprising that application.

Guidance notes

(i) Application forms and guidance notes can be found on the SRA website.

(ii) All parts of the application form must be fully completed. Where forms are only partially complete or where supporting information or documents are still to be provided, the application will not be deemed to have been made and the decision period in Rule 5.2 will not start to run.

RULE 3: APPLICATION INFORMATION AND NOTIFICATION OF ANY CHANGE FOLLOWING APPLICATION

3.1 The *applicant body* must:

(a) ensure that all information given in an application under these rules is correct and complete;

(b) notify the *SRA* as soon as it becomes aware that any information provided in its application under these rules has changed.

Guidance notes

(i) During the application process an applicant body must notify the SRA of any changes to details or information provided as part of the application including notifying new information that the applicant body would have been required to supply if it had been known at the time of the application. It is an offence under the LSA (see Schedule 13 paragraphs 10–12) not to inform the SRA if there is any change to:

(a) the list of non-authorised persons who hold or are expected to hold a material interest in the applicant body, and

(b) the extent or nature of those interests held or to be held.

(ii) Authorised bodies are subject to similar notification requirements under Rule 8.7.

APPENDIX B

PART 2: AUTHORISATION APPLICATIONS AND DECISION PERIOD

RULE 4: APPLICATIONS FOR AUTHORISATION

4.1 A *licensable body* or a *legal services body* may make an application for *authorisation* in accordance with these rules.

4.2 An application by a *licensable body* for *authorisation* must include a statement about what *reserved legal activities* the body seeks *authorisation* for.

4.3 Where an application by a *licensable body* for *authorisation* relates to more than one *reserved legal activity*, the *SRA* may grant the application in relation to all or any of them.

RULE 5: DECISION PERIOD

5.1 The *SRA* must:

 (a) decide an *authorisation* application;
 (b) notify the *applicant body* of its decision;
 (c) if it decides to refuse the application, set out in the notice the reasons for the refusal;

before the end of the *decision period*.

5.2 The *decision period* is the period of 6 months beginning with the day on which the application is made to the *SRA* in accordance with these rules.

5.3 The *SRA* may, on one occasion, give the *applicant body* a notice (an "extension notice") extending the *decision period* by a period specified in the notice.

5.4 But:

 (a) an extension notice must only be given before the time when the *decision period* would end, but for the extension notice; and
 (b) the total *decision period* must not exceed 9 months.

5.5 An extension notice must set out the reasons for the extension.

Guidance notes

(i) See Rule 2.2 above for when an application is made.
(ii) The SRA will extend the period for making a decision if it considers this necessary for the proper consideration of the application (see paragraph 2 of Schedule 11 to the LSA).
(iii) The means of notice or notification can include any form of written electronic communication normally used for business purposes, such as emails.

RULE 6: DETERMINATION OF AUTHORISATION APPLICATIONS

6.1 The *SRA* will determine applications for *authorisation*, so far as is reasonably practicable, in a way:

 (a) which is compatible with the *regulatory objectives* including the objective of improving access to justice; and
 (b) which the *SRA* considers most appropriate for the purpose of meeting those objectives.

SRA AUTHORISATION RULES 2011

6.2 The *SRA* may only grant an application for *authorisation* if the conditions in (a) to (d) below are met:
- (a) if it is an application for recognition, the *applicant body* is a *legal services body*;
- (b) if it is an application for a licence, the *applicant body* is a *licensable body*;
- (c) if it is a *partnership*, the body has adopted a name under which it is to be registered, and which complies with Chapter 8 (Publicity) of the *SRA Code of Conduct*; and
- (d) the *SRA* is satisfied that upon *authorisation*, the body will be in compliance with the following rules:
  - (i) SRA Indemnity Insurance Rules;
  - (ii) Solicitors' Compensation Fund Rules;
  - (iii) Rule 8.5 (compliance officers), including any necessary approval of a *candidate* under Part 4;
  - (iv) Rule 8.6 (management and control) including any necessary approval of a *candidate* under Part 4; and
  - (v) Rules 15 (Formation, registered office and practising address), 16 (Composition of an authorised body) and 12 (Persons who must be "qualified to supervise") of the *SRA Practice Framework Rules*.

6.3 Notwithstanding that the conditions in 6.2 are met, the *SRA* may refuse an application for *authorisation* if:
- (a) it is not satisfied that the *applicant body's managers* and *interest holders* are suitable, as a group, to operate or control a business providing regulated legal services;
- (b) it is not satisfied that the *applicant body's* management or governance arrangements are adequate to safeguard the *regulatory objectives*;
- (c) it is not satisfied that if the *authorisation* is granted, the *applicant body* will comply with the *SRA's regulatory arrangements* including these rules and any conditions imposed on the *authorisation*;
- (d) the *applicant body* has provided inaccurate or misleading information in its application or in response to any requests by the *SRA* for information;
- (e) the *applicant body* has failed to notify the *SRA* of any changes in the information provided in the application in accordance with Rule 3; or
- (f) for any other reason, the *SRA* considers that it would be against the public interest or otherwise inconsistent with the *regulatory objectives* to grant *authorisation*.

6.4 In reaching a decision under this rule, the *SRA* will take into account all the circumstances which the *SRA* considers to be relevant including, for the avoidance of doubt,
- (a) any relevant information regarding:
  - (i) a *manager*, *employee* or *interest holder* of the *applicant body*;
  - (ii) any *persons* that such a *manager*, *employee* or *interest holder* is related to, affiliated with, or acts together with where the *SRA* has reason to believe that such *persons* may have an influence over the way in which the *manager*, *employee* or *interest holder* will exercise their role; and
- (b) any failure or refusal to disclose, or attempts to conceal relevant information.

APPENDIX B

Guidance notes

(i) In considering applications the SRA must comply with the regulatory objectives. Relevant information will therefore be construed widely and the SRA will take account of a broad range of factors. These will include not only issues relevant to the Part 4 approval process, but also factors such as the applicant body's business and governance proposals.
(ii) Where information is provided in respect of an application, the SRA will consider this to be misleading if, despite the fact that the information is accurate, there is a material omission.
(iii) View the forms, Suitability Test and the decision making criteria.

PART 3: CONDITIONS OF AUTHORISATION

RULE 7: TERMS AND CONDITIONS OF AUTHORISATION

7.1 The *authorisation* of a body under these rules entitles:

(a) a *recognised body* to undertake the activities set out in Rule 8.5 (reserved work and immigration work: recognised bodies) of the *SRA Practice Framework Rules*; and
(b) a *licensed body* to undertake the *reserved legal activities* specified in the licence.

7.2 Every *authorisation* is granted by the *SRA* subject to:

(a) the general conditions in Rule 8; and
(b) any further conditions imposed by the *SRA*, at the time of the grant of *authorisation* or at any time subsequently, in accordance with Rule 9.

Guidance notes

(i) Where a firm is authorised by the SRA, as well as undertaking the activities set out in Rule 7, the firm will also be able to carry out other non-reserved legal activities. The SRA's jurisdiction over the firm includes the reserved and other legal activities, as defined under section 12 of the LSA, and other activities which are subject to conditions on the body's licence.
(ii) If a firm carries out a range of legal and non-legal activities (a multi-disciplinary practice or "MDP") the SRA's jurisdiction will not generally extend to cover the "non-legal" activities of the licensed body (unless covered by a specific condition on the licence). Such non-legal activities may be regulated by another regulator, and some activities may not fall within the regulatory ambit of any regulator.

RULE 8: GENERAL CONDITIONS ON AUTHORISATION

8.1 Regulatory compliance

(a) An *authorised body* and its *managers* must ensure that:
  (i) any obligations imposed from time to time on the *authorised body*, its *managers*, *employees* or *interest holders* by or under the *SRA's regulatory arrangements* are complied with; and
  (ii) any other statutory obligations imposed on the *authorised body*, its *managers*, *employees* or *interest holders*, in relation to the body's business of carrying on *authorised activities*, are complied with.

(b) Without prejudice to the generality of sub-rule (a) above, an *authorised body* and its *managers* must agree to be subject to the SRA Disciplinary Procedure Rules 2011 and in particular the power of the *SRA* to:
  (i) impose a written rebuke and publish details of a written rebuke or a decision to impose a penalty, in accordance with Rule 3 of those rules; and
  (ii) conduct an internal appeal of a decision in accordance with Rule 11 of those rules,

  subject to any right of appeal or challenge under those rules or any other enactment in relation to any action taken by the *SRA* under those rules.

(c) Nothing in Rule 8 or any other provision in the *SRA's regulatory arrangements* affects the generality of the condition in Rule 8.1.

8.2 Suitable arrangements for compliance

(a) An *authorised body* must at all times have suitable arrangements in place to ensure that:
  (i) the body, its *managers* and *employees*, comply with the *SRA's regulatory arrangements* as they apply to them, as required under section 176 of the *LSA* and Rule 8.1 above; and
  (ii) the body and its *managers* and *employees*, who are *authorised persons*, maintain the *professional principles*.

(b) A *licensed body* must at all times have suitable arrangements in place to ensure that, as required under section 90 of the *LSA*, the *employees* and *managers* and *interest holders* of that body who are *non-authorised persons* do nothing which causes or substantially contributes to a breach by the *licensed body* or its *employees* or *managers* of the *SRA's regulatory arrangements*.

8.3 Payment of periodical fees

(a) Every *authorised body* must pay to the *SRA* the *prescribed* periodical fees applicable to that body by the *prescribed* date.
(b) The *SRA* shall determine the amount of any fees required under these rules and the *SRA's* decision shall be final.
(c) The *SRA* may prescribe from time to time a fee moderation process under which an *authorised body* may make an application, in accordance with sub-rules (d) to (l) below, for the *prescribed* periodical fees applicable to that body to be varied. A decision under this process shall be final.
(d) The turnover of an *authorised body* for the purpose of determining the *prescribed* periodical fees applicable to that body is based on a historic turnover figure submitted to the *SRA*. Where in the 12 months following the submission of that figure an *authorised*

APPENDIX B

body merges or splits, a notice of succession identifying all *authorised bodies, recognised bodies* and *recognised sole practitioners* affected by the merger or split and any resulting apportionment of the historic turnover figures for those *firms* will enable the *SRA* to ensure that the turnover figure on which the fee is based reflects the impact of the merger or split.

(e) A turnover figure submitted to the *SRA* shall be calculated in accordance with the *SRA's prescribed* method of calculation.

(f) An *authorised body* which has succeeded to the whole or a part of one or more *authorised bodies, recognised bodies* or *recognised sole practitioners* must within 28 days of the change taking place deliver to the *SRA* a notice of succession in the *prescribed* form.

(g) For the purposes of Rule 8.3(f), "succeeded" includes any taking over of the whole or any part of an *authorised body, recognised body* or *recognised sole practitioner*, for value or otherwise.

(h) An *authorised body* which:

    (i) has split or ceded part of the *practice* to an *authorised body* and/or *recognised body* or *recognised sole practitioner*; and

    (ii) wishes this change to be considered by the *SRA* when determining the *authorised body's* next *prescribed* periodical fees applicable to that body

must within 28 days of the change taking place deliver to the *SRA* a notice of succession in the *prescribed* form.

(i) A notice of succession delivered under these rules must:

    (i) identify all *authorised bodies, recognised bodies* and *recognised sole practitioners* affected by the succession; and

    (ii) provide details of any resulting apportionment of the turnover figures for those *authorised bodies, recognised bodies* and *recognised sole practitioners*.

(j) An *authorised body* delivering a notice of succession under these rules must seek the agreement of all affected *authorised bodies, recognised bodies* or *recognised sole practitioners* to the contents of the notice of succession.

(k) Where a notice of succession is delivered to the *SRA* which has not been agreed by all affected *authorised bodies, recognised bodies* or *recognised sole practitioners*, the *authorised body* delivering the notice of succession shall be treated as having made an application for the *SRA* to apportion the turnover figures of the affected *authorised bodies, recognised bodies* or *recognised sole practitioners* for the purposes of determining the periodic fee or the fee for renewal of recognition.

(l) Before apportioning the turnover figures under Rule 8.3(k), the *SRA* will contact any affected *authorised body, recognised body* or *recognised sole practitioner* identified in the notice of succession who has not agreed with the notice of succession and may require the production of additional information.

8.4 Carrying on of activities

(a) An *authorised body* may not carry on an activity unless through a body and individual who is authorised to carry on that activity.

8.5 Compliance officers

(a) An *authorised body* must have suitable arrangements in place to ensure that its *compliance officers* are able to discharge their duties in accordance with these rules.

(b) An *authorised body* must at all times have an individual:

SRA AUTHORISATION RULES 2011

 (i) who is a *manager* or an *employee* of the *authorised body*;
 (ii) who is designated as its *COLP*;
 (iii) who is of sufficient seniority and in a position of sufficient responsibility to fulfil the role; and
 (iv) whose designation is approved by the *SRA*.

(c) The *COLP* of an *authorised body* must:
 (i) take all reasonable steps to:
  (A) ensure compliance with the terms and conditions of the *authorised body's authorisation* except any obligations imposed under the *SRA Accounts Rules*;
  (B) ensure compliance with any statutory obligations of the body, its *managers*, *employees* or *interest holders* in relation to the body's carrying on of *authorised activities*; and
  (C) record any failure so to comply and make such records available to the *SRA* on request; and
 (ii) as soon as reasonably practicable, report to the *SRA* any failure so to comply, provided that:
  (A) in the case of non-material failures, these shall be taken to have been reported as soon as reasonably practicable if they are reported to the *SRA* together with such other information as the *SRA* may require in accordance with Rule 8.7(a); and
  (B) a failure may be material either taken on its own or as part of a pattern of failures so to comply.

(d) An *authorised body* must at all times have an individual:
 (i) who is a *manager* or an *employee* of the *authorised body*;
 (ii) who is designated as its *COFA*;
 (iii) who is of sufficient seniority and in a position of sufficient responsibility to fulfil the role; and
 (iv) whose designation is approved by the *SRA*.

(e) The *COFA* of an *authorised body* must:
 (i) take all reasonable steps to ensure that the body and its *employees* and *managers* comply with any obligations imposed upon them under the *SRA Accounts Rules*;
 (ii) record any failure so to comply and make such records available to the *SRA* on request; and
 (iii) as soon as reasonably practicable, report to the *SRA* any failure so to comply, provided that:
  (A) in the case of non-material failures, these shall be taken to have been reported as soon as reasonably practicable if they are reported to the *SRA* together with such other information as the *SRA* may require in accordance with Rule 8.7(a); and
  (B) a failure may be material either taken on its own or as part of a pattern of failures so to comply.

(f) The *SRA* may approve an individual's designation as a *COLP* or *COFA* if it is satisfied, in accordance with Part 4, that the individual is a suitable person to carry out his or her duties.

(g) A designation of an individual as a *COLP* or *COFA* has effect only while the individual:

APPENDIX B

    (i) consents to the designation;
    (ii) in the case of a *COLP*:

        (A) is not *disqualified* from acting as a *HOLP*; and
        (B) is:

            (I) a *lawyer of England and Wales*;
            (II) an *REL*; or
            (III) registered with the *BSB* under Regulation 17 of the European Communities (Lawyer's Practice) Regulations 2000 (SI 2000/1119);

        and is an *authorised person* in relation to one or more of the *reserved legal activities* which the body is authorised to carry on; and

    (iii) in the case of a *COFA*, is not *disqualified* from acting as a *HOFA*.

8.6 Management and control

(a) An *authorised body* must ensure that:

    (i) any *manager* or *owner* of the *authorised body*; or
    (ii) any *manager* of a *body corporate* which is a *manager* or *owner* of the *authorised body*;

has been approved by the *SRA* under Part 4.

(b) No *manager* of a *licensed body* may be a *person* who is *disqualified* from being a *manager*.

(c) An *authorised body* (or *manager* or *employee* of such a body) must not employ or remunerate a person:

    (i) who is subject to an order under Section 43 of the *SA*, without the *SRA's* written permission;
    (ii) whose name has been struck off the roll, who is suspended from *practising* as a *solicitor*, or whose practising certificate has been suspended whilst he/she is an undischarged bankrupt, without the *SRA's* written permission;
    (iii) if there is a direction in force in respect of that person under section 47(2)(g) of the *SA* (Prohibition on restoration to the roll), without the *SRA's* written permission; or
    (iv) who is *disqualified* from being an *employee*.

(d) No *licensed body* (or *manager* or *employee* of such a body) may, except in accordance with the *SRA's* written permission, permit an individual to be a *manager* or *owner* of the body if:

    (i) that person's name has been struck off the roll;
    (ii) he/she is suspended from *practising* as a *solicitor*;
    (iii) his/her practising certificate has been suspended whilst he/she is an undischarged bankrupt;
    (iv) there is a direction in force in respect of that person under section 47(2)(g) of the *SA* (Prohibition on restoration to the roll); or
    (v) there is an order in force in respect of that individual under section 43 of the *SA* (Control of solicitors' employees and consultants).

(e) No *recognised body* (or *manager* or *employee* of such a body) may, except in accordance with the *SRA's* written permission, permit an individual to be a *manager* or *interest holder* of the body if:

    (i) that person's name has been struck off the roll;

SRA AUTHORISATION RULES 2011

    (ii)   he/she is suspended from *practising* as a *solicitor*;

    (iii)   his/her practising certificate has been suspended whilst he/she is an undischarged bankrupt;

    (iv)   there is a direction in force in respect of that person under section 47(2)(g) of the *SA* (Prohibition on restoration to the roll); or

    (v)   there is an order in force in respect of that person under section 43 of the *SA* (Control of solicitors' employees and consultants).

8.7 Information requirements

(a) An *authorised body* must properly complete and provide to the *SRA* an information report on an annual basis or such other period as specified by the *SRA* in the *prescribed* form and by the *prescribed* date.

(b) An *authorised body* must provide any necessary permissions for information to be given to the *SRA* so as to enable it to:

    (i)   use and prepare a report on the documents produced under (a) above; and

    (ii)   seek verification from *clients, employees, managers* or any other body including banks, building societies or other financial institutions.

(c) An *authorised body* must notify the *SRA* as soon as it becomes aware of any changes to relevant information about itself, its *employees, managers,* or *interest holders* including any non-compliance with these rules and the conditions on the body's *authorisation*.

(d) If an *authorised body* becomes aware or has information that reasonably suggests that it has or may have provided the *SRA* with information which was or may have been false, misleading, incomplete or inaccurate, or has or may have changed in a materially significant way, it must notify the *SRA* immediately.

8.8 Additional conditions for partnerships

(a) If a *partner* in a *partnership* which is an *authorised body*:

    (i)   is committed to prison in civil or criminal proceedings;

    (ii)   becomes and continues to be unable to attend to the *practice* of the body because of incapacity caused by illness, accident or age;

    (iii)   becomes and continues to be a *person who lacks capacity under Part 1 of the Mental Capacity Act 2005*;

    (iv)   abandons the *practice* of the body; or

    (v)   is made subject to a condition on his or her practising certificate, registration or equivalent *authorisation* by an *approved regulator* other than the *SRA* which would be breached by continuing as a *partner*;

and this results in there being only one active *partner*, that *partner* must inform the *SRA* within seven days of the relevant event.

8.9 Additional conditions for recognised bodies

(a) An *interest holder* of a *recognised body* must not create any charge or other third party interest over his or her interest in the *recognised body* except a *member* or *shareowner* of a *company* may hold a share as nominee for a non-*member shareowner* who is able to hold an interest in the body in compliance with Rule 8.6.

(b) If the only, or last remaining, *solicitor* or *REL* whose role in a *recognised body* ensures that the body remains a *legal services body*:

    (i)   is committed to prison in civil or criminal proceedings;

APPENDIX B

      (ii)   becomes and continues to be unable to attend to the *practice* of the body because of incapacity caused by illness, accident or age;

      (iii) becomes and continues to be a *person who lacks capacity under Part 1 of the Mental Capacity Act 2005*;

      (iv) abandons the *practice* of the body; or

      (v)   is made subject to a condition on his or her practising certificate or registration which would be breached by continuing to be a *manager* of the body;

the body must inform the *SRA* within seven days of the relevant event and must within 28 days of the relevant event either ensure that the body becomes a *legal services body* again without reference to that person, or cease to *practise*.

8.10   Additional conditions for licensed bodies

(a)   If the only, or last remaining, *authorised individual* in relation to a reserved legal activity, whose role in a *licensed body* ensures that the body remains a *licensable body*:

      (i)   is committed to prison in civil or criminal proceedings;

      (ii) becomes and continues to be unable to attend to the *practice* of the body because of incapacity caused by illness, accident or age;

      (iii) becomes and continues to be a person who lacks capacity under Part 1 of the Mental Capacity Act 2005;

      (iv) abandons the *practice* of the body; or

      (v)   is made subject to a condition on his/her practising certificate, registration or equivalent *authorisation* by an *approved regulator* other than the *SRA* which would be breached by continuing to be a *manager* of the body;

the body must inform the *SRA* within seven days of the relevant event and must within 28 days of the relevant event either ensure that the body becomes a *licensable body* again without reference to that person, or cease to *practise*.

Guidance notes

(i)   Rule 8.1 is to be read in conjunction with the obligations under sections 90 and 176 of the LSA. These require individuals and bodies regulated by the SRA to comply with its regulatory arrangements (reflected in Rule 19.1 of the SRA Practice Framework Rules), and for non-authorised employees, managers and interest holders of licensed bodies not to do anything which causes or substantially contributes to a breach of that requirement. In addition, Rule 8.2 requires the body to have suitable arrangements in place to ensure compliance with these provisions.

(ii) The SRA's outcomes focused approach to regulation means that the SRA will take into account all of the circumstances relevant to any issue of compliance, whether in relation to the regulatory arrangements or in respect of statutory obligations on firms and those in them. This will include taking into account the evidence that firms and individuals can produce to demonstrate their efforts to ensure compliance (by themselves or others).

(iii) Rule 8.2 deals with the need for firms to have suitable arrangements for compliance (see also Chapter 7 of the SRA Code of Conduct (Management of your business)). What needs to be covered by a firm's compliance plan will depend on factors such as the size and nature of the firm, its work and its areas of risk. Firms will need to analyse the effectiveness of their compliance arrangements before applying for authorisation and monitor effectiveness on an on-going basis once authorised. Common areas for consideration will include:

- (a) clearly defined governance arrangements providing a transparent framework for responsibilities within the firm
- (b) appropriate accounting procedures
- (c) a system for ensuring that only the appropriate people authorise payments from client account
- (d) a system for ensuring that undertakings are given only when intended, and compliance with them is monitored and enforced
- (e) appropriate checks on new staff or contractors
- (f) a system for ensuring that basic regulatory deadlines are not missed e.g. submission of the firm's accountant's report, arranging indemnity cover, renewal of practising certificates and registrations, renewal of all lawyers' licences to practise and provision of regulatory information
- (g) a system for monitoring, reviewing and managing risks
- (h) ensuring that issues of conduct are given appropriate weight in decisions the firm takes, whether on client matters or firm-based issues such as funding
- (i) file reviews
- (j) appropriate systems for supporting the development and training of staff
- (k) obtaining the necessary approvals of managers, owners and COLP/COFA
- (l) arrangements to ensure that any duties to clients and others are fully met even when staff are absent.

(iv) Rule 8.4 confirms the legal position that for a firm to provide services to clients, the services/activities must be covered by the terms of its authorisation and, where it is a reserved legal activity such as litigation, the firm must have a manager or an employee who is authorised to do that work. For example, a firm cannot provide litigation services, even if its licence permits it to, if its only lawyer is a licensed conveyancer. In situations where a firm loses a lawyer who is responsible for supervising the work of non-lawyers, the firm will need to consider whether the reserved legal work can still be carried out until the situation is remedied.

(v) Rule 8.5 requires all authorised bodies to have a COLP and a COFA. For COLPs and COFAs of licensed bodies, compliance with their obligations under Rule 8.5 will assist in complying with their duties as Head of Legal Practice and Head of Finance and Administration under sections 91 and 92 respectively of the LSA.

(vi) The roles of COLP and COFA are a fundamental part of a firm's compliance and governance arrangements. COLPs' and COFAs' ability to take the steps they need to ensure compliance is dependent on the firm having suitable arrangements in place under Rule 8.2. The firm must therefore ensure that any person designated as its COLP or COFA is of sufficient seniority, in a position of sufficient power and responsibility and has clear reporting lines to enable them to have access to all management systems and arrangements and all other relevant information including client files and business information. The existence of compliance officers in a firm and the requirements on them to ensure that the firm, as well as its managers and employees, are complying with the regulatory arrangements (COLP) and the SRA Accounts Rules (COFA) is not a substitute for the firm's and managers' responsibilities and their obligations to comply with Rule 8.1 (Regulatory compliance). Firms and managers need to take care not to obstruct, whether intentionally or unwittingly, a COLP or COFA in fulfilling their role.

(vii) COLPs and COFAs are responsible for ensuring that the firm has systems and controls in place to enable the firm, as well as its managers and employees, to comply with the requirements on them. The firm and its managers are not absolved from any of their own obligations and remain fully responsible for compliance (see Rule 8.1).

APPENDIX B

(viii) Those designated as COLP will need to be in a position to be able to discharge the role. They will need to consider whether they are in a position to, for example:
- (a) take all reasonable steps to ensure compliance with the terms of the firm's authorisation; compliance with the SRA's regulatory arrangements by the firm, its employees and managers; and with relevant statutory obligations e.g.
  - (A) that non-authorised persons comply with the duty imposed by section 90 of the LSA (duty not to do anything which causes or substantially contributes to a breach of the SRA's regulatory arrangements by an authorised body or its employee or manager)
  - (B) that authorised persons and other managers and employees comply with the duty imposed by section 176 of the LSA (duty to comply with the SRA's regulatory arrangements)
  - (C) under the LSA, AJA and the SA in respect of practice matters.
- (b) as soon as reasonably practicable, report to the SRA any failure to comply where such failure is material either on its own or as part of a pattern.

(ix) Those designated as COFA will need to be in a position to be able to discharge the role. They will need to consider whether they are in a position to, for example:
- (a) ensure that they have access to all accounting records
- (b) carry out regular checks on the accounting systems
- (c) carry out file and ledger reviews
- (d) ensure that the reporting accountant has prompt access to all the information needed to complete the accountant's report
- (e) take steps to ensure that breaches of the SRA Accounts Rules are remedied promptly, and report any breach, which is material either on its own or as part of a pattern, to the SRA
- (f) monitor, review and manage risks to compliance with the SRA Accounts Rules.

(x) In considering whether a failure is "material" and therefore reportable, the COLP or COFA, as appropriate, will need to take account of various factors, such as:
- (a) the detriment, or risk of detriment, to clients
- (b) the extent of any risk of loss of confidence in the firm or in the provision of legal services
- (c) the scale of the issue
- (d) the overall impact on the firm, its clients and third parties.

In addition, the COLP/COFA will need to keep appropriate records of failures in compliance to:
- (e) monitor overall compliance with obligations
- (f) assess the effectiveness of the firm's systems
- (g) be able to comply with the duty to report breaches which are material because they form a pattern.

(xi) In developing their governance and administrative arrangements firms will need to consider how they approach unexpected risks such as the absence of key staff, including COLP and COFA, and whether the nature of the absence will trigger the need to notify the SRA (see Rule 8.7) and to obtain approval for a replacement.

(xii) The statutory obligations of a recognised body are contained in the AJA and the SA and for licensed bodies are contained in sections 90 and 176 of the LSA. An important aspect of the roles of COLP and COFA is the need to report breaches to the SRA. Although it will commonly be appropriate for the firm to take steps to remedy breaches immediately, this does not obviate the need for compliance officers to make a report in compliance with Rule 8.5 where appropriate.

(xiii) Approval (see Rules 8.5 and 8.6) relates only to the role for which it is granted. Any change from one role that requires approval to another, will require a further approval. Firms need to ensure that they notify the SRA of any changes and, where necessary, apply for appropriate approval, for example where an employee develops into the role of manager, or an owner's participation amounts to being a manager.

(xiv) The scope of the duty in Rule 8.6(c) is beyond the strict employer-servant relationship (contract of service) and includes a relationship founded on a contract for services or indirect arrangements which are intended to have the effect of frustrating this rule.

(xv) Rule 8.7 imposes information requirements on authorised bodies. As well as the annual information report, firms must update the SRA by giving details of general changes that occur in respect of the firm. For example, if any of the circumstances referred to in Rule 8.8 occur in relation to any manager or person who has a significant role or responsibility in the firm, the SRA should be notified. Reporting and information requirements that apply to individuals or firms include:

    (a) SRA requirements

        (A) Rules 3, 8.7, 8.8, 8.9 and 8.10 and 18, 23, 24 and 25 of these rules
        (B) Rule 18 of the SRA Practice Framework Rules
        (C) Rule 32 of the SRA Accounts Rules
        (D) Regulations 4.3, 4.5 and 15 of the SRA Practising Regulations
        (E) Chapter 10 of the Code of Conduct.

    (b) Statutory requirements

        (A) Section 84 of the SA (notification of a solicitor's place of business)
        (B) Paragraph 21 of Schedule 13 to the LSA (non-authorised persons proposing to acquire an interest in a licensed body have continuing notification requirements. Note, it is an offence to fail to comply with the section 21 notification requirements).

RULE 9: FURTHER CONDITIONS

9.1 The *SRA* may at any time impose one or more further conditions on an *authorisation* if it considers:

    (a) that:

        (i) the condition would limit, restrict, halt or prevent an activity or activities on the part of the body, or of a *manager*, *employee*, or *interest holder* of the body, which is putting or is likely to put at risk the interests of *clients*, third parties or the public;

        (ii) the condition would prevent or limit the activities of a *manager* or *employee* of the body who is considered unsuitable to undertake a particular activity, either at all or save as specified in the condition;

        (iii) the condition would limit, halt or prevent a risk to *clients*, third parties or the public arising from a business agreement or association which the body has or is likely to enter into, or a business practice which the body has or is likely to adopt;

        (iv) a *relevant insolvency event* has occurred in relation to the body but the *SRA* does not propose at that time to suspend or revoke the *authorisation* under Rule 22;

APPENDIX B

> (v) the condition is necessary to facilitate effective monitoring by the *SRA* of compliance with its *regulatory arrangements* on the part of the body, its *managers*, *employees* or *interest holders*;
> (vi) the *SRA* considers that imposing the condition will require the body concerned to take specified steps conducive to the proper, effective or efficient carrying on of a *legal activity* by that body; or
> (vii) the *SRA* considers that imposing a condition is necessary in order to ensure compliance with the *regulatory objectives*;
>
> and
>
> (b) that it is in the public interest to impose the condition.

9.2 A condition imposed under Rule 9.1 takes effect from the date on which the condition is imposed unless otherwise specified by the *SRA*.

Guidance note

(i) Rule 9.1 permits the SRA to impose conditions "at any time", if certain criteria are met. This includes on the approval of a person under Part 4 of these rules or at the time of modification of the terms of an authorisation under Rule 10.

RULE 10: MODIFICATION OF TERMS AND CONDITIONS OF AN AUTHORISATION

10.1 The *SRA* may at any time, modify:

> (a) any terms that specify the *reserved legal activities* that an *authorised body* is entitled to carry on by virtue of the *authorisation*:
>
> > (i) on the application of the *authorised body*; or
> > (ii) if the *SRA* considers it appropriate to do so, without such an application being made; and
>
> having regard to the *regulatory objectives*;
>
> (b) any further conditions of an *authorisation*, imposed under Rule 9:
>
> > (i) on the application of the *authorised body*; or
> > (ii) if the *SRA* considers it appropriate to do so, without such an application being made; and
>
> having regard to the criteria in Rule 9.

Guidance notes

(i) The certificate of authorisation of a licensed body will set out the reserved activities that the body is entitled to carry out. A licensed body may apply to change the categories of those activities at any time, or the SRA may do so (see also Rule 10), for example if the body no longer carries out that type of work or if there is an identified risk to the public in the body continuing to provide certain services (see section 86 of the LSA). Firms are also able to apply for a waiver of these rules, including the general conditions in Rule 8 (except Rule 8.1), under Rule 12 (Waivers).

(ii) Authorised bodies are authorised to carry out non-reserved legal activities as well as the reserved activities for which they are authorised.
(iii) Multi-disciplinary practices which provide a range of different services, some only of which are regulated by the SRA, will need to ensure that it is clear, both within and outside the firm, through which part of the business (and therefore under which regulatory system) non-reserved services are provided. (See Chapter 8 of the SRA Code of Conduct.)

RULE 11: REGULATORY CONFLICT

11.1 If a conflict arises between:

    (a) a requirement imposed:

        (i) on an *authorised body* or on an *employee* or *manager* of the body by the *SRA* as the regulator of that body, and

        (ii) on an individual *manager* or *employee* of that body by another *approved regulator*;

    then the requirement imposed by the *SRA* prevails over the requirement imposed by the other *approved regulator*;

    (b) a requirement imposed:

        (i) on an *authorised non-SRA firm* or on an *employee* or *manager* of the firm by another *approved regulator* as the regulator of that firm, and

        (ii) on an individual *manager* or *employee* of that firm by the *SRA*;

    then the requirement imposed by the other *approved regulator* prevails over the requirement imposed by the *SRA*.

RULE 12: WAIVERS

12.1 Subject to Rule 12.2 below and to provisions in any enactments or the *SRA's regulatory arrangements* affecting its ability to waive any requirements, the *SRA* shall have power to waive in writing the provisions of these rules for a particular purpose or purposes expressed in such waiver, and to attach conditions to or revoke such waiver, at its own discretion.

12.2 The *SRA* shall not have power to waive any of the provisions of Rule 8.1 with respect to any *authorised bodies*.

12.3 The *SRA* shall not have power to grant a waiver under Rule 12 in respect of the *reserved legal activities* that an *authorised body* is entitled to carry on or any conditions of *authorisation* imposed under Rule 9.

Guidance notes

(i) A waiver cannot be granted where to do so would run counter to the overall purpose of the rule. In addition, many of the requirements set out in various Acts such as the LSA and AJA are mandatory provisions which, in spite of Rule 12, the SRA does not have the power to waive. The following are examples from the LSA:

    (a) **Management**

        (A) Schedule 11 para 11–14 – the rules must include that a licensed body

APPENDIX B

must at all times have an individual designated as Head of Legal Practice and one designated as Head of Finance and Administration (in these rules referred to as COLP and COFA). This designation must be approved by the SRA, which must be satisfied that the designated individuals are suitable to carry out the duties. Rule 8.5 reflects this and therefore cannot be waived;

(B) Schedule 11 para 17 – rules must provide that the licensed body must at all times have suitable arrangements in place to ensure that it, its managers and employees comply with the regulatory arrangements, and that any employees carrying out legal activities will maintain the professional principles. Rule 8.1 reflects this and therefore cannot be waived.

(b) **Duration, suspension, modification and revocation of licence**

(A) Schedule 11 para 26(1) – rules must provide criteria for the SRA to use in deciding whether to suspend, revoke or end the suspension of a licence. Rule 22 reflects this and therefore cannot be waived.

(ii) A waiver of these rules "in writing" includes any form of written electronic communication normally used for business purposes, such as emails.

PART 4: APPROVAL OF MANAGERS, OWNERS AND COMPLIANCE OFFICERS

RULE 13: APPLICATION FOR APPROVAL

13.1 This Part governs the *SRA's* determination of applications for:

(a) approval of an *authorised body's managers* and *owners* pursuant to Rule 8.6(a); and

(b) approval of an *authorised body's compliance officers*, pursuant to Rule 8.5(b) and (d).

13.2 The *SRA* will deem a *person* to be approved as suitable to be a *manager* or *owner* of an *authorised body* under this Part if:

(a) that *person* is:

(i) a *solicitor* who holds a current practising certificate; or
(ii) an *authorised body*;

(b) there is no condition on the *person's* practising certificate or *authorisation* as appropriate, preventing or restricting them from being a *manager, owner* or *interest holder* of an *authorised body* or being a *sole practitioner*;

(c) the *SRA* is notified on the *prescribed* form in advance of the *person* becoming a *manager* or *owner* of the *authorised body*; and

(d) the *SRA* has not withdrawn its approval of that *person* to be a *manager* or *owner* under Rule 17.

RULE 14: APPROVAL PROCESS

14.1 An application for approval of a *manager, owner* or *compliance officer* may be made by an *applicant body* or an *authorised body* and must include evidence to satisfy the *SRA* that the *candidate* is suitable to be a *manager, owner* or *compliance officer* of the body, as appropriate.

14.2 The *applicant body* or *authorised body*, as appropriate, must:

    (a) co-operate, and secure the co-operation of the *candidate*, to assist the *SRA* to obtain all information and documentation the *SRA* requires in order to determine the application;

    (b) obtain all other information and documentation in relation to the *candidate* which the *prescribed* form requires the body to obtain and keep; and

    (c) keep all information and documentation under (b) above for a period of not less than 6 years after the *person* concerned has ceased to be a *manager, owner* or *compliance officer* of the body.

14.3 The *candidate* must declare in the application that the information supplied about them is correct and complete.

14.4 The *SRA's* decision to approve or refuse approval must be notified in writing to the *applicant body* or *authorised body* as appropriate, and separately to the *candidate*, as soon as possible.

14.5 The *SRA* may, at the time of granting its approval or at any time subsequently, make its approval of a *person* to be an *owner, manager* or *compliance officer* of an *authorised body* subject to such conditions on the body's *authorisation* as it considers appropriate having regard to the criteria in Rule 9.

14.6 If the *SRA* proposes to object to a *candidate* becoming an *owner* of an *applicant body* or *authorised body*, or to approve such a *person* becoming an *owner* subject to conditions, it must give the *candidate* and the body a warning notice and consider any representations made by them to the *SRA* within the prescribed period.

14.7 The *SRA* may issue a conditional approval or objection without a warning notice under Rule 14.6 if the application for approval has been made after the grant of *authorisation* and the *SRA* considers it necessary or desirable to dispense with the warning notice for the purpose of protecting any of the *regulatory objectives*.

14.8 The *SRA* may at any time require the production of information or documentation from:

    (a) a *person* who has been approved as an *owner, manager* or *compliance officer* under this Part;

    (b) an *authorised body* of which that *person* is a *manager, owner* or *compliance officer*; or

    (c) the body which originally obtained approval for that *person* and holds information and documentation under Rule 14.2(c);

in order to satisfy the *SRA* that the *person* met, meets, or continues to meet the criteria for approval.

Guidance notes

(i) See also the guidance notes to Rule 1 regarding ownership and material interest.

(ii) The SRA's notification "in writing" includes any form of written electronic communication normally used for business purposes, such as emails.

APPENDIX B

RULE 15: CRITERIA FOR APPROVAL

15.1 When considering whether a *candidate* should be approved to be a *manager, owner* or *compliance officer* of the body, as appropriate, the *SRA* will take into account the criteria set out in the SRA Suitability Test and any other relevant information.

Guidance notes

(i) As well as evidence about the candidate, the Suitability Test takes into account evidence about the honesty and integrity of a person that the candidate is related to, affiliated with, or acts together with where the SRA has reason to believe that that person may have an influence over the way in which the candidate will exercise their role.

(ii) See also Regulation 7 of the SRA Practising Regulations under which the SRA has the power to impose conditions on a practising certificate or registration which restrict an individual's ability to be involved in an authorised body.

(iii) Specific provisions exist in the LSA about imposing conditions on the approval of owners of a licensed body:

    (a) For the approval of ownership on an application for a licence, see paragraph 17 of Schedule 13 to the LSA. For the approval of ownership on a change of interests after a licence is issued, see paragraph 28 of that Schedule. These give the SRA the power to approve an owner's or a prospective owner's holding subject to conditions where the Rule 15 criteria are not met in relation to that investment, but only if the SRA considers that, if the conditions are complied with, it will be appropriate for the owner to hold the interest.

    (b) For the imposition of conditions (or further conditions) on an existing ownership interest, see paragraph 33 of Schedule 13 to the LSA. This gives the SRA the power to impose conditions (or further conditions) on a person's holding of an interest, if the SRA is not satisfied that the Rule 15 criteria are met, or if the SRA is satisfied that a condition imposed under paragraphs 17, 28 or 33 of Schedule 13 (see above) on the person's holding of that interest has not been, or is not being, complied with. The SRA may only use the paragraph 33 power if it considers that, if the conditions are complied with, it will be appropriate for the owner to hold the interest without the approval requirements being met.

(iv) Under paragraphs 19 and 20 of Schedule 13 to the LSA the SRA has the power, when dealing with an application for a licence, to object to the holding of an interest if it is not satisfied that the Rule 15 criteria are met in relation to that holding. The mechanism for objecting is set out in those paragraphs.

RULE 16: EFFECT OF APPROVAL

16.1 Approval takes effect from the date of the decision unless otherwise stated and continues until:

    (a) it is withdrawn by the *SRA*; or

    (b) the approved *person* ceases to be a *manager, interest holder* or *compliance officer* of the *authorised body*, as appropriate.

RULE 17: WITHDRAWAL OF APPROVAL

17.1 Where the *SRA* has granted an approval of a *person* to be a *manager*, *owner* or *compliance officer* of a body (including a deemed approval under Rule 13.2), it may subsequently withdraw that approval if:

(a) it is not satisfied that an approved *person* met or meets the criteria for approval in Rule 15;
(b) it is satisfied that a condition imposed on the body's *authorisation* under Rule 14.5 has not been, or is not being complied with;
(c) it is satisfied that the approved *person* has breached a duty or obligation imposed upon them in or under the *SRA's regulatory arrangements* or any enactments; or
(d) information or documentation is not promptly supplied in response to a request made under Rule 14.8.

17.2 Where withdrawal of approval relates to a *director* of a *company*, the *SRA* may set separate dates for that individual ceasing to be a *director* and disposing of his or her shares.

RULE 18: TEMPORARY EMERGENCY APPROVALS FOR COMPLIANCE OFFICERS

18.1 If an *authorised body* ceases to have a *COLP* or *COFA* whose designation has been approved by the *SRA*, the *authorised body* must immediately and in any event within seven days:

(a) notify the *SRA*;
(b) designate another *manager* or *employee* to replace its previous *COLP* or *COFA*, as appropriate; and
(c) make an application to the *SRA* for temporary approval of the new *COLP* or *COFA*, as appropriate.

18.2 The *SRA* may grant a temporary approval under this rule if:

(a) it is satisfied that the *authorised body* could not reasonably have commenced an application for approval of designation in advance of the non-compliance; and
(b) on the face of the application and any other information immediately before the *SRA*, there is no evidence suggesting that the new *compliance officer* is not suitable to carry out the duties imposed on them under these rules.

18.3 Temporary approval under this rule:

(a) may be granted initially for 28 days;
(b) may be granted to have effect from the date the body ceases to have a *COLP* or *COFA* whose designation has been approved;
(c) may be extended in response to a reasonable request by the *authorised body*;
(d) must be extended pending determination of a substantive application for approval commenced in accordance with Rule 18.4;
(e) may be granted or extended subject to such conditions on the *authorised body's authorisation* as the *SRA* thinks fit, having regard to the criteria in Rule 9;
(f) has effect only while the criteria in Rule 8.5(g) are met;

APPENDIX B

(g) if granted, cannot prejudice the discretion of the *SRA* to refuse a substantive application for approval of designation or to impose any conditions on that approval; and

(h) in exceptional circumstances, and for reasonable cause, may be withdrawn at any time.

18.4 If granted temporary approval under Rule 18.3 above for its designation of a new *COLP* or *COFA*, the *authorised body* must:

(a) designate a permanent *COLP* or *COFA*, as appropriate; and

(b) submit a substantive application for approval of that designation under Rule 13;

before the expiry of the temporary approval or any extension of that approval by the *SRA*.

PART 5: NOTIFICATION, EFFECT AND DURATION OF AUTHORISATION

RULE 19: NOTIFICATION OF DECISIONS

19.1 The *SRA* must notify its decision and reasons in writing when it:

(a) refuses an application made under these rules;
(b) grants an application subject to a condition;
(c) refuses a permission required under a condition on a body's *authorisation*; or
(d) withdraws its approval of a *candidate* under Rules 17 and 18.

19.2 The notification in Rule 19.1 must be given:

(a) to the *applicant body* or *authorised body* as appropriate; and
(b) where appropriate, to the *candidate* concerned.

19.3 The *SRA* must give 28 days written notice, with reasons:

(a) to the *authorised body* concerned, when the *SRA* decides to impose a condition on an *authorised body's authorisation* at any time after the grant of the *authorisation*;

(b) to the body and the individual concerned, when the *SRA* decides to withdraw an approval under Rules 17 and 18;

19.4 The *SRA* may shorten or dispense with the 28 day period under Rule 19.3(a) if it is satisfied that it is in the public interest to do so.

Guidance note

(i) The SRA's notification "in writing" may be by any form of written electronic communication normally used for business purposes, such as emails.

RULE 20: NOTIFYING THIRD PARTIES OF DECISIONS

20.1 The *SRA* may, if it considers it in the public interest to do so, publish and notify any *persons* of a decision concerning a body or an individual made under these rules, including but not limited to:

(a) an *authorised person* of which the body or individual concerned is a current, past or prospective *manager*, *employee* or *interest holder*;
(b) any *approved regulator*;
(c) any statutory regulator;
(d) the Legal Services Board;
(e) the *Legal Ombudsman*;
(f) the regulatory body for any profession of which the individual concerned is a member or which regulates the body concerned;
(g) any law enforcement agency.

RULE 21: EFFECT AND VALIDITY OF AUTHORISATION

21.1 A grant of *authorisation* takes effect from the date of the decision unless otherwise stated.

21.2 *Authorisation* continues in force unless it ceases to have effect in accordance with Rule 21.3.

21.3 An *authorised body's authorisation* ceases to have effect so that the body is no longer authorised by the *SRA* under these rules:

(a) from the time that the *authorisation* is revoked under Rule 22;
(b) at any time during which the *authorisation* is suspended;
(c) subject to Part 6, if the body is wound up or for any other reason ceases to exist; or
(d) if in relation to a *licensed body*, the body is issued with a licence by another *approved regulator*.

RULE 22: REVOCATION AND SUSPENSION OF AUTHORISATION

22.1 Subject to Rule 23, the *SRA* may revoke or suspend a body's *authorisation*, where:

(a) in the case of an *authorised body*:

(i) *authorisation* was granted as a result of error, misleading or inaccurate information, or fraud;
(ii) the body is or becomes ineligible to be authorised in accordance with the criteria set out in Rule 6;
(iii) the *SRA* is satisfied that the body has no intention of carrying on the *legal activities* for which it has been authorised under these rules;
(iv) the body has failed to provide any information required by the *SRA* under these rules;
(v) the body has failed to pay any fee payable to the *SRA* under these rules;
(vi) a *relevant insolvency event* has occurred in relation to the body;
(vii) the body makes an application to the *SRA* for its *authorisation* to be revoked or suspended;
(viii) the *SRA* has decided to exercise its intervention powers under section 102 of and Schedule 14 to the *LSA*, Parts I and II of Schedule 1 to the *SA*, paragraph 5 of Schedule 14 to the Courts and Legal Services Act 1990 and Part II of Schedule 1 to the *SA* or paragraph 32 of Schedule 2 to the *AJA* and Part II of Schedule 1 to the *SA*, as appropriate;
(ix) the body, or an *owner*, *interest holder*, *manager* or *employee* of the body

APPENDIX B

                fails to comply with the duties imposed by or under these rules or under any statutory obligations in relation to the body's business of carrying on *authorised activities* including payment of any fine or other financial penalty imposed on the body by the *SRA*, *the Tribunal*, the High Court or the *appellate body*;

        (x)   where:

                (A)   in the case of a *licensed body*, the body fails to comply with Rule 8.6(b) (prohibition on *disqualified managers*); or

                (B)   in the case of an *authorised body*, the body fails to comply with Rule 8.6(c) (employment or remuneration of certain individuals);

                and the *manager* or *employee* concerned was *disqualified* as a result of breach of the duties imposed upon the *manager* or *employee* by sections 176 or 90 of the *LSA*;

        (xi)   the body does not comply with Rule 8.5 (compliance officers);

        (xii)   the body fails to comply with Rule 8.6 (management and control); or

        (xiii)   for any other reason it is in the public interest;

(b)   in the case of a *licensed body*
a *non-authorised person holds an interest* in the *licensed body*:

        (i)   as a result of the *person* taking a step in circumstances where that constitutes an offence under paragraph 24(1) of Schedule 13 to the *LSA* (whether or not the *person* is charged with or convicted of an offence under that paragraph),

        (ii)   in breach of conditions imposed under paragraphs 17, 28 or 33 of that Schedule, or

        (iii)   the *person's* holding of which is subject to an objection by the *licensing authority* under paragraph 31 or 36 of that Schedule.

22.2 The *SRA* must not revoke or suspend an *authorisation* under this rule:

(a)   unless it has first provided the *authorised body* with an opportunity to provide representations to it regarding the issues giving rise to the proposed revocation or suspension;

(b)   unless it has first given the *authorised body* notice of its intention to revoke or suspend the *authorisation*; and

(c)   before the end of the period of 28 days beginning with the day on which the notice in (b) above is given to the body or any longer period specified in the notice.

Guidance notes

(i)   Rule 22.1(a)(x) refers to sections 90 and 176 of the LSA. Section 90 sets out the duty of non-authorised persons, as defined by the LSA, not to do anything which causes or substantially contributes to a breach by a licensed body, or by a manager or an employee of the licensed body who is an authorised person, of the duties imposed on them by section 176. Section 176 imposes the statutory duty on a regulated person to comply with the SRA's regulatory arrangements when practising through an SRA firm. Regulated person includes the firm itself as well as the managers and employees of the firm.

(ii)   Rule 22.1(b)(i) refers to the offence under paragraph 24(1) of Schedule 13 to the LSA. This is the offence of an unauthorised person who is required to notify the licensed body and the SRA of a proposal to take a step leading to acquiring a restricted interest in a licensed body taking the step prior to the SRA's approval. Rule 22.1(b)(ii) refers to breaches of the specific provisions about imposing conditions on approval of owners – see guidance note (ii) to Rule 15 above. Rule 22.1(b)(iii) refers to paragraphs 31 (the SRA having an objection to a notifiable interest) and 36 (the SRA having an objection to an existing restricted interest) of Schedule 13 to the LSA.

(iii) In addition to the power to revoke or suspend authorisation, there are statutory divestiture procedures available to the SRA in respect of owners of licensed bodies. These are set out in Part 5 of Schedule 13 to the LSA. See also the guidance notes to Rule 15 for more information about other statutory powers relating to owners of licensed bodies.

(iv) Revocation and suspension of authorisation is a discretionary power of the SRA. The SRA is unlikely to revoke or suspend authorisation if doing so at that time would present any risk to clients, the public, the protection of public money or to any SRA investigation.

RULE 23: UNFORESEEN TEMPORARY BREACH OF CERTAIN CONDITIONS AND ELIGIBILITY CRITERIA

23.1 Unforeseen breach of eligibility criteria

(a) If due to an event which could not reasonably have been foreseen, a *licensed body* is no longer a *licensable body*:

 (i) because the body no longer has at least one *manager* who is an individual and who is an *authorised person* (other than an *RFL* or an *EEL*) in relation to a *licensed activity*; or

 (ii) because:

 (A) the body no longer has a *manager* or *interest holder* who is a *non-authorised person*; and

 (B) *non-authorised persons* are no longer entitled to exercise, or control the exercise of, at least 10% of the *voting rights* in any body which is a *manager* or *interest holder* of the *licensed body*;

 but the *SRA* is informed of that fact within seven days of the event first occurring and the body becomes a *licensable body* again within 28 days of the event first occurring, then the *licensable body* will be deemed to have remained a *licensable body* and to that extent will not be liable to have its *authorisation* revoked or suspended under Rule 22.

(b) If due to an event which could not reasonably have been foreseen, a *recognised body* is no longer a *legal services body* because the body no longer has at least one *manager* who is:

 (i) a *solicitor*;
 (ii) an *REL*; or
 (iii) a *legally qualified body* with at least one *manager* who is a *solicitor* or an *REL*;

 but the *SRA* is informed of the fact within seven days of the event first occurring and the body becomes a *legal services body* again within 28 days of the event first occurring, then the *recognised body* will be deemed to have remained a *legal services body* and to that extent will not be liable to have its *authorisation* revoked or suspended under Rule 22.

APPENDIX B

23.2 An *LLP* having fewer than two *members*

    (a) If an event which could not reasonably have been foreseen results in an *LLP* having fewer than two *members*, and therefore being in breach of Rule 16.3 (requirement to have at least two *members*) of the *SRA Practice Framework Rules*, but within six months the situation is remedied, and provided the *LLP* has remained in a position to comply with the remainder of the *SRA's regulatory arrangements* including these rules and any conditions imposed on its *authorisation*, the *LLP* will be deemed to have remained in compliance with Rule 16.3 of the *SRA Practice Framework Rules* and to that extent will not be liable to have its *authorisation* revoked under Rule 22.

23.3 Death of *member* or *shareowner* of a *company*

    (a) If an *authorised body* is a *company* with shares and a *member* or *shareowner* dies who had been approved under Part 4 to be a *member* or *shareowner* of the body at the date of death, then, whether or not the personal representatives have been approved under Part 4, the personal representatives may replace the deceased *member* or *shareowner* in their capacity as personal representatives, provided that:

        (i) no vote may be exercised by or on behalf of a personal representative (and no such vote may be accepted) unless all the personal representatives have been approved under Part 4 to be *members* or *shareowners*;

        (ii) no personal representative may hold or own a share in that capacity for longer than 12 months from the date of death;

        (iii) within 12 months of the death the *authorised body* must cancel or acquire the shares or ensure that they are held and owned by *persons* who can *hold the interest* in the body in compliance with Rule 8.6 (management and control), but without this resulting in *RFLs* being the only *shareowners* of a *recognised body*; and

        (iv) no vote may be exercised by or on behalf of any personal representative (and no such vote may be accepted) after the 12 month period has expired.

    (b) If, following the death of a *member* or *shareowner*, a *company* meets the requirements of (a) above, the *company* will be deemed to have remained in compliance with Rule 8.6 (management and control), and to that extent will not be liable to have its *authorisation* revoked under Rule 22.

23.4 *Member* or *shareowner* ceasing to be approved

    (a) If an *authorised body* is a *company* with shares and a *member* or *shareowner* ceases to be approved under Part 4 to be a *member* or *shareowner* of the body, or ceases to exist as a *body corporate*, then provided that:

        (i) no vote is exercised or accepted on the shares held by or on behalf of that *member* or *shareowner*;

        (ii) a trustee in bankruptcy or liquidator (whether approved under Part 4 or not) replaces that *member* or *shareowner* in the capacity of trustee or liquidator for a period not exceeding six months from the date the *member* or *shareowner* ceased to be approved; and

        (iii) the *company* cancels or acquires the shares within six months, or within that time ensures that the shares are held and owned by *persons* in compliance with Rule 8.6, but without this resulting in the body ceasing to be a *licensable body* (in the case of a *licensed body*), or ceasing to be a *legal services body* (in the case of a *recognised body*);

the *company* will be deemed to have remained in compliance with Rule 8.6 (management and control), and to that extent will not be liable to have its *authorisation* revoked under Rule 22.

23.5 *Member* or *shareowner* becoming insolvent but remaining compliant

(a) If an *authorised body* is a *company* with shares and a *member* or *shareowner* becomes insolvent but continues to *hold an interest* in the body in compliance with Rule 8.6, then the trustee in bankruptcy or liquidator (whether approved under Part 4 or not) may replace the insolvent *member* or *shareowner* in the capacity of trustee in bankruptcy or liquidator, provided that:

(i) no vote may be exercised by or on behalf of a trustee in bankruptcy or liquidator (and no such vote may be accepted) unless the trustee or liquidator can *hold the interest* in the *company* in compliance with Rule 8.6;

(ii) no trustee in bankruptcy or liquidator may hold or own a share in that capacity for longer than six months from the date of the insolvency;

(iii) within six months of the insolvency the *company* must cancel or acquire the shares or ensure that they are held and owned by *persons* who can *hold an interest* in the *company* in compliance with Rule 8.6, but without this resulting in the body ceasing to be a *licensable body* (in the case of a *licensed body*), or ceasing to be a *legal services body* (in the case of a *recognised body*); and

(iv) no vote may be exercised by or on behalf of any trustee in bankruptcy or liquidator (and no such vote may be accepted) after the six month period has expired.

(b) If (a) above applies and a *company* meets its requirements, the *company* will be deemed to have remained in compliance with Rule 8.6 (management and control), and to that extent will not be liable to have its *authorisation* revoked under Rule 22.

23.6 Court of Protection deputy

(a) A *Court of Protection deputy* appointed under section 19 of the Mental Capacity Act 2005 may be a *member* or *shareowner* in that capacity, without breaching Rule 8.6 (management and control), provided that:

(i) the person in respect of whom the deputy has been appointed *holds the interest* in compliance with Rule 8.6; and

(ii) if the deputy is not a *member* or *shareowner* in compliance with Rule 8.6, no vote is exercised or accepted on the shares.

(b) If (a) above applies and a *company* meets its requirements, the *company* will be deemed to have remained in compliance with Rule 8.6, and to that extent will not be liable to have its *authorisation* revoked under Rule 22.

Guidance note

(i) The provisions in Rule 23 allow firms time to rectify the position where unexpected changes occur. The effect of the provisions is to allow firms a period to avoid being in breach of SRA rules. Recognised bodies need also to consider the time limit of 90 days

APPENDIX B

to obtain a licence which is imposed by section 18(3) of the LSA on such existing bodies that become licensable.

PART 6: CHANGES IN PARTNERSHIPS

RULE 24: CHANGE TO THE COMPOSITION OF A PARTNERSHIP

24.1 *Authorisation* of a *partnership* may continue despite a change in its composition, subject to Rules 24.2, 24.3, 24.4 and 25.

24.2 If there is a change to an *authorised body*, which is a *partnership*, which results in there being:

    (a)   no remaining *partner* who was a *partner* before the change the *authorised body* must cease to *practise* from the date of the change; the 28 day period under Rule 23.1 does not apply;

    (b)   only one remaining *principal* who needs to be authorised as a *sole practitioner* but could not reasonably have commenced an application in advance of the change:

        (i)   the *firm* may continue to *practise* provided that the remaining *principal*:

            (A)   is a *solicitor* or *REL*;
            (B)   notifies the *SRA* within seven days;
            (C)   is granted temporary emergency recognition under Regulation 4 of the *SRA Practising Regulations*;

        (ii)   during the initial 28 day period, or such extended period as the *SRA* may allow, under any such temporary emergency recognition, the remaining *principal* must:

            (A)   cease to *practise*, and notify the *SRA*; or
            (B)   commence a substantive application for *authorisation* as a *recognised sole practitioner* under the *SRA Practising Regulations*, or if the remaining *principal* has taken on a new *partner*, as an *authorised body*;

    (c)   an *authorised body* which will continue but one or more of the former *partners* intend to carry on as a separate *firm*, which must be authorised as an *authorised body*, a *recognised body* or a *recognised sole practitioner*, but the *principal(s)* in the new firm could not reasonably have commenced an application for *authorisation* in advance of the change:

        (i)   the new *firm* may *practise* from the date of the change provided that the new *firm*:

            (A)   is a *partnership* which complies with Part 3 of the *SRA Practice Framework Rules* in its formation, composition and structure, or is a *solicitor* or *REL sole practitioner*;
            (B)   complies with the SRA Indemnity Insurance Rules;
            (C)   notifies the *SRA* within seven days; and
            (D)   is granted temporary emergency *authorisation* under Rule 25 below or temporary emergency recognition under Regulation 7 of the SRA Recognised Bodies Regulations 2011 or Regulation 4 of the *SRA Practising Regulations*;

(ii) during the initial 28 day period, or such extended period as the *SRA* may allow, the new *firm* must:

 (A) cease to *practise*, and notify the *SRA*; or
 (B) commence a substantive application for *authorisation*;

(d) a failure by:

 (i) a *recognised body* to comply with Rules 13.1 and 16.1 of the *SRA Practice Framework Rules*; or
 (ii) a *licensed body* to comply with Rules 14 and 16 of the *SRA Practice Framework Rules*,

the *firm* must cease to *practise*.

24.3 Following a *partnership* change under Rule 24.2(c), the *SRA* will if necessary decide which of the groups of former *partners* will continue to be covered by the existing *authorisation* and which must apply for a new *authorisation*, and may apportion *authorisation* fees and Compensation Fund contributions between the groups.

24.4 Any decision made under Rule 24.3 will be without prejudice to the outcome of any legal dispute between the former *partners*.

RULE 25: TEMPORARY EMERGENCY AUTHORISATION

25.1 If a *partnership* split brings into being a new *partnership* which is not an *authorised body*:

 (a) the *SRA* must be notified within seven days; and
 (b) temporary emergency *authorisation* may be granted, subject to Rule 25.2 to 25.4 below, so as to enable the *partners* in the new *partnership* to *practise* through the new *firm* for a limited period without breach of these rules and the *SRA Practice Framework Rules*.

25.2 An application for temporary emergency *authorisation* must be made on the *prescribed* form within seven days of the *partnership* split, and must be accompanied by all information and documentation the *SRA* may reasonably require.

25.3 The *SRA* may grant an application for temporary emergency *authorisation* if the following conditions are met.

 (a) The *SRA* must be satisfied that the *partners* could not reasonably have commenced an application for *authorisation* in advance of the change.
 (b) In the case of a *licensable body*, the *partnership* must comply with Rule 14 (Eligibility criteria and fundamental requirements for licensed bodies) of the *SRA Practice Framework Rules*.
 (c) In the case of a *legal services body*, the *partnership* must comply with Rule 13 (Eligibility criteria and fundamental requirements for recognised bodies) of the *SRA Practice Framework Rules*.
 (d) The *partnership* must comply with Rules 12 (Persons who must be "qualified to supervise"), 15 (Formation, registered office and practising address) and 16 (Composition of an authorised body) of the *SRA Practice Framework Rules*.
 (e) The *partnership* must comply with the SRA Indemnity Insurance Rules, and must have adopted a name under which the *firm* is to be registered and which complies with Chapter 8 (Publicity) of the *SRA Code of Conduct*.

25.4 Temporary emergency *authorisation*:

 (a) may be granted initially for 28 days;

APPENDIX B

(b) may be granted to have effect from the date of the *partnership* split or any other appropriate subsequent date;
(c) may be extended in response to a reasonable request by the *applicant body*;
(d) must be extended (subject to (h) below) pending determination of a substantive application for *authorisation* commenced during the currency of a temporary emergency *authorisation*;
(e) is granted or extended subject to the general conditions in Rule 8, unless otherwise specified by the *SRA*, and may be granted or extended subject to such other conditions as the *SRA* sees fit to impose having regard to the criteria in Rule 9;
(f) is to be treated as a new *authorisation* for the purpose of these rules;
(g) if granted, cannot prejudice the discretion of the *SRA* to refuse a substantive application for *authorisation* of the body under Part 2 or to impose any conditions on any such *authorisation*; and
(h) in exceptional circumstances, and for reasonable cause, may be revoked at any time.

PART 7: SPECIAL BODIES, TRANSITIONAL PROVISIONS AND PASSPORTING

RULE 26: SPECIAL KINDS OF LICENSABLE BODIES

26.1 The *SRA* does not accept applications for any order to be made by it under section 106 of the *LSA* from any *licensable body*.

Guidance note

(i) The LSA provides the special kind of licensable bodies mentioned in section 23 with a grace period during which they are not required to apply for authorisation as a licensed body. However, during the grace period (which is expected to end in March 2013), such bodies may apply for authorisation under these rules but will not be able to request special treatment under section 106.

RULE 27: COMMENCEMENT, TRANSITIONAL PROVISIONS AND REPEALS

27.1 These rules shall come into force:

(a) on the designation of the *Society* as a *licensing authority* under Part 1 of Schedule 10 to the *LSA*, in respect of *licensable bodies*;
(b) on 31 March 2012 ("the relevant date"), in respect of *legal services bodies*, and the SRA Recognised Bodies Regulations 2011 (in Rule 27.1 referred to as "the Regulations") shall be repealed, save that:
  (i) applications for initial recognition made under Regulation 2.1 of the Regulations but not decided on the relevant date shall be considered and decided in accordance with the Regulations;
  (ii) applications for approval of an individual as suitable to be a *manager*

made under Regulation 5 of the Regulations but not decided on the relevant date shall be considered and decided in accordance with the Regulations;

(iii) applications for temporary emergency recognition made under Regulation 7.5 of the Regulations, or requests for extension of temporary emergency recognition made under Regulation 7.8(c) of the Regulations, but not decided on the relevant date shall be considered and decided in accordance with the Regulations;

(iv) where a *person* has invoked the internal appeal procedure under Regulation 9 of the Regulations, but the appeal has not been concluded by the relevant date, then the appeal shall be considered and determined in accordance with the Regulations; and

(v) where directions have been issued in respect of a reconsideration under Regulation 18 of the Regulations, the reconsideration shall proceed in accordance with the Regulations,

and for the avoidance of doubt, on the relevant date:

(A) where a notice of succession has been delivered to the *SRA* under Regulation 3.1 or 3.3 of the Regulations in respect of which the *SRA* has made no fee determination, the *SRA* will proceed to consider the matter in accordance with Rule 8.3(d) to (k) above;

(B) where condition(s) have been imposed on a *recognised body's* recognition under Regulation 6 of the Regulations, such condition(s) shall continue to apply as if they had been imposed under Rule 9 above; and

(c) From 31 March 2012 or the date on which an order made pursuant to section 69 of the *LSA* relating to the status of *sole practitioners* comes into force, whichever is the later, ("the relevant date" for the purposes of sub-rules (c) and (d)) the *SRA Practising Regulations* (in Rule 27.1 referred to as "the Practising Regulations") shall have effect with the following amendments:

(i) Regulations 1.6, 4, 5, 8.2(b), 8.4(d), 8.4(j), 8.4(l), 9.1(d), 9.2(d), 10.1(d), 10.2(b), 11.2(g), 12.2(h) and 14.1(d) shall be repealed;

(ii) in Regulation 8.4(e), "13ZA(6)," shall be omitted;

(iii) in Regulation 8.5(a)(ii) the words "including, where applicable, the renewal of an existing authorisation as a *recognised sole practitioner* endorsed on the practising certificate or registration," shall be omitted;

(iv) in Regulation 10.2(c) the word "or" shall be substituted for the ";" between "practising certificate" and "registration" and the words ", or authorisation as a *recognised sole practitioner*" shall be omitted;

(v) in Regulation 10.3(a) the word "or" shall be substituted for the ";" between "practising certificate" and "registration" and for the ";" between "practising certificate" and "renew a registration", and the words ", or authorisation as a *recognised sole practitioner*" and the words "or renew an authorisation" shall be omitted;

(vi) in Regulation 11.2(k) the words "or suspension of the *solicitor* from practice as a *sole practitioner*, or suspension of the *solicitor's authorisation* as a *recognised sole practitioner*," shall be omitted;

(vii) in Regulation 12.2(k) the words "or suspension of the *lawyer* from practice as a *sole practitioner*, or suspension of the *lawyer's* authorisation as a *recognised sole practitioner*," shall be omitted;

(viii) in Regulation 13.2(h) and 16.1(b) the words "*recognised sole practitioner*," shall be omitted;

APPENDIX B

(d) Notwithstanding the provisions of sub-rule (c) above:
- (i) applications for authorisation as a *recognised sole practitioner* made under Regulation 4.1 of the Practising Regulations but not decided on the relevant date shall be considered and decided in accordance with the Practising Regulations;
- (ii) applications for temporary emergency recognition made under Regulation 4.4(a) or for recognition made under Regulation 4.5(b) of the Practising Regulations, or requests for extension of temporary emergency recognition made under Regulation 4.4(c)(iii) of the Practising Regulations, but not decided on the relevant date shall be considered and decided in accordance with the Practising Regulations;

and, for the avoidance of doubt, where on the relevant date, a notice of succession has been delivered to the *SRA* under Regulation 5.1 or 5.3 of the Practising Regulations in respect of which the *SRA* has made no fee determination, the *SRA* will proceed to consider the matter in accordance with Rule 8.3(d) to (l) above.

27.2 From 31 March 2012 these rules shall have effect subject to the following amendments:
- (a) in Rule 8.3(d), 8.3(i)(i) and 8.3(i)(ii) the words ", *recognised bodies*" shall be omitted;
- (b) in Rule 8.3(f), 8.3(j) and 8.3(k) the words ", *recognised bodies*" shall be omitted;
- (c) in Rule 8.3(g) and 8.3(l), the words ", *recognised body*" shall be omitted;
- (d) in Rule 8.3(h)(i), the words "*recognised body* or" shall be omitted;
- (e) in Rule 24.2(c), the words ", a *recognised body*" shall be omitted; and
- (f) in Rule 24.2(c)(i)(D), the words "Regulation 7 of the SRA Recognised Bodies Regulations 2011 or" shall be omitted.

27.3 From 31 March 2012 or the date on which an order made pursuant to section 69 of the Legal Services Act relating to the status of *sole practitioners* comes into force, whichever is the later, these rules shall have effect subject to the following amendments:
- (a) in Rule 6.3(a) the words ", as a group, are, or the *sole practitioner* is, suitable" shall be substituted for the words "are suitable, as a group";
- (b) in Rule 8.3(d), 8.3(i)(i) and 8.3(i)(ii) the words "and *recognised sole practitioners*" shall be omitted;
- (c) in Rule 8.3(f), 8.3(j) and 8.3(k) the words "or *recognised sole practitioners*" shall be omitted;
- (d) in Rule 8.3(g) and 8.3(l), the words "or *recognised sole practitioner*" shall be omitted;
- (e) in Rule 8.3(h)(i), the words "and/or *recognised sole practitioner*" shall be omitted;
- (f) Rule 24.2(b) shall be omitted;
- (g) in Rule 24.2(c), the words "or a *recognised sole practitioner*" shall be omitted;
- (h) in Rule 24.2(c)(i)(D), the words "or temporary emergency recognition under Regulation 4 of the *SRA Practising Regulations*" shall be omitted;
- (i) Rule 25.1 shall have effect as if the words "or a new *sole practitioner firm*" were inserted after the word "*partnership*";
- (j) Rule 25.1(b) shall have effect as if the words ", or the new *sole principal*," were inserted after the words "the new *partnership*";
- (k) Rule 25.3(a) shall have effect as if the words "or sole *principal*" were inserted after the word "*partners*";

(l) Rule 25.3(c), 25.3(d) and 25.3(e) shall have effect as if the words "or sole *principal*" were inserted after the word "*partnership*"; and

(m) Rule 25 shall have effect as if the following provisions were inserted:

25.5 Sole practitioners

(a) If a sole practitioner dies:

(i) the *SRA* must be notified within seven days;

(ii) within 28 days of the death an emergency application may be made, on the *prescribed* form, for recognition as a *recognised body* in the capacity of personal representative, practice manager or *employee* by a *solicitor* or an *REL* who is:

(A) the sole practitioner's executor;

(B) practice manager appointed by the sole practitioner's personal representatives; or

(C) an employee of the firm.

(b) If the application for recognition in the capacity of personal representative, practice manager or *employee* is granted:

(i) recognition will be deemed to run from the date of death;

(ii) recognition will not be renewed for any period after the winding up of the estate or 12 months from the date of death, whichever is the earlier.

27.4 From 31 March 2012, a *legal services body* which does not comply with Rule 8.5 above may be treated as an *authorised body* for the purposes of these rules and the *SRA's regulatory arrangements*, until 31 October 2012, at which time a *legal services body* shall be required to comply with Rule 8.5 in order to be authorised under these rules.

27.5 Unless the context otherwise requires, references in these rules to:

(a) these rules, or a provision of these rules; and

(b) the *SRA Code of Conduct*, rules, regulations or *regulatory arrangements*, or a provision of the same,

include a reference to the equivalent rules, regulations or provisions previously in force.

RULE 28: TRANSITION OF RECOGNISED BODIES AND SOLE PRACTITIONERS

28.1 From 31 March 2012:

(a) the recognition of a body recognised under section 9 of the *AJA*, shall have effect as if it were *authorisation* granted under these rules; and

(b) all *managers* and *owners* of bodies falling within sub-rule (a) shall be deemed to have been approved under Part 4 of these rules, as applicable, including those approved under Rule 27.1(b)(ii) above.

28.2 From 31 March 2012 or the date on which an order made pursuant to section 69 of the Legal Services Act relating to the status of *sole practitioners* comes into force, whichever is the later, these rules shall have effect subject to the following amendments:

(a) a sole *solicitor* or *REL* who has been recognised as a *sole practitioner* by way of an endorsement under section 1B of the *SA* shall be deemed to have been recognised as a *legal services body* under section 9 of the *AJA*; and

(b) all sole *solicitors* and *RELs* falling within sub-rule (a) shall be deemed to have been approved under Part 4 of these rules, as applicable.

APPENDIX B

PART 8: RECONSIDERATION AND APPEALS

RULE 29: RECONSIDERATION

29.1 The *SRA* may reconsider a decision made under these rules when it appears that the decision maker:

    (a)   was not provided with material evidence that was available to the *SRA*;
    (b)   was materially misled;
    (c)   failed to take proper account of material facts or evidence;
    (d)   took into account immaterial facts or evidence;
    (e)   made a material error of law;
    (f)   made a decision which was otherwise irrational or procedurally unfair;
    (g)   made a decision which was otherwise ultra vires; or
    (h)   failed to give sufficient reasons.

29.2 A decision may be reconsidered under Rule 29.1 only on the initiative of the *SRA*.

29.3 The *SRA*, when considering the exercise of its powers under this rule, may also give directions for:

    (a)   further investigations to be undertaken;
    (b)   further information or explanation to be obtained from any *person*; and
    (c)   the reconsideration to be undertaken by the original decision maker or by a different decision maker or panel.

RULE 30: APPEALS BY LEGAL SERVICES BODIES

30.1 A *legal services body* which is the subject of any decision in (a)–(b) below may invoke the *SRA's* own appeals procedure:

    (a)   against the *SRA's* decision to modify or refuse an application for modification of the terms and conditions of an *authorisation* under Rule 10;
    (b)   before exercising its right of appeal to the High Court:

        (i)   against refusal of *authorisation*, under paragraph 2(1)(a) of Schedule 2 to the *AJA*;
        (ii)   against the imposition of a condition on its *authorisation*, under paragraph 2(1)(b) or (c) of that Schedule; or
        (iii)   against refusal by the *SRA* to approve a step which, under a condition on the body's *authorisation*, requires such prior approval, under paragraph 2(2) of that Schedule.

30.2 A *legal services body* which is the subject of any decision in (a)–(c) below and/or the *person* who is the subject of any decision in (a)–(c) below, may invoke the *SRA's* own appeals procedure against the *SRA's* decision:

    (a)   not to approve the *person* to be an *owner* or *compliance officer* of a *legal services body* under Rules 8.5(b) or (c) or 8.6(a);
    (b)   to approve the *person* to be a *manager*, *owner* or *compliance officer* of a *legal services body* under Rules 8.5(b) or (d) or 8.6(a) subject to conditions on the body's *authorisation*; or
    (c)   to withdraw its approval of the *person* to be an *owner* or *compliance officer* of the body under Rule 17 or Rule 18.

30.3 A *legal services body* may appeal to the High Court against the *SRA's* decision to suspend or revoke the body's *authorisation*, but must first invoke the *SRA's* own appeals procedure.

30.4 A *legal services body* which is the subject of any decision in (a)–(b) below and/or the *person* who is the subject of any decision in (a)–(b) below, may appeal to the High Court against the *SRA's* decision:

(a) not to approve the *person* to be a *manager* of the body under Rule 8.6(a); and

(b) to withdraw its approval of the *person* to be a *manager* of the body under Rule 17;

but must first invoke the *SRA's* own appeals procedure.

30.5 Deemed refusal

(a) An application by a *legal services body* for *authorisation* under Rule 4 is deemed, for the purpose of any appeal under Rule 30.1(b) above, to be refused on the day of the expiry of the *decision period*, if by the end of that day the *SRA* has not notified the *applicant body* of its decision.

(b) An application for approval of a *person* under Part 4 is deemed, for the purpose of any appeal under Rule 30.4(a) above, to be refused on the day of the expiry of the *decision period*, if by the end of that day the *SRA* has not notified the *applicant body* or *authorised body* as appropriate, and the *person* who is the subject of the approval, of its decision.

30.6 If an appeal is made to the High Court in relation to a decision made in respect of a *legal services body* to:

(a) impose conditions on an *authorisation* under Rule 9;

(b) modify terms and conditions of an *authorisation* under Rule 10;

(c) withdraw approval of an *owner*, *manager*, *COLP* or *COFA*; or

(d) revoke or suspend a body's *authorisation*;

the appellant may apply to the High Court for a stay of the decision pending the determination or discontinuance of the appeal, and if the High Court imposes an order for a stay in relation to a decision, the *SRA* shall stay the decision accordingly.

Guidance note

(i) Rule 30.5 allows an applicant body or authorised body to regard their application as refused on certain dates to allow an appeal to be commenced. However, this is only for the purpose of ensuring the body has appeal rights and despite the deemed refusal the SRA may still determine the application.

RULE 31: APPEALS BY LICENSABLE BODIES

31.1 A *licensable body* which is the subject of any decision in (a)–(b) below may appeal to the *appellate body* against:

(a) the *SRA's* decision to:

(i) refuse an application for *authorisation*;

(ii) impose a condition on an *authorisation*;

(iii) revoke or suspend a body's *authorisation*;

APPENDIX B

(iv) refuse to approve a step which, under a condition on the body's *authorisation*, requires such prior approval;
(v) modify or refuse an application for modification of the terms and conditions of an *authorisation* under Rule 10; or

(b) the *SRA's* failure to make a decision within the *decision period*;

but must first invoke the *SRA's* own appeal procedure.

31.2 A *licensable body* which makes the application for approval pursuant to Rule 8.5 or 8.6 and/or the *person* who is the subject of the application for approval may appeal to the *appellate body* against the *SRA's* decision:

(a) not to approve the *person* to be a *manager* or *compliance officer* of the body under Rules 8.5(b) or (d) or 8.6(a);
(b) to approve the *person* to be a *manager* or *compliance officer* of the body under Rules 8.5(b) or (d) or 8.6(a) subject to conditions on the body's *authorisation*; or
(c) to withdraw its approval of the *person* to be a *manager* or *compliance officer* of the body under Rule 17;

but must first invoke the *SRA's* own appeals procedure.

31.3 Any *person* who is the subject of any decision in (a)–(c) below may invoke the *SRA's* own appeals procedure, before exercising their right of appeal to the *appellate body*:

(a) against the *SRA's* imposition of a financial penalty, under section 96 of the *LSA*;
(b) against the *SRA's* imposition of conditions on an *authorisation* in connection with its approval of a *person* being an *owner* of a *licensed body*, under paragraphs 18, 29 or 34 of Schedule 13 to the *LSA*; or
(c) against the *SRA's* decision not to approve, or its decision to withdraw its approval of, a *person* being an *owner* of a *licensed body*, under paragraphs 20, 32 or 37 of Schedule 13 to the *LSA*.

31.4 If an appeal is made to the *appellate body* in relation to a decision in respect of a *licensable body* to:

(a) impose conditions on an *authorisation* under Rule 9;
(b) modify terms and conditions of an *authorisation* under Rule 10;
(c) withdraw approval of an *owner*, *manager*, *COLP* or *COFA*;
(d) revoke or suspend a body's *authorisation*; or
(e) impose conditions on the holding of an interest under paragraph 28 or 33 of Schedule 13 of the *LSA*;

the appellant may apply to the *appellate body* for a stay of the decision pending the determination or discontinuance of the appeal, and if the *appellate body* imposes an order for a stay in relation to a decision, the *SRA* shall stay the decision accordingly.

RULE 32: APPEALS – GENERAL PROVISIONS

32.1 Appeals under the *SRA's* own appeals procedure in respect of a decision made under these rules must be made within 28 days of:

(a) notification of the *SRA's* decision and reasons;
(b) deemed refusal under Rule 30.5 above; or
(c) expiry of the *decision period* or extension notice under Rule 5;

as applicable.

32.2 Unless otherwise provided in rules of the High Court or the Legal Services Board or in the relevant decision, an appeal to the High Court or *appellate body* in respect of a decision made under these rules must be made:
- (a) within the period of 28 days from the date on which the notice of the decision that is subject to appeal is given to the appellant;
- (b) within the period of 28 days from the date on which the notice of the refusal of an appeal under the *SRA's* own appeals procedure is given; or
- (c) within the period of 28 days from the date on which the notice of the decision to impose a condition under the *SRA's* own appeals procedure is given;

as appropriate.

32.3 An appeal under the *SRA's* own appeals procedure under Rules 30.2(a), 30.4(a) or 31.2(a), or against the *SRA's* decision to refuse an approval under Rule 31.3(c), shall be treated as an application for the purpose of these rules.

32.4 If an appeal is made under:
- (a) Rules 30.2(c), 30.4(b), 31.2(c) or 31.3(c), against the *SRA's* decision to withdraw an approval; or
- (b) Rules 30.3 or 31.1(a)(iii), against the *SRA's* decision to revoke or suspend an *authorisation* under Rule 22;

before the decision takes effect, the decision shall not take effect pending the determination or discontinuance of the appeal, unless in the opinion of the *SRA* the proceedings on that appeal have been unduly protracted by the appellant or are unlikely to be successful.

32.5 Any decision referred to in Rule 30.6 and 31.4 which is made by the *SRA* may include a direction that the condition, modification, withdrawal, revocation or suspension shall not take effect until the determination or discontinuance of any appeal.

PART 9: REGISTER AND CERTIFICATE OF AUTHORISATION

RULE 33: NAME OF AN AUTHORISED BODY

33.1 A *body corporate* will be authorised under its corporate name.
33.2 A *partnership* must elect to have a name under which it is to be authorised.

RULE 34: THE REGISTER OF AUTHORISED BODIES

34.1 The *SRA* must keep a register of all *authorised bodies* authorised by the *SRA*, which may be kept in electronic form.

34.2 The register must contain, for each *authorised body*:
- (a) the name and number under which the body is authorised;
- (b) whether the *authorised body* is a *recognised body* or a *licensed body*;
- (c) any other *practising* styles used by the body;
- (d) the *authorised body's* registered office and registered number, if it is an *LLP* or *company*;
- (e) the *authorised body's* main *practising address* in England and Wales;
- (f) all the *authorised body's* other *practising addresses*;
- (g) whether the *authorised body* is a *partnership*, an *LLP* or a *company*;
- (h) if the *authorised body* is a *company*, whether it is:

APPENDIX B

(i) a *company* limited by shares;
(ii) a *company* limited by guarantee;
(iii) an unlimited *company*;
(iv) an overseas company registered in England and Wales;
(v) an overseas company registered in Scotland;
(vi) an overseas company registered in Northern Ireland; or
(vii) a *societas Europaea*;

(i) a list of the *authorised body's managers*, and in respect of each *manager*, whether that *manager* is:

(i) a *lawyer of England and Wales*, and if so the nature of his or her qualification;
(ii) an *REL*, and if so his or her professional title and jurisdiction of qualification;
(iii) an *EEL* registered with the *BSB*, and if so his or her professional title and jurisdiction of qualification;
(iv) an *EEL* based entirely at an office or offices outside England and Wales, and if so his or her professional title and jurisdiction of qualification;
(v) an *RFL*, and if so his or her professional title and jurisdiction of qualification;
(vi) any other individual approved under Part 4;
(vii) a *company* approved under Part 4, and if so whether it is a *licensed body*, a *recognised body*, a *European corporate practice* or an *authorised non-SRA firm*;
(viii) an *LLP* approved under Part 4, and if so whether it is a *licensed body*, a *recognised body*, a *European corporate practice* or an *authorised non-SRA firm*; or
(ix) a *partnership* with separate legal personality approved under Part 4, and if so whether it is a *licensed body*, a *recognised body*, a *European corporate practice* or an *authorised non-SRA firm*;

(j) the name of the individual who is the *firm's COLP*, and the name of the *approved regulator* which authorises that individual as an *authorised person*;
(k) the name of the individual who is the *firm's COFA*;
(l) any condition to which the body's *authorisation* is subject;
(m) if the *authorised body's authorisation* is for the time being suspended, a note to state that fact; and
(n) any other information considered necessary by the *SRA* for carrying out its statutory functions in the public interest, as may from time to time be *prescribed*.

34.3 Public information

(a) Entries in the register must be available for inspection by any member of the public except that the *SRA* may withhold a *recognised body's* address in exceptional circumstances where the *SRA* considers that to do so would be in the public interest.
(b) The date on which, and the circumstances in which, an *authorised body's authorisation* expired or was revoked must be made available to a member of the public on request.

RULE 35: CERTIFICATES OF AUTHORISATION

35.1 When a body is granted an *authorisation*, the *SRA* must issue a *certificate of authorisation*.
35.2 Each *certificate of authorisation* must state, in respect of the *authorised body*:
- (a) whether it is a licence or a certificate of recognition;
- (b) the name and number under which the body is authorised;
- (c) its registered office, if it is an *LLP* or *company*;
- (d) its main *practising address* in England and Wales;
- (e) whether it is a *partnership*, an *LLP* or a *company*; and
- (f) if it is a *company*, whether it is:
    - (i) a *company* limited by shares;
    - (ii) a *company* limited by guarantee;
    - (iii) an unlimited *company*;
    - (iv) an overseas company registered in England and Wales;
    - (v) an overseas company registered in Scotland;
    - (vi) an overseas company registered in Northern Ireland; or
    - (vii) a *societas Europaea*;
- (g) the date from which *authorisation* is granted; and
- (h) the terms and conditions to which the body's *authorisation* is subject.

APPENDIX C

SRA Practice Framework Rules 2011

Rules dated 17 June 2011 commencing on 6 October 2011
made by the Solicitors Regulation Authority Board, under sections 31, 79 and 80 of the Solicitors Act 1974, sections 9 and 9A of the Administration of Justice Act 1985 and section 83 and Schedule 11 to the Legal Services Act 2007, with the approval of the Legal Services Board under paragraph 19 of Schedule 4 to the Legal Services Act 2007.

INTRODUCTION

Part 1 of these rules sets out the types of business through which *solicitors*, *RELs*, *RFLs* and *authorised bodies* may *practise*. It restricts the types of business available in order to reflect statutory provisions and to ensure that *clients* and the public have the protections provided for by statute.

Part 2 permits *authorised bodies*, *solicitors*, *RELs* and *RFLs* to carry out certain types of work, including *immigration work*.

Part 3 governs the formation and practice requirements which must be satisfied by bodies to be eligible for authorisation by the *SRA*, and is based on the requirements of sections 9 and 9A of the *AJA* and section 72 of the *LSA*.

Part 4 sets out certain requirements relating to compliance with these rules and the *SRA's regulatory arrangements*.

PART 1: FRAMEWORK OF PRACTICE

RULE 1: SOLICITORS

Practice from an office in England and Wales

1.1 You may *practise* as a *solicitor* from an office in England and Wales in the following ways only:

    (a) as a *recognised sole practitioner* or the *employee* of a *recognised sole practitioner*;

    (b) as a *solicitor* exempted under Rule 10.2 from the obligation to be a *recognised sole practitioner*;

    (c) as a *manager*, *employee*, *member* or *interest holder* of:

        (i) an *authorised body*; or

        (ii) a *body corporate* which is a *manager*, *member* or *interest holder* of an *authorised body*,

    provided that in the case of both (i) and (ii) all work you do is:

SRA PRACTICE FRAMEWORK RULES 2011

(A) carried out through the *authorised body* and of a sort the body is authorised by the *SRA* to carry out; or

(B) done for the body itself, or falls within Rule 4.1 to 4.11 (In-house practice: Work colleagues, Related bodies and Pro bono work), and where this sub-paragraph applies, references in Rule 4 to *"employer"* shall be construed as referring to that body, accordingly;

(d) as a *manager, employee, member* or *interest holder* of:

(i) an *authorised non-SRA firm*; or

(ii) a *body corporate* which is a *manager, member* or *interest holder* of an *authorised non-SRA firm*,

provided that in the case of both (i) and (ii) all work you do is:

(A) carried out through the *authorised non-SRA firm* and of a sort the firm is authorised by the firm's *approved regulator* to carry out; or

(B) done for the firm itself, or falls within Rule 4.1 to 4.11 (In-house practice: Work colleagues, Related bodies and Pro bono work), and where this sub-paragraph applies, references in Rule 4 to *"employer"* shall be construed as referring to that firm, accordingly;

(e) as the *employee* of another *person*, business or organisation, provided that you undertake work only for your *employer*, or as permitted by Rule 4 (In-house practice).

Practice from an office outside England and Wales

1.2 You may *practise* as a *solicitor* from an office outside England and Wales in the following ways only:

(a) as a *sole practitioner* (including a *recognised sole practitioner*);

(b) as the *employee* of a sole *principal* who is a *lawyer*;

(c) as a *manager, employee, member* or *interest holder* of an *authorised body*, provided that if any of the body's *managers* or *interest holders* are non-lawyers and the office is in an *Establishment Directive state* other than the *UK*, the rules for local *lawyers* would permit a local *lawyer* to practise through a business of that composition and structure;

(d) as an *employee* of a business which is not required to be an *authorised body*, provided that it meets all the following conditions:

(i) the business carries on the provision of legal advice or assistance, or representation in connection with the application of the law or resolution of legal disputes;

(ii) a controlling majority of the *managers* and the *interest holders* are *lawyers* and/or *bodies corporate* in which *lawyers* constitute a controlling majority of the *managers* and *interest holders*;

(iii) if any of the business's *managers* or *interest holders* are non-lawyers and any *manager* or *interest holder* is subject to the rules for local *lawyers*, the composition and structure of the business complies with those rules; and

(iv) if any of the business's *managers* or *interest holders* are non-lawyers and the office is in an *Establishment Directive state*, the rules for local *lawyers* would permit a local *lawyer* to practise through a business of that composition and structure;

(e) as *manager, member* or *interest holder* of a business which is not required to be

APPENDIX C

an *authorised body*, provided that it does not practise from an office in England and Wales, and that it meets all the conditions set out in sub-paragraph (d)(i) to (iv) above;

(f) as the *employee* of another *person*, business or organisation, provided that you undertake work only for your *employer*, or as permitted by Rule 4.22 to 4.25 (In-house practice overseas).

Guidance notes

(i) See also Rules 10 (Sole practitioners), 13 (Eligibility criteria and fundamental requirements for recognised bodies), 14 (Eligibility criteria and fundamental requirements for licensed bodies), 15 (Formation, registered office and practising address), 16 (Composition of an authorised body) and 17 (Authorised bodies which are companies) below, the SRA Recognised Bodies Regulations 2011, Chapter 13 of the SRA Code of Conduct (Application and waivers provisions) and the SRA Practising Regulations.

(ii) See Rule 4.3 below and the definition of "in-house practice" in the SRA Code of Conduct, in relation to in-house work that you carry out for clients which is outside of your firm's authorisation.

RULE 2: RELS

Practice from an office in England and Wales

2.1 You may *practise* as an *REL* from an office in England and Wales in the following ways only:

(a) as a *recognised sole practitioner* or the *employee* of a *recognised sole practitioner*;

(b) as an *REL* exempted under Rule 10.2 from the obligation to be a *recognised sole practitioner*;

(c) as a *manager*, *employee*, *member* or *interest holder* of:

(i) an *authorised body*; or
(ii) a *body corporate* which is a *manager*, *member* or *interest holder* of an *authorised body*,

provided that in the case of both (i) and (ii) all work you do is:

(A) carried out through the *authorised body* and of a sort the body is authorised by the *SRA* to carry out; or
(B) done for the body itself, or falls within Rule 4.1 to 4.11 (In-house practice: Work colleagues, Related bodies and Pro bono work), and where this sub-paragraph applies, references in Rule 4 to "*employer*" shall be construed as referring to that body, accordingly;

(d) as a *manager*, *employee*, *member* or *interest holder* of:

(i) an *authorised non-SRA firm*; or
(ii) a *body corporate* which is a *manager*, *member* or *interest holder* of an *authorised non-SRA firm*,

provided that in the case of both (i) and (ii) all work you do is:

SRA PRACTICE FRAMEWORK RULES 2011

    (A) carried out through the *authorised non-SRA firm* and of a sort the firm is authorised by the firm's *approved regulator* to carry out; or

    (B) done for the firm itself, or falls within Rule 4.1 to 4.11 (In-house practice: Work colleagues, Related bodies and Pro bono work), and where this sub-paragraph applies, references in Rule 4 to "*employer*" shall be construed as referring to that firm, accordingly;

(e) as the *employee* of another *person*, business or organisation, provided that you undertake work only for your *employer*, or as permitted by Rule 4 (In-house practice).

Practice from an office in Scotland or Northern Ireland

2.2 You may *practise* as an *REL* from an office in Scotland or Northern Ireland in the following ways only:

(a) as a *sole practitioner* (including a *recognised sole practitioner*);
(b) as the *employee* of a sole *principal* who is a *lawyer*;
(c) as a *manager, employee, member* or *interest holder* of an *authorised body*;
(d) as an *employee* of a business which is not required to be an *authorised body* provided that it meets all the following conditions:

    (i) the business carries on the provision of legal advice or assistance, or representation in connection with the application of the law or resolution of legal disputes;

    (ii) a controlling majority of the *managers* and the *interest holders* are *lawyers* and/or *bodies corporate* in which *lawyers* constitute a controlling majority of the *managers* and *interest holders*; and

    (iii) if any of the business's *managers* or *interest holders* are non-lawyers, the professional rules governing a solicitor of that jurisdiction would allow such a solicitor to practise through a business of that composition and structure;

(e) as *manager, member* or *interest holder* of a business which is not required to be an *authorised body*, provided that it does not practise from an office in England and Wales, and that it meets all the conditions set out in sub-paragraph (d)(i) to (iii) above;

(f) as the *employee* of another *person*, business or organisation, provided that you undertake work only for your *employer*, or as permitted by Rule 4.22 to 4.25 (In-house practice overseas).

Guidance notes

(i) The overseas provisions for an REL are the same as those for a solicitor practising overseas except that they apply only in Scotland and Northern Ireland. RELs are not subject to Rule 2 in relation to practice from an office outside the UK.

(ii) See Rule 4.3 and the definition of "in-house practice" in the SRA Code of Conduct, in relation to in-house work that you carry out for clients which is outside of your firm's authorisation.

APPENDIX C

RULE 3: RFLS

Practice in the capacity of an RFL

3.1 Your *practice* as a *foreign lawyer* in the capacity of an *RFL* is confined to *practice* as:
    (a) the *employee* of a *recognised sole practitioner*;
    (b) a *manager, employee, member* or *interest holder* of:
        (i) an *authorised body*; or
        (ii) a *body corporate* which is a *manager, member* or *interest holder* of an *authorised body*,

        provided that in the case of both (i) and (ii) all work you do is:

        (A) carried out through the *authorised body* and of a sort the body is authorised by the *SRA* to carry out; or
        (B) done for the body itself, or falls within Rule 4.1 to 4.11 (In-house practice: Work colleagues, Related bodies and Pro bono work), and where this sub-paragraph applies, references in Rule 4 to "*employer*" shall be construed as referring to that body, accordingly;

    (c) a *manager, employee, member* or *interest holder* of:
        (i) an *authorised non-SRA firm*; or
        (ii) a *body corporate* which is a *manager, member* or *interest holder* of an *authorised non-SRA firm*,

        provided that in the case of both (i) and (ii) all work you do is:

        (A) carried out through the *authorised non-SRA firm* and of a sort the firm is authorised by the firm's *approved regulator* to carry out; or
        (B) done for the firm itself, or falls within Rule 4.1 to 4.11 (In-house practice: Work colleagues, Related bodies and Pro bono work), and where this sub-paragraph applies, references in Rule 4 to "*employer*" shall be construed as referring to that firm, accordingly.

Practice in another capacity than as an RFL

3.2 If you provide services as a *foreign lawyer* in any of the following ways in England and Wales or elsewhere, you will not be *practising* in the capacity of an *RFL* and you must not be held out or described in that context as an *RFL*, or as regulated by or registered with the *Society* or the *SRA*:
    (a) as a sole *principal*; or
    (b) as a *manager, member* or *interest holder* of any business or organisation other than an *authorised body* or an *authorised non-SRA firm*; or
    (c) as a *manager, member* or *interest holder* of a *body corporate* which is a *manager, member* or *interest holder* of any business or organisation other than an *authorised body* or an *authorised non-SRA firm*; or
    (d) as the *employee* of any business or organisation other than a *recognised sole practitioner*, an *authorised body* or an *authorised non-SRA firm*.

3.3 If you have a *practice* under Rule 3.1 above, and another business under Rule 3.2 above, the latter is a *separate business* for the purpose of these rules and you must therefore comply with Chapter 12 (Separate businesses) of the *SRA Code of Conduct*.

Scope of practice

3.4 Whether or not you are *practising* in the capacity of an *RFL* you must not:

(a) be held out in any way which suggests that you are, or are entitled to *practise* as, a *lawyer of England and Wales*;

(b) undertake the following *reserved work* in England and Wales:

  (i) advocacy in open *court*;
  (ii) the conduct of *court* litigation;
  (iii) the administration of oaths and statutory declarations;

(c) undertake advocacy in chambers in England and Wales, except under instructions given by a person qualified to supervise that *reserved work*;

(d) undertake the following *reserved work* in England and Wales, except at the direction and under the supervision of a person qualified to supervise that *reserved work*:

  (i) the preparation of *court* documents;
  (ii) the preparation of instruments and the lodging of documents relating to the transfer or charge of land;
  (iii) the preparation of papers on which to found or oppose a grant of probate or a grant of letters of administration;
  (iv) the preparation of trust deeds disposing of capital, unless you also are eligible to act as a *lawyer of England and Wales*;

(e) If you are not *practising* in the capacity of an *RFL* you must not carry out *immigration work* in the *UK* unless you are entitled to do so by virtue of being a qualified person within the meaning of section 84 of the Immigration and Asylum Act 1999, whether this is as a result of being entitled to do the work in your own right, doing so under supervision, or otherwise.

Guidance notes

(i) A foreign lawyer must be registered with the SRA as an RFL to be a manager, member or owner of a recognised body, with the following exceptions:

(a) a foreign lawyer who is also qualified as a lawyer of England and Wales does not have to be an RFL;

(b) a member of an Establishment Directive profession – except that if the lawyer is not a national of an Establishment Directive state and will be based, or partly based, in England and Wales, he or she does have to be an RFL in order to be a manager, member or owner of a recognised body. See our website for additional guidance on RFLs and multi-national practice [**www.sra.org.uk/solicitors/code-of-conduct/guidance.page**].

(ii) There is no requirement to register as an RFL in order to be employed by a recognised body or sole practitioner or to be a manager or owner of, or employed by, a licensed body but, if you are registered as an RFL, you will be subject to SRA regulation in this capacity when working for an SRA firm or an authorised non-SRA firm.

(iii) An RFL is subject to the same restrictions as a solicitor or REL in relation to practice from an office in England and Wales with two exceptions. Your registration as an RFL does not entitle you to practise:

(a) as an RFL sole practitioner; or

APPENDIX C

(b) as an in-house RFL (subject to note (iv) below).

(iv) Registration as an RFL is portable to the extent that it will enable you to be a manager, employee, member or owner of an authorised non-SRA firm, although your ability to work within such a firm will depend on the framework of practice requirements of the relevant approved regulator. You will be able to undertake work authorised by the firm's approved regulator (subject to any statutory limitations or requirements). Additionally you will be able to function as an in-house lawyer under Rule 4, doing other work for the employer, related bodies, work colleagues and pro bono clients under the SRA's rules.

(v) Your registration as an RFL will not be relevant in the role of owner or employee of a business in England and Wales which is not regulated by the SRA or one of the other approved regulators. The SRA does not regulate any practice you might have outside the framework established under the LSA, so there must be no implication in such a context that you are an RFL, or that you or the business are regulated by or registered with the SRA or the Society.

(vi) Where, in order to satisfy statutory requirements, there is a need for an RFL doing reserved work to be supervised or directed by someone in the firm, this can only be undertaken by a person of equivalent or higher status.

(vii) See the application provisions in 4.2 of the SRA Principles. Also see the provisions relating to practice from an office outside England and Wales in Chapter 13 of the SRA Code of Conduct.

(viii) See Rule 4.3 and the definition of "in-house practice" in the SRA Code of Conduct, in relation to in-house work that you carry out for clients which is outside of your firm's authorisation.

RULE 4: IN-HOUSE PRACTICE

4.1 If you are employed in house, you must not act for *clients* other than your *employer* except in the following circumstances and where you are able to act without compromising the *Principles* or your obligations under the *SRA Code of Conduct*.

4.2 Indemnity

(a) In order to act for a *client* other than your *employer* under Rule 4.10, 4.14, 4.16 and 4.19, you must have professional indemnity insurance cover.

(b) In all other cases you must consider whether your *employer* has appropriate indemnity insurance or funds to meet any award made as a result of a claim in professional negligence against you, for which your *employer* might be vicariously liable. If not, you must inform the *client* in writing that you are not covered by the compulsory insurance scheme.

4.3 If you are a *solicitor*, *REL* or *RFL* in an *authorised body* or an *authorised non-SRA firm*, you must comply with this rule as if you were an in-house *solicitor* or *REL* when, as:

(a) a *manager* or *employee*; or

(b) a *manager* or *employee* of a body which is a *manager* of the firm,

you do work of a type which is outside the scope of the firm's authorisation in accordance with Rules 1, 2 or 3, either for the firm itself or within 4.4 to 4.6 (Work colleagues), 4.7 to 4.9 (Related bodies) or 4.10 to 4.11 (Pro bono work).

Work colleagues

4.4 Subject to Rule 4.5 below, you may act for a *person* who is, or was formerly:

(a) an *employee*, a *manager*, the company secretary, a board member or a trustee of your *employer*;
(b) an *employee*, a *manager*, the company secretary, a board member or a trustee of a *related body* of your *employer*; or
(c) a contributor to a programme or periodical publication, broadcast or published by your *employer* or by a *related body*, but only where the contributor is a defendant or potential defendant in a defamation case.

4.5 You may act under Rule 4.4 above only if:

(a) the matter relates to and arises out of the work of the *employee*, *manager*, company secretary, board member, trustee or contributor in that capacity;
(b) the matter does not relate to a claim arising as a result of a personal injury to the *employee*, *manager*, company secretary, board member, trustee or contributor;
(c) you are satisfied that the *employee*, *manager*, company secretary, board member, trustee or contributor does not wish to instruct some other *lawyer*; and
(d) no charge is made for your work unless those costs are recoverable from another source.

4.6 Where acting in a conveyancing transaction under Rule 4.4(a) or (b) above you may also act for a joint owner or joint buyer of the property and for a mortgagee.

Related bodies

4.7 You may act for:

(a) your *employer's* holding, associated or *subsidiary company*;
(b) a *partnership*, syndicate, *LLP* or *company* by way of joint venture in which your *employer* and others have an interest;
(c) a trade association of which your *employer* is a member; or
(d) a club, association, pension fund or other scheme operated for the benefit of *employees* of your *employer*.

4.8 If you are employed in local government, Rule 4.7(a) and (b) above do not apply.
4.9 For the purpose of Rule 4.10 to 4.14 references to your *employer* include *related bodies* of the *employer*, and "employment" and "employed" must be construed accordingly.

Pro bono work

4.10 You may, in the course of your *practice*, conduct work on a pro bono basis for a *client* other than your *employer* provided:

(a) the work is covered by an indemnity reasonably equivalent to that required under the SRA Indemnity Insurance Rules;
(b) either:
  (i) no fees are charged; or
  (ii) a conditional fee agreement is used and the only fees charged are those which you receive by way of costs from your *client's* opponent or other third party and all of which you pay to a *charity* under a fee sharing agreement; and
(c) you do not undertake any *reserved legal activities*, unless the provision of relevant services to the public or a section of the public (with or without a view to profit) is not part of your employer's business.

APPENDIX C

4.11 Rule 4.10 above does not permit you to conduct work on a pro bono basis in conjunction with services provided by your *employer* under Rule 4.12 (Associations), Rule 4.13 (Insurers), Rule 4.14 (Commercial legal advice services) or Rule 4.19 to 4.21 (Foreign law firms).

Associations

4.12 If you are employed by an association you may act for a member of that association provided:

(a) you do not undertake any *reserved legal activities*;
(b) the membership of the association is limited to *persons* engaged or concerned in a particular trade, occupation or specialist activity or otherwise having a community of interest, such interest being a specialist interest;
(c) the association is one formed bona fide for the benefit of its members and not formed directly or indirectly for your benefit or primarily for securing assistance in legal proceedings;
(d) there is no charge to the member in non-contentious matters, and in contentious matters the association indemnifies the member in relation to your costs and disbursements insofar as they are not recoverable from any other source; and
(e) you act only in matters that relate to or arise out of the particular trade, occupation or specialist activity of the association or otherwise relate to the specialist community of interest, for which the association is formed.

Insurers

4.13 If you are employed by an insurer subrogated to the rights of an insured in respect of any matter you may act on behalf of the insurer in relation to that matter in the name of the insured, and also:

(a) act on behalf of the insured in relation to uninsured losses in respect of the matter;
(b) act in proceedings both for the insured and for a defendant covered by another insurer where the insurers have agreed an apportionment of liability; and/or
(c) act in the matter on behalf of the *employer* and another insurer in the joint prosecution of a claim.

Commercial legal advice services

4.14 If you are employed by a commercial organisation providing a telephone legal advice service you may advise *persons* making enquiries of that organisation, provided:

(a) the advice comprises telephone advice only, together with a follow up letter to the enquirer when necessary;
(b) you are satisfied that there is indemnity cover reasonably equivalent to that required under the SRA Indemnity Insurance Rules; and
(c) you do not undertake any *reserved legal activities*.

Local government

4.15 If you are employed in local government you may act:

(a) for another organisation or *person* to which or to whom the *employer* is statutorily empowered to provide legal services, subject to the conditions in (b) to (g) below;
(b) for a member or former member of the local authority, provided that:
  (i) the matter relates to or arises out of the work of the member in that capacity;
  (ii) the matter does not relate to a claim arising as a result of a personal injury to the member;
  (iii) you are satisfied that the member does not wish to instruct some other *lawyer*; and
  (iv) no charge is made for your work unless those costs are recoverable from some other source;
(c) for a *company* limited by shares or guarantee of which:
  (i) the *employer* or nominee of the *employer* is a shareholder or guarantor; or
  (ii) you are, or an officer of the *employer* is, appointed by the *employer* as an officer of the *company*,

  provided the *employer* is acting in pursuance of its statutory powers;
(d) for lenders in connection with new mortgages arising from the redemption of mortgages to the local authority, provided:
  (i) neither you nor any other *employee* acts on behalf of the borrowers; and
  (ii) the borrowers are given the opportunity to be independently advised by a qualified conveyancer of their choice;
(e) for a *charity* or voluntary organisation whose objects relate wholly or partly to the *employer's* area, provided that there is no charge to the *charity* or voluntary organisation in non-contentious matters, and in contentious matters the *employer* indemnifies the *charity* or voluntary organisation in relation to your costs insofar as they are not recoverable from any other source;
(f) for a patient who is the subject of a Court of Protection Order where you are acting for a work colleague (under Rule 4.4 to 4.6 above) who is appointed as deputy for the patient; or
(g) for a child or young person subject to a Care Order in favour of the *employer* on an application to the Criminal Injuries Compensation Authority.

Law Centres, charities and other non-commercial advice services

4.16 If you are employed by a law centre or advice service operated by a charitable or similar non-commercial organisation you may give advice to and otherwise act for members of the public, provided:

(a) no funding agent has majority representation on the body responsible for the management of the service, and that body remains independent of central and local government;
(b) no fees are charged save:
  (i) where the *client* is publicly funded; or
  (ii) where the organisation indemnifies the *client* in relation to your costs insofar as they are not recoverable from any other source;
(c) all fees you earn and costs you recover are paid to the organisation for furthering the provision of the organisation's services;

APPENDIX C

(d) the organisation is not described as a law centre unless it is a member of the Law Centres Federation; and

(e) the organisation has indemnity cover in relation to the *legal activities* carried out by you, reasonably equivalent to that required under the SRA Indemnity Insurance Rules.

4.17 Rule 4.16 above does not apply to an association formed for the benefit of its members.

The Crown, non-departmental public bodies and the Legal Services Commission

4.18 If you are employed by the Crown, a non-departmental public body or the Legal Services Commission (or any body established or maintained by the Legal Services Commission), you may give legal advice to, and act for, *persons* other than your *employer* if in doing so you are carrying out the lawful functions of your *employer*.

Foreign law firms

4.19 You may provide legal services to your *employer's clients*, subject to the conditions set out in Rule 4.20 below, if you are a *solicitor* or an *REL* employed by:

(a) a practising lawyer of another jurisdiction who:

(i) is not struck off or suspended from the *register of foreign lawyers* or the *register of European lawyers*; and

(ii) is not *practising* in that context as a *solicitor* or as an *REL*; or

(b) a business whose *managers* and owners are all practising through that business as lawyers of jurisdictions other than England and Wales, and do not include any person who:

(i) is struck off or suspended from the *register of foreign lawyers* or the *register of European lawyers*; or

(ii) is *practising* through or in the context of that business as a *solicitor* or as an *REL*.

4.20 You must meet the following conditions if acting, under Rule 4.19 above, for anyone other than your *employer*.

(a) Even if you are qualified to do such work for your *employer*, you must not do, or supervise or assume responsibility for doing any of the following:

(i) drawing or preparing any instrument or papers comprising *reserved legal activities* under section 12(1)(c) or (d) of the *LSA*;

(ii) exercising any right of audience, or right to conduct litigation (including making any application or lodging any document relating to litigation), before a *court* or immigration tribunal; or

(iii) providing any immigration advice or immigration services, unless the *employer*, or a senior fellow *employee*, is registered with the Immigration Services Commissioner.

(b) You must ensure that the work you do is covered by professional indemnity insurance reasonably equivalent to that required under the SRA Indemnity Insurance Rules.

(c) You must:

(i) inform your *client* that your *employer* is not regulated by the *SRA* and that the *SRA's* compulsory insurance scheme does not apply, and either give or confirm this information in writing, if you are a *solicitor*, and you

are held out to a *client* as a *solicitor* (or as an English or Welsh *lawyer*) in connection with work you are doing for that *client*; and
    (ii) ensure that if you are identified on the notepaper as a *solicitor* (or as an English or Welsh *lawyer*) the notepaper also states that your *employer* is not regulated by the *SRA*.

4.21 Rule 4.20(c) above should also be read as referring to an *REL* being held out or identified as a *lawyer*, or under the *REL's* title from their home state.

In-house practice overseas

4.22 Rules 4.10 and 4.11 (Pro bono work) apply to your *overseas practice*.

4.23 The other provisions of Rule 4 (In-house practice) do not apply to your *overseas practice*, but you must comply with Rules 4.24 and 4.25 below.

4.24 Subject to 4.25 below, you may act as an in-house *lawyer*, but only for:

(a) your *employer*;
(b) a *company* or organisation controlled by your *employer* or in which your *employer* has a substantial measure of control;
(c) a *company* in the same group as your *employer*;
(d) a *company* which controls your *employer*; or
(e) an *employee* (including a *director* or a company secretary) of a *company* or organisation under (a) to (d) above, provided that the matter relates to or arises out of the work of that *company* or organisation, does not relate to a claim arising as a result of a personal injury to the *employee*, and no charge is made for your work unless those costs are recoverable from another source.

4.25 If you are a *solicitor* registered in another state under the *Establishment Directive* with the professional body for a local legal profession you may *practise* in-house to the extent that a member of that legal profession is permitted to do so.

Regulatory bodies

4.26 If you are employed by a regulatory body you may in carrying out the function of the *employer* give legal advice to other *persons* and, where those functions are statutory, may act generally for such *persons*.

Guidance notes

(i) The general principle, subject to limited exceptions, is that your employer itself will need to be authorised if, in your capacity as an employee, you wish to provide reserved legal services to the public.

(ii) If you are a solicitor working in-house (whether in or outside England and Wales) you must comply with Rule 9 (Practising certificates). For further guidance on the need for a practising certificate see our website. Examples of situations where you will be practising as a solicitor, and will therefore need a practising certificate, include:

(a) you are employed as a solicitor;
(b) you are held out, on stationery or otherwise, as a solicitor for your employer;
(c) you administer oaths;
(d) you appear before a court or tribunal in reliance upon your qualification as a solicitor;
(e) you instruct counsel;

APPENDIX C

    (f)   you undertake work which is prohibited to unqualified persons under the provisions of Part 3 of the LSA, unless you are supervised by, and acting in the name of, a solicitor with a practising certificate or another qualified person;

    (g)   your only qualification as a lawyer is that you are a solicitor, and:

        (A)   you are employed or held out as a lawyer;
        (B)   you undertake work in another jurisdiction which is reserved to lawyers;
        (C)   you are registered in a state other than the UK under the Establishment Directive; or
        (D)   you are a registered foreign legal consultant in another jurisdiction.

(iii) In England and Wales a number of statutory exceptions apply to qualify (ii). Certain in-house government solicitors are allowed to practise as solicitors without practising certificates. Some reserved work can be undertaken by non-solicitors working for local government, and therefore by non-practising solicitors working for local government. See also Rules 9, 10 and 11.

(iv) A solicitor acting only as a justices' clerk in England and Wales is not practising as a solicitor and can instruct counsel without a practising certificate.

(v) If you are an in-house solicitor the address of your employer's legal department is the place (or one of the places) where you practise and must therefore be notified to the SRA.

(vi) If you handle client money, the SRA Accounts Rules will apply to you unless you are exempted under Rule 5 of those rules.

(vii) If you are working in-house as the senior legal adviser of a company or a local authority you should have direct access to the board or to the council and its committees, and should try to ensure that your terms of employment provide for such access. "Direct access" does not mean that all instructions and advice must pass directly to and from the council, committee or board, but you must have direct access where necessary.

(viii) An in-house solicitor may act for work colleagues, subject to certain safeguards, provided the matter relates to and arises out of the person's work for the employer. This will cover matters that relate directly to the fellow employee's work but would not, for example, permit reserved legal services to be offered as a benefit under an employment package. Those working in-house will need to consider whether they are allowed to act on a case by case basis and, in particular, the extent to which there is a direct relationship between the work colleague's employment and the reserved legal activity.

(ix) The ability of in-house solicitors to act for clients on a pro bono basis is limited by the LSA, which requires that, in general, the provision of reserved legal services to the public is carried out through an authorised body. There is no such limitation under the LSA in respect of unreserved services, such as providing legal advice. Rule 4.10 sets out the parameters within which in-house solicitors may provide reserved services on a pro bono basis, reflecting the position under the LSA. To determine whether you can undertake reserved legal activities within 4.10, one question will be whether the activities to be undertaken can be regarded as part of the business of the employer. Relevant factors are likely to be:

    (a)   relevancy of such work to the employer's business;
    (b)   whether the work is required of the employee by the employer;
    (c)   how often such work is carried out;
    (d)   where such work is carried out;
    (e)   when such work is carried out;
    (f)   whether such work is explicitly carried out on the employer's behalf;
    (g)   who provides the necessary professional indemnity insurance;
    (h)   the extent to which the employer relies on or publicises such work;

(i) whether the employer provides management, training or supervision in relation to such work;
(j) whether the employer specifically rewards the employee in any way in relation to such work;
(k) how many employees carry out the work, and the overall proportion of their time spent on such work;
(l) the extent to which such work complements or enhances the employer's business.

All the circumstances, and the context, will be critical to your decision about whether you may act, for example the work will not necessarily be part of the employer's business merely because it is carried out in office hours, or at the employer's premises.

There will be some situations which are likely to be easier to judge. If there is a clear relationship with the employer's business, acting will not be permissible. For example, you are likely to be prevented from acting:

(A) where the employer describes its business as including the provision of pro bono services;
(B) where the work may boost the employer's business by providing extra business opportunities or creating contacts.

(x) If you are employed as a solicitor or REL by an insurer which runs a commercial legal telephone advice service, the restrictions in Rule 4.14 will not apply to prevent you acting for an insured in accordance with Rule 4.13.

(xi) If you are employed as a solicitor or REL by a law centre or advice service operated by a charitable or similar non-commercial organisation, you can advise and act for members of the public provided you comply with Rule 4.16 and 4.17. A solicitor or REL who works as a volunteer for such an advice service must comply with the SRA Indemnity Insurance Rules unless exempted by a waiver. If your employer obtains authorisation as a licensed body you will not need to rely on the exceptions in Rule 4.

(xii) As the in-house employee of a foreign law firm under Rule 4.19 and 4.20 you may not do reserved work for clients or (unless your employer is separately authorised) immigration work. You must also comply with special requirements as to insurance and "health warnings". Note also, that if you are employed by a foreign law firm and a principal, owner or director of the firm is a solicitor, Rule 4.19 and 4.20 will not apply unless the solicitor is dually qualified and is practising only as a lawyer of another jurisdiction in the context of that business.

(xiii) By contrast, employment overseas by a foreign law firm will not usually fall within the definition of in-house practice in Chapter 14 of the SRA Code of Conduct (Interpretation) if your employer is a lawyer or a law firm.

(xiv) If you are a solicitor, REL or RFL practising as a manager, employee, member or owner of an authorised non-SRA firm, neither Rule 4, nor the bulk of the SRA Code of Conduct, nor the SRA Accounts Rules, will be relevant to you when you do work of a type that is within the scope of the firm's authorisation. See Chapter 13 of the SRA Code of Conduct (Application and waivers provisions).

(xv) If you are a solicitor, REL or RFL practising as a manager, employee, member or owner of an authorised non-SRA firm, you must comply with Rule 4, with the SRA Code of Conduct, and with the SRA Accounts Rules, as if you were an in-house solicitor or REL when you do work of a type which is outside the scope of the firm's authorisation – see Rule 4.3 and the definition of "in-house practice" in the SRA Code of Conduct.

(xvi) Note that if you are a solicitor, REL or RFL and you are a manager, member or owner of an authorised non-SRA firm, or employed in such a firm in connection with the provision of any legal services, it must be:

(a) in your capacity as a solicitor, REL or RFL, or

APPENDIX C

(b) in the capacity of an individual authorised by an approved regulator other than the SRA, if you are so authorised, or
(c) in both such capacities;

except that if you are a solicitor who is a director of an authorised non-SRA firm or employed in such a firm in connection with the provision of any legal services, you must be practising in your capacity as a solicitor, even if also in some other capacity. See Rule 11.2 and 11.3, as well as section 1A(d) of the SA.

RULE 5: AUTHORISED BODIES

Practice from an office in England and Wales

5.1 An *authorised body* may *practise* from an office in England and Wales in the following ways only:

(a) as a stand-alone *firm*;
(b) as a *manager*, *member* or *interest holder* of another *authorised body*;
(c) as a *manager*, *member* or *interest holder* of an *authorised non-SRA firm*, in which case you must comply with any terms and requirements imposed on that firm's authorisation; or
(d) as an executor, trustee or nominee *company*, or a *company* providing company secretarial services, wholly owned and operated by another *authorised body* or by a *recognised sole practitioner*.

Practice from an office outside England and Wales

5.2 An *authorised body* may *practise* from an office outside England and Wales in the following ways only:

(a) as a stand-alone *firm*, provided that if any of the body's *managers* or *interest holders* are non-lawyers and the office is in an *Establishment Directive state* other than the *UK*, the rules for local *lawyers* would permit a local *lawyer* to practise through a business of that composition and structure;
(b) as a *manager*, *member* or *interest holder* of a business which has no office in England and Wales and meets all the following conditions:

(i) the business carries on the provision of legal advice or assistance, or representation in connection with the application of the law or resolution of legal disputes;
(ii) a controlling majority of the *managers* and the *interest holders* are *lawyers* and/or *bodies corporate* in which *lawyers* constitute a controlling majority of the *managers* and *interest holders*;
(iii) if any of the business's *managers* or *interest holders* are non-lawyers and any *manager* or *interest holder* is subject to the rules for local *lawyers*, the composition and structure of the business complies with those rules; and
(iv) if any of the business's *managers* or *interest holders* are non-lawyers and the office is in an *Establishment Directive state* other than the *UK*, the rules for local *lawyers* would permit a local *lawyer* to practise through a business of that composition and structure;

(c) as an executor, trustee or nominee *company*, or a *company* providing company secretarial services, wholly owned and operated by another *authorised body* or by a *recognised sole practitioner*.

Guidance notes

(i) See Part 3 of these rules for the formation and eligibility criteria for recognised bodies and licensed bodies.
(ii) Authorised bodies can have a complex structure, involving multi-layered ownership. But note that a partnership cannot be a partner in another partnership which is an authorised body because a partnership does not have separate legal identity (although, as an exception, an overseas partnership with separate legal identity could be a partner in a partnership which is an authorised body).

RULE 6: MANAGERS AND EMPLOYEES AUTHORISED BY ANOTHER APPROVED REGULATOR

6.1 If you are a *manager* or *employee* of an *authorised body* or an *employee* of a *recognised sole practitioner* and you are not a *solicitor* but you are authorised by an *approved regulator* other than the *SRA*, you must not:

(a) be held out in any way which suggests that you are, or are entitled to *practise* as, a *solicitor*;
(b) undertake the following *reserved work* in England and Wales, unless authorised by your *approved regulator* to do so:
 (i) advocacy in open *court*;
 (ii) the conduct of *court* litigation;
 (iii) the administration of oaths and statutory declarations;
(c) undertake advocacy in chambers in England and Wales, unless authorised by your *approved regulator* or acting under instructions given by a person qualified to supervise that *reserved work*;
(d) undertake the following *reserved work* in England and Wales, unless authorised by your *approved regulator* or acting under the supervision of a person qualified to supervise that *reserved work*:
 (i) the preparation of *court* documents;
 (ii) the preparation of instruments and the lodging of documents relating to the transfer or charge of land;
 (iii) the preparation of papers on which to found or oppose a grant of probate or a grant of letters of administration;
 (iv) the preparation of trust deeds disposing of capital;
(e) undertake the conduct of immigration tribunal proceedings in the *UK* or advocacy before an immigration tribunal in the *UK* unless you are authorised by your *approved regulator* or the Immigration Services Commissioner to do that work;
(f) prepare documents in the *UK* for immigration tribunal proceedings unless you are authorised by your *approved regulator* or the Immigration Services Commissioner to do that work or acting under the supervision of a person qualified to supervise that *reserved work*; or
(g) carry out *immigration work* in the *UK* which is not within (b) to (f) above,

APPENDIX C

unless you are authorised by your *approved regulator* or the Immigration Services Commissioner to do that work, or acting under the supervision of an individual working in the *firm* who is authorised under statute to do that work.

Guidance notes

(i) Rule 16 permits lawyers and firms authorised by another approved regulator to be owners and managers of an authorised body.
(ii) An individual authorised by another approved regulator cannot practise as a sole practitioner regulated by the SRA as the SRA can only authorise and regulate sole solicitors and RELs.
(iii) Where, in order to satisfy statutory requirements, there is a need for an individual doing reserved work to be supervised or directed by someone in the firm, this can only be undertaken by a person of equivalent or higher status.
(iv) A lawyer of England and Wales who is an individual authorised by another approved regulator is subject to the SRA's regulatory arrangements in relation to practice outside England and Wales if he or she is a manager of an authorised body.

RULE 7: MANAGERS AND EMPLOYEES WHO ARE NOT LAWYERS

7.1 If you are a *manager* or *employee* of an *authorised body* or an *employee* of a *recognised sole practitioner* and you are not a *lawyer of England and Wales*, an *RFL* or a *lawyer* of an *Establishment Directive profession*, you must not:

(a) be held out in any way which suggests that you are, or are entitled to *practise* as, a *lawyer of England and Wales*;
(b) undertake the following *reserved work* in England and Wales:

(i) advocacy in open *court*;
(ii) the conduct of *court* litigation;
(iii) the administration of oaths and statutory declarations;

(c) undertake advocacy in chambers in England and Wales, except under instructions given by a person qualified to supervise that *reserved work*;
(d) undertake the following *reserved work* in England and Wales, except at the direction and under the supervision of a person qualified to supervise that *reserved work*:

(i) the preparation of *court* documents;
(ii) the preparation of instruments and the lodging of documents relating to the transfer or charge of land;
(iii) the preparation of papers on which to found or oppose a grant of probate or a grant of letters of administration;
(iv) the preparation of trust deeds disposing of capital;

(e) undertake the conduct of immigration tribunal proceedings in the *UK* or advocacy before an immigration tribunal in the *UK* unless you are authorised by the Immigration Services Commissioner to do that work;
(f) prepare documents in the *UK* for immigration tribunal proceedings unless you are authorised by the Immigration Services Commissioner to do that work, or acting under the supervision of a person qualified to supervise that *reserved work*; or

SRA PRACTICE FRAMEWORK RULES 2011

(g) carry out *immigration work* in the *UK* which is not within (b) to (f) above, unless you are authorised by the Immigration Services Commissioner to do that work or you do the work under the supervision of an individual working in the *firm* who is authorised under statute to do that work.

Guidance note

(i) A non-lawyer manager is subject to the SRA's regulatory arrangements in relation to legal practice outside England and Wales if he or she is a manager of an authorised body.

PART 2: RIGHTS OF PRACTICE

RULE 8: RESERVED WORK AND IMMIGRATION WORK

Solicitors

8.1 As a *solicitor*, provided that you comply with Rule 9.1, you are authorised by the *SRA*:

(a) to undertake the following *reserved work*:

 (i) the exercise of any right of audience which *solicitors* had immediately before 7 December 1989;
 (ii) the exercise of any additional right of audience if you have a relevant higher courts advocacy qualification awarded by the *SRA* or another *approved regulator*;
 (iii) the conduct of, and the preparation of documents in, *court* and immigration tribunal proceedings;
 (iv) the preparation of instruments and the lodging of documents relating to the transfer or charge of land;
 (v) the preparation of trust deeds disposing of capital;
 (vi) the preparation of papers on which to found or oppose a grant of probate or a grant of letters of administration;
 (vii) the administration of oaths and statutory declarations; and

(b) to undertake *immigration work* not included under (a) above.

RELs

8.2 As an *REL*, you are authorised by the *SRA*:

(a) to undertake the following *reserved work*:

 (i) the exercise of any right of audience which *solicitors* had immediately before 7 December 1989;
 (ii) the exercise of any additional right of audience provided that you have a relevant higher courts advocacy qualification awarded by the *SRA* or another *approved regulator*;
 (iii) the conduct of, and the preparation of documents in, *court* and immigration tribunal proceedings;
 (iv) the preparation of instruments and the lodging of documents relating to the transfer or charge of land, provided you are a member of a profession

APPENDIX C

(iv) listed under regulation 12 of the European Communities (Lawyer's Practice) Regulations 2000;
(v) the preparation of trust deeds disposing of capital;
(vi) the preparation of papers on which to found or oppose a grant of probate or a grant of letters of administration, provided you are a member of a profession listed under regulation 13 of the European Communities (Lawyer's Practice) Regulations 2000;
(vii) the administration of oaths and statutory declarations; and

(b) to undertake *immigration work* not included under (a) above.

8.3 When as an *REL* you exercise a right of audience before a *court* under 8.2(a)(i) or (ii), conduct *court* litigation under 8.2(a)(iii) or prepare *court* documents under 8.2(a)(iii) you must act in conjunction with a *solicitor* or barrister authorised to do that work.

RFLs

8.4 As an *RFL* working within Rule 3 you are authorised by the *SRA*:

(a) to undertake the following *reserved work*:

(i) advocacy before immigration tribunals; and
(ii) the conduct of, and the preparation of documents in, immigration tribunal proceedings; and

(b) to undertake immigration services which are not *reserved work* and are not included under (a) above, and to provide immigration advice.

Recognised bodies

8.5 Recognised bodies

(a) A *recognised body* is authorised by the *SRA* to undertake the following *reserved work*:

(i) advocacy before a *court* or immigration tribunal provided the *manager* or *employee* exercising the right of audience is authorised by the *SRA*, or otherwise entitled, to do so;
(ii) the conduct of proceedings in a *court* or immigration tribunal;
(iii) the preparation of documents in proceedings before a *court* or immigration tribunal;
(iv) the preparation of instruments and the lodging of documents relating to the transfer or charge of land, provided the body has a *manager* who is:

(A) an individual who is authorised to do that work, or
(B) a *body corporate* which has a *manager* who is authorised to do that work;

(v) the preparation of trust deeds disposing of capital;
(vi) the preparation of papers on which to found or oppose a grant of probate or a grant of letters of administration, provided the body has a *manager* who is an individual authorised to do that work, or a *body corporate* with a *manager* who is authorised to do that work; and
(vii) the administration of oaths and statutory declarations.

(b) A *recognised body* is authorised to undertake immigration services which are not within (a) above, and to provide immigration advice.

Licensed bodies

8.6 A *licensed body* is authorised by the *SRA* to undertake the *reserved legal activities* which are specified in the authorisation granted to the body under Rule 6 of the *SRA Authorisation Rules*.

Sole practitioner firms

8.7 Sole practitioner firms

    (a) A *recognised sole practitioner* who is a *solicitor* is authorised by the *SRA*:

        (i) to provide any *reserved work* which the *solicitor* is authorised to provide under Rule 8.1 above, and any other advocacy service through an *employee* of the *sole practitioner's firm* exercising a right of audience as authorised by the *SRA*, or otherwise entitled, to do; and

        (ii) to undertake immigration services which are not within (i) above, and provide immigration advice.

    (b) A *recognised sole practitioner* who is an *REL* is authorised by the *SRA*:

        (i) to provide any *reserved work* which the *REL* is authorised to provide under Rule 8.2 above, and any other advocacy service through an *employee* of the *sole practitioner's firm* exercising a right of audience as authorised by the *SRA*, or otherwise entitled, to do; and

        (ii) to undertake *immigration work* which is not within (i) above.

Guidance notes

(i) Reserved work is work that is defined in Schedule 2 to the LSA as a "reserved legal activity". Certain categories of reserved work (rights of audience in chambers, reserved instrument activities and probate activities) can be done by an unqualified person under the supervision of a manager or fellow employee qualified to do that work – see Schedule 3 to the LSA.

(ii) Immigration work (immigration advice and immigration services) is restricted to certain persons under the Immigration and Asylum Act 1999. Immigration services relating to courts or immigration tribunals are reserved work – advocacy, the conduct of cases, and the preparation of papers. The court work is subject to the normal restriction on court work. Immigration Tribunal work can be done by RFLs who are practising as such. Other immigration work is not reserved work, but can only be done by an authorised person such as a solicitor, a barrister, a legal executive, a member of an Establishment Directive profession, or an RFL practising as such, or under the supervision of an authorised person, or under an exemption given by the Office of the Immigration Services Commissioner.

(iii) The Financial Services and Markets Act 2000 reserves the provision of "regulated activities" to persons authorised by the Financial Services Authority (FSA). Certain "regulated activities", ancillary to the provision of a professional service, are exempt from regulation by the FSA when carried out by firms authorised by the SRA – see the SRA Financial Services (Scope) Rules. For the definition of "regulated activity" see the activities specified in the Financial Services and Markets Act 2000 (Regulated Activities) Order 2001 (SI 2001/544).

(iv) From 31 March 2012 or the date on which an order made pursuant to section 69 of the LSA relating to the status of sole practitioners comes into force, whichever is the later, a

APPENDIX C

sole practitioner's firm will be regulated as a type of authorised body and will be authorised under the SRA Authorisation Rules.
(v) The SRA does not authorise notarial activities. This does not prevent individuals, in an SRA authorised firm, providing notarial services where personally authorised to do so by the Master of the Faculties within paragraph 7 of Schedule 2 to the LSA.
(vi) See also Rule 8.4 of the SRA Authorisation Rules which provides that an authorised body may not carry on an activity unless through a body and individual who is authorised to carry on that activity.

RULE 9: PRACTISING CERTIFICATES

9.1 If you are *practising* as a *solicitor* (including in-house), whether in England and Wales or overseas, you must:
    (a) have in force a practising certificate issued by the *SRA*; or
    (b) be exempt under section 88 of the *SA* from holding a practising certificate.

9.2 You will be *practising* as a *solicitor* if you are involved in legal practice and:
    (a) your involvement in the firm or the work depends on your being a *solicitor*;
    (b) you are held out explicitly or implicitly as a *practising solicitor*;
    (c) you are employed explicitly or implicitly as a *solicitor*; or
    (d) you are deemed by section 1A of the *SA* to be acting as a *solicitor*.

9.3 In 9.2 above "legal practice" includes not only the provision of legal advice or assistance, or representation in connection with the application of the law or resolution of legal disputes, but also the provision of other services such as are provided by *solicitors*.

9.4 If you are a *solicitor* who was formerly an *REL*, and you are *practising* from an office in the *UK* as a *lawyer* of an *Establishment Directive profession*, you must have in force a practising certificate issued by the *SRA*, even if you are not *practising* as a *solicitor*.

Guidance notes

(i) Rule 9 includes, in rule form, the requirements of section 1 of the SA. The issuing of practising certificates under that Act is the responsibility of the SRA. For further guidance on the need for a practising certificate see our website.
(ii) If you practise as a solicitor, whether in a firm or in-house, without having a practising certificate, you will commit a criminal offence, as well as a breach of the rules, unless you are entitled to rely on the exemption in section 88 of the SA.

RULE 10: SOLE PRACTITIONERS

10.1 If you are a *solicitor* or *REL* you must not *practise* as a *sole practitioner* unless:
    (a) the *SRA* has first authorised you as a *recognised sole practitioner* by endorsing your practising certificate or certificate of registration to that effect;
    (b) your *practice* falls within 10.2 below and you are therefore exempt from the obligation to be a *recognised sole practitioner*; or

(c) you are authorised to *practise* as a *sole practitioner* by an *approved regulator* other than the *SRA*.

10.2 For the purpose of 10.1(b) above you are exempt from the obligation to be a *recognised sole practitioner* if:

    (a) your *practice* is conducted entirely from an office or offices outside England and Wales;

    (b) your *practice* consists entirely of work as a temporary or permanent *employee* and any *firm* which employs you takes full responsibility for you as an *employee*; or

    (c) your *practice* consists entirely of:

        (i) providing professional services without remuneration for friends, relatives, companies wholly owned by you or your family, or registered *charities*; and/or

        (ii) administering oaths and statutory declarations; and/or

        (iii) activities which could constitute *practice* but are done in the course of discharging the functions of any of the offices or appointments listed in paragraph (c) of the definition of "Private practice" in Appendix 4 to the SRA Indemnity Insurance Rules.

Guidance note

(i) Until 31 March 2012 or the date on which an order made pursuant to section 69 of the LSA relating to the status of sole practitioners comes into force, whichever is the later, see regulation 4 of the SRA Practising Regulations. After that, see the SRA Authorisation Rules.

RULE 11: PARTICIPATION IN LEGAL PRACTICE

11.1 If you are a *solicitor*, *REL* or *RFL* and you are:

    (a) a *manager*, *member* or *interest holder* of:

        (i) a *recognised body*; or

        (ii) a *body corporate* which is a *manager* of a *recognised body*; or

    (b) a *manager*, *member* or owner of:

        (i) a *licensed body*; or

        (ii) a *body corporate* which is a *manager* of a *licensed body*;

    it must be in your capacity as a *solicitor*, *REL* or *RFL* (whether or not you are held out as such);

    (c) employed in connection with the provision of legal services in England and Wales, by:

        (i) a *recognised sole practitioner*;

        (ii) an *authorised body*; or

        (iii) a *body corporate* which is a *manager* of an *authorised body*;

    it must be in your capacity as a *solicitor*, in accordance with section 1A of the *SA*, an *REL* or an *RFL* (whether or not you are held out as such);

APPENDIX C

(d) *Practising* in accordance with (a), (b) or (c) above does not prevent you from *practising* also as an individual authorised by an *approved regulator* other than the *SRA* or providing services as a member of a non-lawyer profession.

11.2 Subject to 11.3 below, if you are a *solicitor*, *REL* or *RFL* and you are:

(a) a *manager, member* or *interest holder* of:

  (i) an *authorised non-SRA firm* of which all the *managers* and *interest holders* are *lawyers*; or
  (ii) a *body corporate* which is a *manager* of such an *authorised non-SRA firm*;

(b) a *manager, member* or owner of:

  (i) an *authorised non-SRA firm* which is a *licensable body*; or
  (ii) a *body corporate* which is a *manager* of such an *authorised non-SRA firm*; or

(c) an *employee* who is employed in connection with the provision of legal services in England and Wales, by:

  (i) an *authorised non-SRA firm*; or
  (ii) a *body corporate* which is a *manager* of an *authorised non-SRA firm*;

it must be in your capacity as a *solicitor*, *REL* or *RFL* or as an individual authorised by an *approved regulator* other than the *SRA* (whether or not you are held out as such) but this does not prevent you from *practising* in both capacities or providing services as a member of a non-lawyer profession in addition to *practising* as a *lawyer*.

11.3 If you are a *solicitor* who is employed by, or is a *director* of, an *authorised non-SRA firm*, section 1A of the *SA* will require you to *practise* through that firm in the capacity of *solicitor*, even if also *practising* in some other capacity.

11.4 No *solicitor* or *REL*, while a prisoner in any prison, may commence, prosecute or defend any action, suit or other contentious proceedings, or appear as an advocate in any such proceedings, unless he or she does so as a litigant in person and not as a *solicitor* or *REL*.

Guidance note

(i) A solicitor, REL or RFL is required to be involved in a recognised body in that capacity even if they merely have a small interest in the firm. There is greater flexibility in licensed bodies where a solicitor, REL or RFL is permitted to have a small share in a licensed body without being treated as practising merely because of that involvement. For example, a solicitor could have a small interest in a licensed body through a pension fund even though not practising.

RULE 12: PERSONS WHO MUST BE "QUALIFIED TO SUPERVISE"

12.1 The following persons must be "*qualified to supervise*":

(a) a *recognised sole practitioner*;

(b) one of the *lawyer managers* of an *authorised body* or of a *body corporate* which is a *legally qualified body* and which is a *manager* of the *authorised body*;
(c) one of the *solicitors* or *RELs* employed by a law centre in England and Wales; or
(d) one in-house *solicitor* or in-house *REL* in any department in England and Wales where *solicitors* and/or *RELs*, as part of their employment:
  (i) do publicly funded work; or
  (ii) do or supervise advocacy or the conduct of proceedings for members of the public before a *court* or immigration tribunal.

12.2 To be "*qualified to supervise* " under this rule a person must:
  (a) have completed the training specified from time to time by the *SRA* for this purpose; and
  (b) have been entitled to practise as a *lawyer* for at least 36 months within the last ten years; and

must be able to demonstrate this if asked by the *SRA*.

Guidance notes

(i) The person "qualified to supervise" under Rule 12 does not have to be personally entitled by law to supervise all work undertaken by the firm. However, an important part of that person's responsibilities is to ensure that unqualified persons do not undertake reserved work except under the supervision of a suitably qualified person.
(ii) In satisfying the requirement for 36 months entitlement to practise you can for example rely on a period as a lawyer of another jurisdiction. In calculating the 36 months, any period of entitlement to practise as a lawyer of another jurisdiction can be taken into account in addition to your time entitled to practise as a solicitor.
(iii) Waivers may be granted in individual cases. See Rule 21.
(iv) The training presently specified by the SRA is attendance at or participation in any course(s), or programme(s) of learning, on management skills involving attendance or participation for a minimum of 12 hours. The courses or programmes do not have to be CPD accredited in order to satisfy the requirement. It is not normally necessary to check with the SRA before undertaking a course or programme unless the course is unusual and outside the mainstream of management training. Advice may be sought from the Professional Ethics Guidance Team.

PART 3: FORMATION AND ELIGIBILITY CRITERIA FOR RECOGNISED BODIES AND LICENSED BODIES

RULE 13: ELIGIBILITY CRITERIA AND FUNDAMENTAL REQUIREMENTS FOR RECOGNISED BODIES

13.1 To be eligible to be a *recognised body*, a body must be a *legal services body* namely a *partnership*, *company* or *LLP* of which:
  (a) at least one *manager* is:

APPENDIX C

    (i) a *solicitor* with a current practising certificate issued under the *SRA Practising Regulations*, or
    (ii) an *REL*, or
    (iii) (in the case of a *partnership* or *LLP*) a *body corporate* which is a *legally qualified body* with at least one *manager* who is a *solicitor* with a current practising certificate or an *REL*; and

  (b) all of the *managers* and *interest holders* are *legally qualified*, save that where another body ("A") is a *manager* of or has an interest in the body, *non-authorised persons* are entitled to exercise, or control the exercise of, less than 10% of the *voting rights* in A.

Services requirement

13.2 The business of a *recognised body* may consist only of the provision of:

  (a) professional services of the sort provided by individuals *practising* as *solicitors* and/or *lawyers* of other jurisdictions; and
  (b) professional services of the sort provided by notaries public, but only if a notary public is a *manager* or *employee* of a *recognised body*,

but this does not prevent a *recognised body* providing services within Chapter 12 (Separate businesses) of the *SRA Code of Conduct*, or holding an interest in a *company* which is a *separate business*.

Guidance notes

(i) Although most organisations which involve non-lawyers as managers or owners must be licensed bodies, the limited exception in Rule 13.1(b) (following the terms of the LSA) permits a small degree of non-lawyer involvement in recognised bodies. Where one or more bodies are involved in a firm as a manager or owner/interest holder, then the firm will remain a legal services body requiring recognition under the AJA, rather than a licensable body requiring a licence under the LSA, where non-authorised persons have only a de minimis (less than 10%) control by way of voting rights over each (manager/owner) body.

(ii) The services requirement in 13.2 should be read in conjunction with Chapter 12 of the SRA Code of Conduct. Certain services which could be offered through a "permitted separate business" (see Chapter 12) can also be provided in conjunction with a firm or in-house practice whilst still complying with the services requirement in 13.2. These services, which extend or fall outside the scope of the professional services mentioned in 13.2, are:

  (a) education and training activities; and
  (b) authorship, journalism and publishing.

RULE 14: ELIGIBILITY CRITERIA AND FUNDAMENTAL REQUIREMENTS FOR LICENSED BODIES

14.1 To be eligible to be a *licensed body*, a body must comply with the *lawyer manager* requirement set out in Rule 14.2 below and be a "licensable body", as defined under section 72 of the *LSA*, and as set out in Rule 14.3 to 14.6 below.

14.2 At all times at least one *manager* of a *licensed body* must be an individual who is:
  (a) a *solicitor* with a current practising certificate;
  (b) an *REL*;
  (c) a *lawyer of England and Wales* and who is authorised by an *approved regulator* other than the *SRA*; or
  (d) registered with the *BSB* under regulation 17 of the European Communities (Lawyer's Practice) Regulations 2000 (SI 2000/1119).

14.3 A body ("B") is a *licensable body* if a *non-authorised person*:
  (a) is a *manager* of B, or
  (b) is an *interest holder* of B.

14.4 A body ("B") is also a *licensable body* if:
  (a) another body ("A") is a *manager* of B, or is an *interest holder* of B, and
  (b) *non-authorised persons* are entitled to exercise, or control the exercise of, at least 10% of the *voting rights* in A.

14.5 A body may be a *licensable body* by virtue of both 14.3 and 14.4.

14.6 For the purposes of this rule, a *non-authorised person* has an indirect interest in a *licensable body* if the body is a *licensable body* by virtue of 14.4 and the *non-authorised person* is entitled to exercise, or control the exercise of, *voting rights* in A.

RULE 15: FORMATION, REGISTERED OFFICE AND PRACTISING ADDRESS

15.1 An *authorised body* which is a *partnership* may be formed under the law of any country and may be a legal *person*.

15.2 An *authorised body* which is an *LLP* must be incorporated and registered in England and Wales, Scotland or Northern Ireland under the Limited Liability Partnerships Act 2000.

15.3 An *authorised body* which is a *company* must be:
  (a) incorporated and registered in England and Wales, Scotland or Northern Ireland under Parts 1 and 2 of the Companies Act 2006;
  (b) incorporated in an *Establishment Directive state* and registered as an overseas company under Part 34 of the Companies Act 2006; or
  (c) incorporated and registered in an *Establishment Directive state* as a *societas Europaea*.

15.4 An *authorised body* must have at least one *practising* address in England and Wales.

15.5 An *authorised body* must have its registered office at a *practising* address in England and Wales if the *authorised body* is registered in England and Wales:
  (a) under Parts 1 and 2 of the Companies Act 2006;
  (b) under the Limited Liability Partnerships Act 2000; or
  (c) as a *societas Europaea*.

RULE 16: COMPOSITION OF AN AUTHORISED BODY

16.1 Provided that the requirements for all *authorised bodies* set out in Rule 13 or Rule 14, as appropriate, are met, an *authorised body* may have all or any of the following as a *partner* (if it is a *partnership*), a *member* (if it is an *LLP*), or a *director, member* or *shareowner* (if it is a *company*):

APPENDIX C

(a) a *lawyer of England and Wales* (including a *solicitor* with a current practising certificate);
(b) an *REL*;
(c) an *RFL*;
(d) an *EEL*;
(e) a *body corporate* which is a *legally qualified body*, save that a *legally qualified body* may not be a *director* of a *recognised body* which is a *company*;

provided that, where necessary, they comply with the approval requirements in Part 4 of the *SRA Authorisation Rules*.

16.2 If the *authorised body* is a *licensed body*, then the list of permitted *partners*, *members* of an *LLP* or, in the case of a *company directors*, registered *members* or *shareowners* at 16.1(a) to (e) shall include:

(a) a *licensed body*; and
(b) any other individual or *body corporate*, subject to any necessary approval as a *manager* or owner under Part 4 (Approval of managers, owners and compliance officers) of the *SRA Authorisation Rules*, save that a *body corporate* may not be a *director* of a *licensed body* which is a *company*.

16.3 An *authorised body* which is an *LLP* must have at least two *members*.

Guidance notes

(i) See 22.3 below regarding the position of firms which have non-lawyer managers prior to 6 October 2011.
(ii) Although a legal services body can have a variety of types of manager, only a solicitor or an REL may be a sole practitioner.
(iii) Where, in line with Rule 16, a firm has persons other than solicitors as managers (in particular where European lawyers are involved), any list of the managers will need to:

    (a) identify any solicitor as a solicitor;
    (b) in the case of any lawyer or notary of an Establishment Directive state other than the UK:

        (A) identify the jurisdiction(s) – local or national as appropriate – under whose professional title the lawyer or notary is practising;
        (B) give the professional title(s), expressed in an official language of the Establishment Directive state(s) concerned; and
        (C) if the lawyer is an REL, refer to that lawyer's registration with the SRA;

    (c) indicate the professional qualification(s) of any other lawyer and the country or jurisdiction of qualification of any RFL not included in (b) above;
    (d) identify any individual non-lawyer as a non-lawyer; and
    (e) identify the nature of any body corporate, if this is not clear from its name.

In addition, whenever an REL (whether or not a manager) is named on letterhead used by any firm or in-house practice, the firm or the employer will need to follow the guidance in (iii)(b) above.

RULE 17: AUTHORISED BODIES WHICH ARE COMPANIES

Record of non-member shareowners

17.1 Keeping a record

    (a) A *recognised body* which is a *company* with shares must keep a record of any non-*member interest holders*, and retain the record for at least three years after their interest ceases;

    (b) A *licensed body* which is a *company* with shares must keep a record of any non-*member* owners, and retain the record for at least three years after their ownership ceases and for the purpose of this rule the term "owner" shall be defined as in Rule 1.2 of the *SRA Authorisation Rules*.

17.2 A *member* who holds a share as nominee for a non-*member shareowner* in an *authorised body* must keep the *authorised body* informed of all facts necessary to keep an accurate and up-to-date record.

RULE 18: INFORMATION AND DOCUMENTATION

18.1 An *authorised body* must supply any information and documentation relating to its composition and structure or to any of its *managers*, *employees*, *members* or *shareowners*, as and when requested to do so by the *SRA*.

18.2 Notwithstanding any requirement to obtain approval of a *manager*, owner, *COLP* or *COFA* under Part 4 of the *SRA Authorisation Rules*, an *authorised body* must notify the *SRA* within seven days of any change to its:

    (a) name;
    (b) registered office and/or any of its *practising* addresses;
    (c) *managers*;
    (d) *members*, if it is a *company*;
    (e) *interest holders*, if it is a *recognised body*;
    (f) owners, if it is a *licensed body* and for the purpose of this rule the term "owner" shall be defined as in Rule 1.2 of the *SRA Authorisation Rules*;
    (g) *COLP*; or
    (h) *COFA*.

18.3 An *authorised body* must notify the *SRA* within seven days if it is an unlimited *company* and it is re-registered as limited under the *Companies Acts*.

18.4 If a *relevant insolvency event* occurs in relation to an *authorised body* its *managers*, or in the case of an *authorised body* which is an overseas company, its *directors*, must notify the *SRA* within seven days.

Guidance notes

(i) There are other SRA reporting and information requirements that apply to individuals or firms. See for example:

    (a) Rules 3, 8.7, 8.8, 8.9 and 8.10 and 18, 23, 24 and 25 of the SRA Authorisation Rules
    (b) Rule 32 of the SRA Accounts Rules
    (c) Regulations 4.3, 4.5, and 15 of the SRA Practising Regulations
    (d) Chapter 10 of the SRA Code of Conduct.

APPENDIX C

(ii) In addition to the requirement to inform the SRA when certain persons leave the firm, there are the requirements in Rule 8 of the SRA Authorisation Rules for firms to seek approval, where necessary, before certain persons join the firm. This is more onerous than simply informing the SRA of changes that have taken place.

PART 4: COMPLIANCE WITH PRACTICE REQUIREMENTS

RULE 19: COMPLIANCE WITH PRACTICE REQUIREMENTS

19.1 An *authorised body* and its *managers* and *employees* must at all times ensure that they act in accordance with the requirements of the *SRA's regulatory arrangements* as they apply to them.

19.2 A *solicitor*, *REL* or *RFL* who is a *member* or *shareowner* of an *authorised body* which is a *company* must not cause, instigate or connive at any breach of the requirements imposed under the *SRA's regulatory arrangements* by the *authorised body* or any of its *managers* or *employees*.

19.3 An *employee* of an *authorised body* must not cause, instigate or connive at any breach of any requirements imposed under the *SRA's regulatory arrangements*.

19.4 The *partners* in an *authorised body* which is a *partnership* are responsible not only as *managers* but also, jointly and severally, as the *authorised body*.

RULE 20: OVERSEAS PRACTICE

20.1 Subject to Rule 20.2 to 20.4, the requirements in these rules apply to the *overseas practice* of a *solicitor*, *REL*, *RFL* or *authorised body*.

20.2 The rules in Part 2 and Rules 17.2, 18.4, 19 and 21 apply to your *overseas practice* as:

(a) a *manager* of an *authorised body*, if you are a *lawyer of England and Wales* or an individual non-lawyer;

(b) a *member* or *shareowner* of an *authorised body* which is a *company*, if you are a *solicitor* or (in relation to *practice* from an office in Scotland or Northern Ireland) an *REL*,

except that Rule 19 applies only to the extent that it applies to the *authorised body*, *manager* or *employee* by virtue of these rules or Chapter 13 (Application and waivers provisions) of the *SRA Code of Conduct*.

20.3 If you are a *solicitor* or an *REL* you are not required to comply with Rule 13 or Rule 14, as appropriate, in order to *practise* through a firm which has no office in England and Wales, but you must comply with Rule 1 and Rule 2.

20.4 If compliance with any applicable provision of these rules would result in your breaching local law, you may disregard that provision to the extent necessary to comply with that local law.

RULE 21: WAIVERS

21.1 Subject to provisions relating to any statutory obligations or the *SRA's regulatory arrangements* affecting its ability to waive any requirements, the *SRA* Board shall have power to waive in writing the provisions of these rules for a particular purpose or purposes expressed in such waiver, and to attach conditions to or revoke such waiver, at its own discretion.

Guidance note

(i) An applicant for a waiver must satisfy the SRA that the circumstances are sufficiently exceptional to justify a departure from the requirements of the rule in question, bearing in mind its purpose. Applications should be made to the Professional Ethics Guidance Team.

RULE 22: TRANSITIONAL PROVISIONS AND GRACE PERIOD

22.1 From 31 March 2012 or the date on which an order made pursuant to section 69 of the *LSA* relating to the status of *sole practitioners* comes into force, whichever is the later, these rules shall have effect subject to the following amendments:

    (a) Rules 1.1(a), 2.1(a), 3.1(a), 8.7, 11.1(c)(i) and 12.1(a) shall be omitted;

    (b) In Rules 1.1(b) and 2.1(b) the words, "authorised as a *sole practitioner*" shall be substituted for the words "a *recognised sole practitioner*";

    (c) In Rules 1.2(a) and 2.2(a) the words "as a *recognised body*" shall be substituted for the words "a *recognised sole practitioner*";

    (d) In Rule 3.2(d) the words "a *recognised sole practitioner*," shall be omitted;

    (e) In Rules 5.1(d) and 5.2(c) the words "or by a *recognised sole practitioner*" shall be omitted;

    (f) In Rules 6.1 and 7.1 the words "or an *employee* of a *recognised sole practitioner*" shall be omitted;

    (g) In Rule 10.1(a) the word "*recognised*" shall be omitted and the words "by endorsing your practising certificate or certificate of registration to that effect" shall be omitted;

    (h) In Rules 10.1(b) and 10.2 the words "authorised as a" shall be substituted for the words "a *recognised*";

    (i) In Rule 12.1(b), the words "a *lawyer manager*" shall be substituted for the words "one of the *lawyer managers*"; and

    (j) Rule 13.1 shall have effect as if the words "*sole practitioner*," were inserted after the words "namely a".

22.2 Unless the context otherwise requires, references in these rules to:

    (a) these rules, or a provision of these rules; and

    (b) the *SRA Code of Conduct*, rules, regulations or *regulatory arrangements*, or a provision of the same,

include a reference to the equivalent rules, regulations or provisions previously in force.

22.3 A body that has, at the time these rules come into force, been recognised by the *SRA* under section 9 *AJA* and that does not comply with Rule 13.1(b) above shall continue to be treated as a *legal services body* for the purposes of these rules and the *SRA's regulatory arrangements* until:

    (a) such time as it ceases to comply with the management and control requirements set out in Rule 22.4 below; or

APPENDIX C

 (b) the end of the transitional period under Part 2 of Schedule 5 to the *LSA*, or such earlier time as the body may elect,

at which time it shall be a *licensed body* for the purposes of these rules and the *SRA's regulatory arrangements*.

22.4 The management and control requirements referred to in Rule 22.3 above are:

 (a) At least 75% of the body's *managers* must be:

  (i) individuals who are, and are entitled to *practise* as, *lawyers of England and Wales*, lawyers of *Establishment Directive professions* or *RFLs*; or

  (ii) *bodies corporate* which are *legally qualified bodies*;

 although a *legally qualified body* cannot be a *director* of a body which is a *company*;

 (b) Individuals who are, and are entitled to *practise* as, *lawyers of England and Wales*, lawyers of *Establishment Directive professions* or *RFLs* must make up at least 75% of the ultimate beneficial ownership of the body; and

 (c) Individuals who are, and are entitled to *practise* as, *lawyers of England and Wales*, lawyers of *Establishment Directive professions* or *RFLs*, and/or *legally qualified bodies*, must:

  (i) exercise or control the exercise of at least 75% of the *voting rights* in the body; and

  (ii) if the body is a *company* with shares, hold (as registered *members* of the *company*) at least 75% of the shares.

 (d) Subject to Rule 13.1(b) above, every owner of the *recognised body*, and every *person* who exercises or controls the exercise of any *voting rights* in the body, must be:

  (i) an individual who is, and is entitled to *practise* as, a *lawyer of England and Wales*, a *lawyer* of an *Establishment Directive profession* or an *RFL*;

  (ii) a *legally qualified body*; or

  (iii) an individual who is approved under regulation 5 of the SRA Recognised Bodies Regulations and, subject to (e) below, is a *manager* of the body.

 (e) An individual who is not entitled under (d)(i) above may be an owner of a *recognised body* without being a *manager* of the body if:

  (i) the *recognised body* is a *company* which is wholly or partly owned by a *partnership* or *LLP* which is a *legally qualified body*;

  (ii) the individual is approved under regulation 5 of the SRA Recognised Bodies Regulations and is a *manager* of the *partnership* or *LLP*; and

  (iii) the individual is precluded under the *partnership* agreement or *members'* agreement from exercising or authorising any vote in relation to the *company*.

22.5 These rules shall not apply to *licensable bodies* until such time as the *Society* is designated as a *licensing authority* under Part 1 of Schedule 10 to the *LSA* and all definitions shall be construed accordingly.

22.6 In these rules references:

 (a) in the preamble to the rules being made under section 83 and Schedule 11 to the Legal Services Act 2007;

 (b) to *COLPs* and *COFAs*; and

 (c) to the approval of *managers*, owners, *COLPs* and *COFAs*;

SRA PRACTICE FRAMEWORK RULES 2011

shall have no effect until such time as the *Society* is designated as a *licensing authority* under Part 1 of Schedule 10 to the *LSA*.

22.7 Until the 180th day after the date on which the *Society* is designated as a *licensing authority* under Part 1 of Schedule 10 to the *LSA*:

(a) Rule 4.12(a) shall have no effect;
(b) Rule 4.13 (insurers) shall have no effect;
(c) Rule 13.06 (insurers) of the Solicitors' Code of Conduct 2007 shall continue to have effect; and
(d) references to Rule 4.13 shall be treated as references to Rule 13.06 of the Solicitors' Code of Conduct 2007.

PART 5: INTERPRETATION

RULE 23: INTERPRETATION

23.1 All italicised terms in these rules are to be interpreted in accordance with Chapter 14 (Interpretation) of the *SRA Code of Conduct*, unless they are defined as follows:

authorised person(s) means a *person* who is authorised by the *SRA* or another *approved regulator* to carry on a *legal activity* and for the purpose of these rules includes a *solicitor*, a *sole practitioner*, an *REL*, an *EEL*, an *RFL*, an *authorised body*, an *authorised non-SRA firm* and a *European corporate practice* and the terms "authorised individual" and "non-authorised person" shall be construed accordingly;

BSB means the Bar Standards Board;

charity has the meaning given in section 96(1) of the Charities Act 1993;

EEL means exempt European *lawyer*, namely a member of an *Establishment Directive profession*:

(i) registered with the *BSB*; or
(ii) based entirely at an office or offices outside England and Wales,

who is not a *lawyer of England and Wales* (whether entitled to *practise* as such or not);

European corporate practice means a *lawyers'* practice which is a body incorporated in an *Establishment Directive state*, or a *partnership* with separate legal identity formed under the law of an *Establishment Directive state*:

(i) which has an office in an *Establishment Directive state* but does not have an office in England and Wales;
(ii) whose ultimate beneficial owners include at least one individual who is not a *lawyer of England and Wales* but is, and is entitled to practise as, a *lawyer* of an *Establishment Directive profession*; and
(iii) whose *managers* include at least one such individual, or at least one *body corporate* whose *managers* include at least one such individual;

foreign lawyer means an individual who is not a *solicitor* or barrister of England and Wales, but who is a member and is entitled to practise as such, of a legal profession regulated within a jurisdiction outside England and Wales;

interest holder means a *person* who has an interest or an indirect interest, or holds a *material interest*, in a body (and "indirect interest" and "interest" have the same meaning as in the *LSA*), and references to "holds an interest" shall be construed accordingly;

legal activity has the meaning given in section 12 of the *LSA* and includes any reserved legal activity and any other activity which consists of the provision of legal advice or assistance, or representation in connection with the application of the law or resolution of legal disputes;

legally qualified means any of the following:

(i) a *lawyer*;
(ii) a *recognised body*;
(iii) an *authorised non-SRA firm* of which all the *managers* and *interest holders* are *lawyers* save that where another body ("A") is a *manager* of or has an interest in the firm, *non-authorised persons* are entitled to exercise, or control the exercise of, less than 10% of the *voting rights* in A;
(iv) *European corporate practice* of which all the *managers* and *interest holders* are *lawyers*;

and references to a "legally qualified body" shall be construed accordingly;

legal services body means a body which meets the criteria in Rule 13 (Eligibility criteria and fundamental requirements for recognised bodies);

licensing authority means an *approved regulator* which is designated as a licensing authority under Part 1 of Schedule 10 to the *LSA*, and whose licensing rules have been approved for the purposes of the *LSA*;

principal means a *sole practitioner* or a *partner* in a *partnership*;

qualified to supervise means a person complying with the requirements of Rule 12.2;

register of European lawyers means the register of European lawyers maintained by the *SRA* under regulation 15 of the European Communities (Lawyer's Practice) Regulations 2000 (SI 2000/1119);

register of foreign lawyers means the register of foreign lawyers maintained by the *SRA* under the Courts and Legal Services Act 1990;

regulatory arrangements has the meaning given to it by section 21 of the *LSA*, and includes all rules and regulations of the *SRA* in relation to the authorisation, practice, conduct, discipline and qualification of *persons* carrying on *legal activities* and the accounts rules and indemnification and compensation arrangements in relation to their *practice*;

related body in relation to *in-house practice* means a body standing in relation to your *employer* as specified in Rule 4.7(a) to (d) or 4.15(c);

relevant insolvency event a relevant insolvency event occurs in relation to a body if:

(i) a resolution for a voluntary winding-up of the body is passed without a declaration of solvency under section 89 of the Insolvency Act 1986;
(ii) the body enters administration within the meaning of paragraph 1(2)(b) of Schedule B1 to that Act;
(iii) an administrative receiver within the meaning of section 251 of that Act is appointed;
(iv) a meeting of creditors is held in relation to the body under section 95 of that Act (creditors' meeting which has the effect of converting a *members'* voluntary winding up into a creditors' voluntary winding up);
(v) an order for the winding up of the body is made;
(vi) all of the *managers* in a body which is unincorporated have been adjudicated bankrupt; or
(vii) the body is an overseas company or a *societas Europaea* registered outside England, Wales, Scotland and Northern Ireland and the body is subject to an event in its country of incorporation analogous to an event as set out in paragraphs (i) to (vi) above;

reserved work means activities which *persons* are authorised by the *SRA* to carry out, or prohibited from carrying out, under these rules;
shareowner means:

   (i)   a *member* of a *company* with a share capital, who owns a share in the body; or

   (ii)   a *person* who is not a *member* of a *company* with a share capital, but owns a share in the body, which is held by a *member* as nominee;

SRA Accounts Rules means the SRA Accounts Rules 2011;
SRA Code of Conduct means the SRA Code of Conduct 2011;
SRA Practising Regulations means the SRA Practising Regulations 2011.

APPENDIX D
SRA Suitability Test 2011

INTRODUCTION TO THE SUITABILITY TEST

PREAMBLE

Authority: Made on 17 June 2011 by the Solicitors Regulation Authority Board under sections 28, 79 and 80 of the Solicitors Act 1974 with the approval of the Legal Services Board under paragraph 19 of Schedule 4 to the Legal Services Act 2007
    Date: These regulations came into force on 6 October 2011
    Replacing: The SRA guidelines on the assessment of character and suitability
    Applicability: Students and trainee solicitors under the SRA Training Regulations; Qualified lawyers under the QLTSR;
    Those seeking admission as solicitors under the Admission Regulations, fulfilling the duties under section 3 of the Solicitors Act 1974;
    Those seeking to become authorised role holders in accordance with rules 8.5 and 8.6 of the SRA Authorisation Rules.

OVERVIEW

Outcomes-focused regulation concentrates on providing positive outcomes which when achieved will benefit and protect *clients* and the public. *We* must ensure that any individual admitted as a *solicitor* has, and maintains, the level of honesty, integrity and the professionalism expected by the public and other stakeholders and professionals, and does not pose a risk to the public or the profession.

The Suitability Test will apply the same high standards to all those seeking admission as a *solicitor*, as well as legally qualified and non-legally qualified applicants for roles in authorised bodies as *authorised role holders*.

The test is the same for non-solicitors as they will be working within the profession and must meet the same high standards that the general public expect of *solicitors*. This document is intended to make it clear to *you* what this standard is in terms of *your* character, suitability, fitness and propriety.

No applicant has the automatic right of admission or authorisation and it will always be for *you* to discharge the burden of satisfying suitability under this test. Any application that requires *us* to be satisfied as to character, suitability, fitness and propriety will be determined by reference to this test.

THE PRINCIPLES

The Suitability Test forms part of the Handbook, in which the 10 mandatory *Principles* are all-pervasive. They apply to all those *we* regulate and to all aspects of practice.
    You must:

1   uphold the rule of law and the proper administration of justice;
2   act with integrity;
3   not allow *your* independence to be compromised;
4   act in the best interests of each *client*;
5   provide a proper standard of service to *your clients*;
6   behave in a way that maintains the trust the public places in *you* and in the provision of legal services;
7   comply with *your* legal and regulatory obligations and deal with *your* regulators and ombudsmen in an open, timely and co-operative manner;
8   run *your* business or carry out *your* role in the business effectively and in accordance with proper governance and sound financial and risk management principles;
9   run *your* business or carry out *your* role in the business in a way that encourages equality of opportunity and respect for diversity; and
10   protect *client money* and *assets*.

OUTCOMES

The outcomes which apply to this test are as follows:

O(SB1) if *you* are a *solicitor*, *you* are of the required standard of *character and suitability*;

O(SB2) if *you* are an *authorised role holder*, *you* are *fit and proper*; and

O(SB3) *you* act so that *clients*, and the wider public, have confidence that O(SB1) has been demonstrated.

The outcomes, and the criteria that flow from them, apply to all those who are intending to become *solicitors* – i.e. *students*, *trainee solicitors*, and qualified lawyers from other jurisdictions seeking qualification via transfer – at the point of *student enrolment*, admission, and throughout the pre-qualification period. They also apply to *compliance officers*, *owners*, and/or *managers* at the point of and throughout their period of authorisation.

INTERPRETATION AND DEFINITIONS

1   Unless the context otherwise requires, the definitions and interpretation provisions as set out within the SRA Glossary shall apply to the SRA Suitability Test.
2   In this test:

    academic stage of training means that stage of the training of an entrant to the *solicitors'* profession which is completed by satisfying regulation 3 of the *SRA Training Regulations* Part 1 – Qualification Regulations, and "academic stage" should be construed accordingly;

    assets includes money, documents, wills, deeds, investments and other property;

    authorised role holder means *COLP*, *COFA*, *owner* or *manager* under rules 8.5 and 8.6 of the *SRA Authorisation Rules*, and "authorised role" should be construed accordingly;

    bodies corporate means a company, an LLP, or a partnership which is a legal person in its own right, and "bodies corporate" should be construed accordingly;

    character and suitability satisfies the requirement of section 3 of the *SA* in order that an individual shall be admitted as a *solicitor*;

    client means the person for whom *you* act and where the context permits, includes prospective and former clients;

    client money has the meaning given in Rule 12 of the SRA Accounts Rules, save that for the purposes of Part 7 (Overseas practice) of the SRA Accounts Rules, means

APPENDIX D

money received or held for or on behalf of a *client* or trust (but excluding money which is held or received by a multi-disciplinary practice – a licensed body providing a range of different services – in relation to those activities for which it is not regulated by the *SRA*);

COFA means *compliance officer* for finance and administration in accordance with rule 8.5 of the *SRA Authorisation Rules*, and in relation to a licensable body is a reference to its HOFA;

COLP means *compliance officer* for legal practice in accordance with rule 8.5 of the *SRA Authorisation Rules* and in relation to a licensable body is a reference to its HOLP;

compliance officer is a reference to a body's *COLP* or its *COFA*;

court means any court, tribunal or enquiry of England and Wales, or a British court martial, or any court of another jurisdiction;

discrimination has the meaning set out in the Equality Act 2010, being when person (A) discriminates against another (B) if, because of a protected characteristic, A treats B less favourably than A treats or would treat others;

fit and proper satisfies the requirement of Schedule 13 of the *LSA* in order that an individual may be an *authorised role holder*;

LSA means the Legal Services Act 2007;

manager means:

    (i)   a member of an LLP;
    (ii)   a director of a company;
    (iii)   a partner in a partnership; or
    (iv)   in relation to any other body, a member of its governing body;

save that for the purposes of:

    (v)   Part 7 (Overseas practice) of the SRA Accounts Rules "a manager" includes the director of any company, and is not limited to the director of a company as defined herein; and
    (vi)   the SRA Cost of Investigations Regulations and the SRA Disciplinary Procedure Rules where in (iii) above terms partner and partnership are to be given their natural meaning;

owner means, in relation to a body, a person with any ownership interest in the body, save that:

    (i)   in the SRA Authorisation Rules owner means any person who holds a material interest in an authorised body, and in the case of a partnership, any partner regardless of whether they hold a material interest in the partnership; and
    (ii)   for the purposes of Chapter 12 of the SRA Code of Conduct means a person having a substantial ownership interest in a separate business and "own" and "owned by" shall be construed accordingly; and
    (iii)   for the purposes of the Suitability Test includes owners who have no active role in the running of the business as well as owners who do;

Principles means the Principles in the SRA Handbook;

QLTSR means the SRA Qualified Lawyers Transfer Scheme Regulations 2010 and 2011;

SA means the Solicitors Act 1974;

solicitor means a person who has been admitted as a solicitor of the Senior Courts of England and Wales and whose name is on the roll kept by the Society under section 6 of the *SA*, save that in the SRA Indemnity Insurance Rules includes a person who practises as a solicitor whether or not he or she has in force a practising certificate and also includes practice under home title of a former REL who has become a solicitor;

SRA means the Solicitors Regulation Authority, and reference to the SRA as an approved regulator or licensing authority means the SRA carrying out regulatory functions assigned to the Society as an approved regulator or licensing authority;

SRA Authorisation Rules means the SRA Authorisation Rules for Legal Services Bodies and Licensable Bodies 2011;

SRA Training Regulations means the SRA Training Regulations 2011;

student enrolment means the process where *we* satisfy ourselves that a student who intends to proceed to the vocational stage of training has satisfactorily completed the academic stage of training and is of the appropriate *character and suitability*; "*enrolment*" should be construed accordingly, and "*certificate of enrolment*" should be construed as evidence *of student enrolment*;

trainee solicitor means any person receiving workplace training with the express purpose of qualification as a *solicitor*, at an authorised training establishment, under a training contract; and "trainee" should be construed accordingly;

UK means United Kingdom;

us means the *SRA*, and "we", "our" and "ourselves" should be construed accordingly;

you means any individual intending to be a *solicitor*, and any person seeking authorisation as an *authorised role holder* under the *Authorisation Rules*, and "your" and "yourself" should be construed accordingly.

3 In this test, the reference in the preamble to those seeking to become authorised role holders in accordance with rules 8.5 and 8.6 of the *SRA Authorisation Rules*, fulfilling the duties under Sections 89, 90, 91 and 92 of the *LSA* shall have no effect until such time as the Society is designated as a licensing authority under Part 1 of Schedule 10 to the *LSA*.

4 This test shall not apply to licensed bodies until such time as the Society is designated as a licensing authority under Part 1 of Schedule 10 to the *LSA* and all definitions shall be construed accordingly.

5 Part 2 of this test shall have no effect until such time as the Society is designated as a licensing authority under Part 1 of Schedule 10 to the *LSA*.

PART 1: BASIC REQUIREMENTS

If *you* are applying for *student enrolment* or admission, *you* must comply with Part 1. If *you* are applying for authorisation as an *authorised role holder* then *you* must comply with Part 1 and Part 2.

When considering any application under this test, *we* will take the following actions:

1: CRIMINAL OFFENCES

1.1 Unless there are exceptional circumstances, *we* will refuse *your* application if *you* have been convicted by a *court* of a criminal offence:

    (a) for which *you* received a custodial or suspended sentence;
    (b) involving dishonesty, fraud, perjury and/or bribery;
    (c) specifically in relation to which *you* have been included on the Violent and Sex Offender Register;
    (d) associated with obstructing the course of justice;

APPENDIX D

(e) which demonstrated behaviour showing signs of *discrimination* towards others;
(f) associated with terrorism;
(g) which was racially aggravated;
(h) which was motivated by any of the "protected" characteristics defined within the Equality Act 2010;
(i) which in *our* judgement is so serious as to prevent *your student enrolment*, admission as a *solicitor*, or approval as an *authorised role holder*; and/or
(j) *you* have been convicted by a *court* of more than one criminal offence.

Guidance note

(i) The provisions in 1.1(a) will not be relevant to entities because *bodies corporate*, and other unincorporated bodies and bodies of persons, cannot themselves receive custodial sentences.

1.2 *We* are more likely than not to refuse *your* application if *you* have:

(a) been convicted by a *court* of a criminal offence not falling within 1.1 above but which has an impact on *your character and suitability*;
(b) been included on the Violent and Sex Offender Register but in relation to *your* inclusion on the Register, *you* have not been convicted by a *court* of a criminal offence; and/or
(c) accepted a caution for an offence involving dishonesty.

1.3 *We* may refuse *your* application if *you* have:

(a) received a local warning from the police;
(b) accepted a caution from the police for an offence not involving dishonesty;
(c) received a Penalty Notice for Disorder (PND) from the police;
(d) received a final warning or reprimand from the police (youths only); and/or
(e) received a referral order from the *courts* (youths only).

Guidance note

(i) Where a criminal conviction, warning, simple caution, PND and/or inclusion on the Violent and Sex Offender Register has been disclosed, *we* will not look behind the decision made by the police or the finding made by a *court*. However, *we* will take into account material such as sentencing remarks and any other independent information. See also Section 7 Evidence.
(ii) *You* should disclose details of any criminal charge(s) *you* may be facing. *We* will not determine *your* application until *you* can confirm that the charge(s) has/have either been dropped or the outcome of *your* case is known.
(iii) Cautions and local warnings issued by the police may be subsequently recorded on the Police National Computer (PNC) and these will be shown on a PNC printout, which *you* may be required to submit to *us*.
(iv) Police can only issue a caution if there is evidence that *you* are guilty of an offence and if *you* admit that *you* committed the offence. Therefore, by accepting a caution, please bear in mind that *you* are making an admission of guilt.

(v) On Penalty Notices for Disorder no admission of guilt is required, and by paying the penalty, a recipient discharges liability for conviction for the offence – however, *you* should still disclose such matters as *we* will need to consider them.
(vi) Serious motoring offences that result in a criminal conviction must be disclosed. Motoring offences that do not result in a criminal conviction do not need to be disclosed.

2: DISCLOSURE

2.1 All material information relating to *your* application must be disclosed. Failure to disclose material information will be treated as prima facie evidence of dishonest behaviour.

2.2 *You* must disclose any matters that have occurred in the *UK* and/or overseas.

Guidance note

(i) *You* should bear in mind that Regulation 35 of the *SRA Training Regulations* Part 1 – Qualification Regulations requires all those seeking admission as *solicitors* to apply for a standard disclosure from the Criminal Records Bureau (CRB). *We* will also perform a PNC check at the *student enrolment* stage and have reciprocal arrangements with other jurisdictions in order to gather similar information on lawyers from other countries.

(ii) If *you* are seeking approval as an *authorised role holder*, *you* should bear in mind that Rule 14 of the *Authorisation Rules* allows *us* to seek other information relating to *your* application and this would normally include CRB disclosure.

(iii) It is therefore highly likely that matters will come to light.

3: BEHAVIOUR NOT COMPATIBLE WITH THAT EXPECTED OF A PROSPECTIVE SOLICITOR OR AUTHORISED ROLE HOLDER

3.1 Unless there are exceptional circumstances *we* will refuse *your* application if *you* have:

    (a) been responsible for behaviour:

        (i) which is dishonest;
        (ii) which is violent;
        (iii) where there is evidence of *discrimination* towards others;

    (b) misused *your* position to obtain pecuniary advantage;
    (c) misused *your* position of trust in relation to vulnerable people; and/or
    (d) been responsible for other forms of behaviour which demonstrate that *you* cannot be relied upon to discharge *your* regulatory duties as a *solicitor* or *authorised role holder*.

4: ASSESSMENT OFFENCES

4.1 Unless there are exceptional circumstances *we* will refuse *your* application if *you* have committed and/or have been adjudged by an education establishment to have committed a deliberate assessment offence which amounts to plagiarism or cheating to gain an advantage for *yourself* or others.

APPENDIX D

Guidance note

(i) Exceptional circumstances may include where the finding does not amount to cheating or dishonesty, e.g. incorrect referencing, or failure to attribute correctly, in an essay or paper.

5: FINANCIAL EVIDENCE

5.1 Unless there are exceptional circumstances *we* will refuse *your* application if:
   (a) there is evidence that *you* cannot manage *your* finances properly and carefully;
   (b) there is evidence that *you* have deliberately sought to avoid responsibility for *your* debts; and/or
   (c) there is evidence of dishonesty in relation to the management of *your* finances.

5.2 If *you* have been declared bankrupt, entered into any individual voluntary arrangements (IVA) or have had a County Court Judgement issued against *you* it will raise a presumption that there has been evidence that *you* cannot manage *your* finances properly and carefully.

Guidance note

(i) The following might help to establish confidence in *your* ability to run *your* business/carry out *your* role in the business effectively and in accordance with proper governance and sound financial and risk management principles:
   (a) the bankruptcy/IVA/County Court Judgement occurred many years ago and there is evidence of subsequent sound financial management and conduct to show that creditors have been repaid;
   (b) *you* were affected by exceptional circumstances beyond *your* control which *you* could not have reasonably foreseen.

6: REGULATORY HISTORY

6.1 Unless there are exceptional circumstances *we* will refuse *your* application if *you*:
   (a) have been made the subject of a serious disciplinary finding, sanction or action by a regulatory body and/or any *court* or other body hearing appeals in relation to disciplinary or regulatory findings;
   (b) have failed to disclose information to a regulatory body when required to do so, or have provided false or misleading information;
   (c) have significantly breached the requirements of a regulatory body;
   (d) have been refused registration by a regulatory body; and/or
   (e) have failed to comply with the reasonable requests of a regulatory body.

6.2 *We* may refuse *your* application if *you* have been rebuked, reprimanded or received a warning about *your* conduct by a regulatory body, unless there are exceptional circumstances.

Guidance note

(i) "Regulatory body" includes *us* and the Solicitors Disciplinary Tribunal, approved regulators under the Legal Services Act 2007, as well as any other body responsible for regulation of a profession.
(ii) *You* should disclose details of any disciplinary proceeding(s) or investigation(s) *you* may be facing. *We* will not determine *your* application until *you* can confirm that the matter(s) has/have either been dropped or the outcome of *your* case is known.

7: EVIDENCE

7.1 To help *us* consider an application where a disclosure has been made, *you* should include the following evidence, where relevant:

(a) at least one independent report relating to the event(s), such as sentencing remarks following a criminal conviction;
(b) references from at least two independent professional people (of which one should preferably be from an employer or tutor) who know *you* well and are familiar with the matters being considered;
(c) evidence of any rehabilitation (e.g. probation reports, references from employers and/or tutors);
(d) documentary evidence in support of *your* case and where possible, an independent corroboration of *your* account of the event(s);
(e) *your* attitude towards the event(s);
(f) the extent to which *you* were aware of the rules and procedures governing the reference of material, or the use of group work or collaborative material;
(g) the extent to which *you* could reasonably have been expected to realise that the offence did not constitute legitimate academic practice;
(h) credit check information (in the relevant circumstances); and/or
(i) actions *you* have taken to clear any debts, satisfy any judgements and manage *your* finances.

7.2 The onus is on *you* to provide any evidence *you* consider necessary and/or appropriate. However, should *we* consider that *you* have provided insufficient evidence, *we* reserve the right to carry out our own investigation and/or refuse the application if further evidence is not forthcoming.

8: REHABILITATION

8.1 It is for *you* to demonstrate that *you* have undergone successful rehabilitation, where relevant. The individual circumstances *you* put forward must be weighed against the public interest and the need to safeguard members of the public and maintain the reputation of the profession. However, *we* will consider each application on its own merits.
8.2 If the Rehabilitation of Offenders Act 1974 (Exceptions) Order 1975 (as amended) is

APPENDIX D

applicable to *your* occupation, profession or role, *you* must declare all convictions and cautions, even if they are deemed to be spent in accordance with the Act.

8.3 In accordance with paragraph 2 above (disclosure), if *you* fall within the Rehabilitation of Offenders Act 1974 (Exceptions) Order 1975 and *you* fail to disclose information about convictions and/or cautions for criminal offences, whether they are spent or unspent, *we* will consider this as amounting to prima facie evidence of dishonest behaviour.

Guidance note

(i) The provisions of the Rehabilitation of Offenders Act 1974 (as amended) and the Rehabilitation of Offenders Act 1974 (Exceptions) Order 1975 (as amended) will be taken into account by *us* in considering any application *you* make.
(ii) If *you* fall within the Rehabilitation of Offenders Act 1974 (Exceptions) Order 1975 (as amended), the fact that the conviction is spent, and the time that has passed since the conviction was given, together with any other material circumstances will be taken into account by *us* when determining any application made by *you*.
(iii) A period of rehabilitation, particularly after *we* have decided to refuse *your* application, will not in itself result in automatic admission/authorisation. *We* need *you* to show, through a period of good behaviour, that *you* have taken steps to rehabilitate *yourself* by *your* own volition.

PART 2: ADDITIONAL REQUIREMENTS TO BECOME AUTHORISED UNDER THE AUTHORISATION RULES

9: ALL APPLICANTS MUST COMPLY WITH PART 1

9.1 Under this test, when considering any application by an individual seeking to become an *authorised role holder*, all of the tests set out in Part 1 will apply in addition to this Part.

10: ADDITIONAL REQUIREMENTS

10.1 Unless there are exceptional circumstances *we* may refuse *your* application if:

(a) *you* have been removed from the office of trustee for a charity by an order imposed by the Charities Act 1993;
(b) *you* have been removed and/or disqualified as a company director;
(c) any body corporate of which *you* are/were a *manager* or *owner* has been the subject of a winding up order, an administrative order or an administrative receivership, or has otherwise been wound up or put into administration in circumstances of insolvency;
(d) *you* have a previous conviction which is now spent for a criminal offence relating to bankruptcy, IVAs or other circumstances of insolvency;
(e) *you* are a corporate person/entity subject to a relevant insolvency event defined in rule 1.2 of the *Authorisation Rules*;
(f) *you* are a corporate person/entity and other matters that call *your* fitness and propriety into question are disclosed or come to light;

(g) *you* have committed an offence under the Companies Act 2006; and/or

(h) *we* have evidence reflecting on the honesty and integrity of a person *you* are related to, affiliated with, or act together with where *we* have reason to believe that the person may have an influence over the way in which *you* will exercise *your authorised role*.

Guidance note

(i) The provisions of the Rehabilitation of Offenders Act 1974 (as amended) and the Rehabilitation of Offenders Act 1974 (Exceptions) Order 1975 (as amended) do not apply to corporate persons/entities. Therefore, corporate convictions cannot become spent, so if *you* are a corporate person/entity *you* must disclose any and all matters in *your* application.

(ii) Other matters under 10.1(f) include but are not limited to debts, corporate criminal matters, Companies Act transgressions such as late submission of accounts, and taking steps without submitting proper documents to Companies House.

APPENDIX E

Law Society Practice Notes

E1   ALTERNATIVE BUSINESS STRUCTURES
4 May 2011

1   Introduction

1.1   Who should read this practice note?

This practice note should be read by all those who are interested in the opportunities offered by and the rules governing alternative business structures (ABS).

1.2   What's the issue?

Subject to any administrative delay, part 5 of the Legal Services Act 2007 is expected to come into force on 6 October 2011, allowing the licensing of ABS.

The changes will allow non-lawyers to own and invest in law firms. The present limit on the number of non-lawyer managers within a law firm will also be removed.

In the future, legal disciplinary practices (LDPs) with non-lawyer managers will be regulated as ABS. LDPs with lawyer managers only may remain as LDPs (see the practice note on LDPs for more information [**www.lawsociety.org.uk/productsandservices/practicenotes/ldp.page**]).

This practice note provides details on the changes relating to ABS.

2   What is an ABS?

An ABS is a firm where a non-lawyer:

- is a manager of the firm, or
- has an ownership-type interest in the firm

A firm may also be an ABS where another body:

- is a manager of the firm, or
- has an ownership-type interest in the firm

and at least 10 per cent of that body is controlled by non-lawyers.

A non-lawyer is a person who is not authorised under the Legal Services Act 2007 to carry out reserved legal activities.

3 Potential benefits and risks of becoming an ABS

3.1 *Potential benefits*

Many of the benefits of becoming an ABS are benefits that also applied to becoming an LDP:

1. equity can be raised from a broader base of potential partners, members or directors for example from:
   - other professionals
   - non-solicitor employees

2. Non-solicitor employees may be rewarded by partner, member or director status, with a direct stake in the firm, thus enabling a practice to both:
   - retain high-performing non-solicitor employees
   - attract outside legal talent

3. The ability to diversify the range of legal services provided by the practice either through:
   - becoming a 'one stop shop', or
   - consolidating a specialism in a particular area of the market.

There are, however, some additional potential benefits to becoming an ABS:

4. Equity can be raised from outside the legal sector without the need for non-lawyer involvement at the management level. This has the potential to allow firms to attract new investment from different markets.
5. You may provide a wider range of services to clients through an ABS than you can through an ordinary law firm.

3.2 *Potential risks*

You should be aware of how the ABS structure may affect your firm. You should consider the following questions in your assessment:

1. What impact will non-lawyer managers or owners have on the culture of the firm?
2. How will the changes affect the firm's business plan and what benefits are they likely to achieve?
3. How far will non-lawyers understand the culture and obligations of solicitors?
4. Will becoming an ABS change the firm's perceived risk profile? The SRA does not believe that ABS are inherently more risky but changes to your firm may still alter the perceived risk. This may alter the way a firm is regulated by the SRA under its new system of risk based regulation and the ability of, and terms on which, a firm can obtain professional indemnity insurance.
5. Do you want to provide services through an office overseas? Many foreign jurisdictions may not accept ABS.

3.2.1 STAFF

Elevating suitable, existing, non-solicitor employees to partner, member or director status should be a fairly straight-forward process if there is consensus about this within the firm. Merging practices or bringing in a range of non-solicitor managers from diverse backgrounds carries an elevated degree of risk that will require a greater level of planning and risk assessment.

APPENDIX E

3.2.2 OUTSIDE INVESTMENT

If you plan to accept outside investment then there will be more complex considerations particularly regarding how the firm will ensure compliance with principles and the new code of conduct. You should think about:

1. the purpose of the investment
2. the level of control that the owner will have over your business
3. whether the owner could sell on their interest or withdraw their investment and the potential consequences to the firm of such an occurrence
4. if the owner's control could interfere with the firm's ability to act in the best interests of clients and, if so, how this risk can be mitigated

4 Services an ABS may provide

Under the proposed rules, ABS are not limited in the services that they can offer to the public. However, you will need to consider whether offering certain services may conflict with the duties owed to a solicitor's client. For instance, duties of different professionals within an ABS may conflict. One example of this is auditors, who are often under a duty to disclose information while lawyers are on the whole required to keep information provided by clients confidential.

You may not be able to accept instructions from some clients where aims of different parts of an ABS may conflict with a client's best interests. For instance, an ABS with an insurance arm would probably be unable to offer legal services to a client whose claim was against an organisation or individual insured by that ABS. This is because, it would be in the interest of part of the ABS (the insurance arm) for the client to lose the case and this creates a conflict which would normally preclude the ABS from acting for the client.

It will be important that an ABS that plans to offer additional services considers the potential conflicts that may arise and how they can be mitigated. There may be some cases where the risks cannot be mitigated and therefore a particular service might not be capable of being offered.

In general, the SRA do not plan to regulate non-legal services carried out within a multidisciplinary practice (MDP). However, it should be noted that the Code applies to individuals working within the MDP as well as the MDP itself and individuals carrying out non-legal activities may still be subject to the Code. However, if such services are not regulated and are not covered by the ABS's indemnity insurance or the compensation fund, this must be made clear to the client.

5 'Jumping the gun'

Practices must also ensure they do not breach the existing rules, for example by appointing managers or ceding control of the law firm to a non-lawyer in anticipation of the emergence of ABSs.

Read the SRA's guidance [**www.sra.org.uk/solicitors/code-of-conduct/guidance/abs/preparing-for-alternative-business-structures-info.page**]

6 How does a practice become an ABS?

6.1 Fundamental requirements

To be eligible to be an ABS, a body must:

1. at all times have at least one manager who must be an individual and who is:
    - a solicitor with a current practising certificate

- a registered European lawyer (REL), or
- a lawyer of England and Wales and who is authorised by an approved regulator other than the SRA, or
- registered with the Bar Standards Board under regulation 17 of the European Communities (Lawyer's Practice) Regulations 2000 (SI 2000/1119)

2. meet the requirements for an ABS set out in section 2 of this practice note
3. have a practising address in England or Wales

6.2 Existing practices

Existing practices that wish to become ABS will need to apply to the SRA under the new authorisation rules. Existing LDPs with non-lawyer managers will be 'passported' to ABS status. However, this will involve an application procedure.

6.3 New firms

New firms will need to apply for approval to become licensed as an ABS under the new authorisation rules. The SRA plans to accept applications from firms wishing to become ABS in August 2011. Firms who plan to apply to become ABS should contact the SRA ahead of this time to begin discussing their plans.

6.4 Approval of a body under the Authorisation Rules

6.4.1 APPLICATION

A firm wishing to become an ABS will need to:

- complete the SRA's application form (still under development)
- provide any additional information required by the SRA
- and pay the application fee (to be determined)

The application must set out which reserved activities the applicant wishes to be licensed to carry out.

If any of the information provided changes, the SRA should be informed. It should be noted that failure to do so or providing inaccurate or misleading information can lead to an application being refused or a licence being withdrawn.

6.4.2 DECISION TO GRANT A LICENCE

The SRA will only grant a licence where it is satisfied, among other things, that:

- the firm is an ABS
- the firm will comply with the requirements relating to professional indemnity insurance and the compensation fund
- compliance officers have been appointed (see further information on compliance officers in section 6.5.1.3)
- all authorised role holders are approved, and
- that one of the lawyer managers is qualified to supervise

The SRA may refuse a licence application if:

- it is not satisfied that the managers and owners are suitable as a group to operate the ABS
- it is not satisfied that the management and governance arrangements are adequate

APPENDIX E

- it is not satisfied that the ABS will comply with the SRA's requirements, including any conditions imposed on a licence
- the applicant has provided inaccurate or misleading information, or failed to inform the SRA of a change to the information provided, or
- it believes it is against the public interest or inconsistent with the regulatory objectives set out in the Legal Services Act 2007

It is the responsibility of the applicant to show that they meet the SRA's requirements.

6.4.3 GRANTING A LICENCE

All licences will be granted subject to the general conditions set out in the authorisation rules. These relate to various aspects of the running of an ABS and include:

- compliance with the SRA's requirements
- payment of fees
- the role of compliance officers, and
- provision of information to the SRA

Licences may also be granted subject to further conditions which may:

- limit the activities of the ABS, or a particular manager, or employee, in order to protect clients or the public interest
- prevent the ABS from entering into particular business agreements or adopting particular business practices in order to protect clients or the public interest
- facilitate the SRA's monitoring of a business, in order to help the SRA ensure regulatory compliance, or
- make the ABS take specific actions to ensure that they provide legal services in a suitable manner.

The SRA will normally be required to make any licensing decision within six months of application though it can extend this period to nine months. If it refuses an application it must set out its reasons for refusal.

6.4.4 APPEALING AGAINST DECISIONS

The SRA can decide to:

- grant a licence
- grant a licence subject to conditions
- refuse an application

The licences have no specific end date so they do not have to be renewed.

The applicant can appeal against the SRA's decision to refuse an application and to grant a licence subject to conditions. In the first instance, the appeal must be to the SRA within 28 days of the decision. A further appeal can be made to the appellate body. This body has yet to be appointed.

6.4.5 EFFECTS OF REFUSAL

The SRA may, if it considers it in the public interest to do so, publish and notify any persons of a decision including a decision to refuse a licence application. These persons include but are not limited to:

- an authorised person of which the body or individual concerned is a past, current or prospective manager, employee or interest holder
- other approved regulators
- other professional regulators
- the Legal Ombudsman

It is not clear how the SRA intends to use this power. However, a publication policy is under development.

6.5 Approval of authorised role holders under the Authorisation Rules

Under the Authorisation Rules, those undertaking certain roles within an ABS will require approval from the SRA. Approval will need to be sought in the first instance as part of the application to become an ABS. As the ABS grows and changes it is likely role holders will change and new approvals will need to be sought.

6.5.1 AUTHORISED ROLE HOLDERS

Authorised role holders are managers, owners and compliance officers.

6.5.1.1 Managers

Managers are defined as:

- partners of a general partnership
- members of a limited liability partnership
- directors of a company, or
- in relation to any other body, a member of its governing body

A manager can be an individual or a corporate body.

6.5.1.2 Owners

The term 'owner' is not specifically defined in the Legal Services Act 2007, the act makes references to restricted interests, therefore 'owner' has been defined by the SRA. It considers an owner to be any person who holds a material interest in a body or a partner where the body in question is a partnership. A 'material interest' is defined in the Legal Services Act 2007. In essence it is an interest of ten per cent in a corporate body or an interest that allows a significant influence over a corporate body. Those with a lesser stake will not be considered 'owners' by the SRA and will not need to be authorised. An owner can be an individual or a corporate body.

6.5.1.3 Compliance officers

A compliance officer is either a compliance officer for legal practice (COLP) or a compliance officer for finance and administration (COFA). Compliance officers will need to be individuals who are employees or managers of the ABS. A COLP must also be a lawyer of England or Wales, or a REL, or a person who is registered with the Bar Standard Board under Regulation 17 of the European Communities (Lawyer's Practice) Regulations 2000. Both a COLP and a COFA will need to be in a position of sufficient seniority and responsibility to fulfil their role.

The roles of COLPs and COFAs are set out in the authorisation rules. COLPs will need to take all reasonable steps to ensure the ABS complies with the SRA's regulatory arrangements (except those relating to accounts rules) and any statutory obligations of the body. They will also need to report any failure to comply to the SRA.

The COFA will need to take all reasonable steps to ensure that the body complies with the SRA Accounts Rules and report to the SRA any failure to comply.

APPENDIX E

The SRA has clarified that the ultimate responsibility for compliance still remains with the governing body of a firm. However, it will expect compliance officers to ensure firms put in place systems and controls for compliance and to oversee those controls.

6.5.1.4 Approval process for authorised role holders

The SRA must normally approve all authorised role holders. However, a practising solicitor with no conditions on their practising certificate or authorised body is deemed to be approved for the roles of owner or manager (but not for the roles of COLP or COFA) provided the appropriate notification requirements put in place by the SRA are met.

When approving persons for an authorised role, the SRA will consider:

- the criteria set out in the SRA suitability test, and
- any other relevant information

6.5.2 THE SUITABILITY TEST

All managers, owners and compliance officers will need to meet the suitability requirements that a solicitor would need to meet on entry to the profession. In assessing a person's suitability the SRA will consider:

- any criminal offences
- any behaviour not compatible with that expected of a prospective solicitor eg behaviour which is dishonest or violent in nature
- regulatory history
- financial behaviour

There are also additional requirements for authorised role holders. In these cases, when assessing a person's suitability the SRA will also consider:

- corporate or professional history
- a person's affiliates

The SRA will normally refuse an application where it has evidence that reflects on the honesty and integrity of a person who an authorised role holder is affiliated with and who the SRA believe would influence how the role holder would carry out their role.

6.5.3 APPLICATION PROCESS

The ABS or potential ABS will need to apply on behalf of the candidate who wishes to fulfil an authorised role. The obligation falls on the applicant to satisfy the SRA that the candidate is suitable to fulfil the role. The candidate will need to declare that all the information provided is accurate.

The applicant must cooperate with the SRA with regard to supplying information, answering queries and securing the cooperation of the candidate for the role.

6.5.4 RETENTION OF INFORMATION

The Authorisation Rules require that practices retain information and documentation pertaining to the application for the approval of an authorised role holder for not less than six years after the person ceases to carry out the authorised role.

6.5.5 APPEALING AGAINST DECISIONS

The SRA will notify both the applicant and candidate of their decision. The SRA can decide to:

- grant approval
- grant approval subject to conditions
- refuse approval

If the SRA intends to refuse to approve an owner or grant conditional approval then they are normally obliged to warn the applicant and the candidate, to allow them the opportunity to make representations within a prescribed period. If the application is made once a body has been granted authorisation, this warning may be dispensed with. Any person can also appeal against the decision to the SRA. The appeal will normally need to be made within 28 days of the notification of the SRA's decision and reasons. Any person may make a further appeal against the decision to the appellate body.

The applicant or the candidate can also appeal against the SRA's decision to refuse to approve a manager or compliance officer or to grant conditional approval. In the first instance, the appeal must be to the SRA within 28 days of the decision. A further appeal can be made to the appellate body.

6.5.6 EFFECT OF REFUSAL

It should be noted that where the SRA refuses approval for a solicitor to fulfil an authorised role then regulation 3 of the Practising Regulations will be triggered and the solicitor will need to submit their next application for a practising certificate early (ie at least six weeks before the replacement or renewal date).

The SRA may also, if it considers it in the public interest to do so, publish and notify any persons of a decision, including a decision to refuse to approve a potential authorised role holder. These persons include but are not limited to:

- an authorised individual or body of which the person concerned is a past, current or prospective manager, employee or interest holder
- other approved regulators
- other professional regulators
- the Legal Ombudsman

It is not clear to what extent the SRA plans to use this power. However, a publication policy is under development.

7 Becoming recognised as an ABS

The SRA website [**www.sra.org.uk**] will provide full information on the application process.

ABS will not formally exist until 6 October 2011. Before this date practices may apply for a licence to become an ABS.

8 Costs and renewal

For details of current fees for see the SRA website [**www.sra.org.uk**].

9 Further considerations

9.1 Disciplinary powers

The SRA will have new enforcement powers against ABS. These include the power to impose significant fines and to disqualify Heads of Legal Practice (HOLPs), Heads of

APPENDIX E

Finance Administration (HOFAs), managers and employees of ABS. The appeal provisions will also differ from those applicable to non-ABS.

9.2 International operations

Practices with offices in overseas jurisdictions should consider the potential impact that ABS status may have on non-UK operations.

Some jurisdictions do not permit non-lawyer owners or managers of the type permitted by the ABS rules. Some jurisdictions' local regulations may also not recognise as lawyers some people who are not solicitors and barristers, even though they may be considered as such under the Legal Services Act 2007.

You should therefore make a careful analysis of any local regulations which may affect your firm. The Law Society's International Department can offer background information on many foreign jurisdictions. See the International Practice section [**http://international.lawsociety.org.uk/ip/practise**] of the department website or contact the department directly on +44 (0)20 7242 1222.

10 Further information

10.1 Professional conduct

The following parts of the SRA Handbook [**www.sra.org.uk/handbook**] are relevant:

- Practice Framework Rules – Rule 14
- Authorisation Rules

10.2 Statutory provisions

- Legal Services Act 2007

10.3 Status of this note

Practice notes are issued by the Law Society for the use and benefit of its members. They represent the Law Society's view of good practice in a particular area. They are not intended to be the only standard of good practice that solicitors can follow. You are not required to follow them, but doing so will make it easier to account to oversight bodies for your actions.

Practice notes are not legal advice, nor do they necessarily provide a defence to complaints of misconduct or of inadequate professional service. While care has been taken to ensure that they are accurate, up to date and useful, the Law Society will not accept any legal liability in relation to them.

For queries or comments on this practice note contact the Law Society's Practice Advice Service.

10.4 Terminology

Must – a specific requirement in the Solicitor's Code of Conduct or legislation. You must comply, unless there are specific exemptions or defences provided for in the code of conduct or relevant legislation.

Should – good practice for most situations in the Law Society's view. If you do not follow this, you must be able to justify to oversight bodies why this is appropriate, either for your practice, or in the particular retainer.

May – a non-exhaustive list of options for meeting your obligations. Which option you choose is determined by the risk profile of the individual practice, client or retainer. You must be able to justify why this was an appropriate option to oversight bodies.

A glossary of other terms used throughout this practice note is available on the SRA website

10.5   More information and products

10.5.1   LAW SOCIETY PRACTICE NOTES

- Firm based regulation
- LDPs

10.5.2   SRA GUIDANCE

See the SRA website [**www.sra.org.uk**].

10.5.3   LAW SOCIETY INTERNATIONAL DEPARTMENT

Information on foreign jurisdictions is available via the department website [**http://international.lawsociety.org.uk**], or you can contact the department directly on +44 (0)20 7242 1222.

10.5.4   LAW SOCIETY PRACTICE ADVICE SERVICE

Support for solicitors on a wide range of areas of practice. Practice advice can be contacted on 0870 606 2522 from 9:00 to 17:00 on weekdays

E2   COMPLIANCE OFFICERS

8 September 2011

1   Introduction

1.1   Who should read this practice note?

Solicitors involved in the appointment of a compliance officer for legal practice (COLP) or compliance officer for finance and administration (COFA) and those fulfilling the role of COLP and COFA.

1.2   What's the issue?

The Solicitors Regulation Authority (SRA) is implementing outcomes-focused regulation (OFR) in October 2011. OFR is a move away from a rules-based approach to one that focuses on high-level outcomes governing practice and the quality of outcomes for clients.

An overview of OFR can be found on the Law Society's website [**www.lawsociety.org.uk/practicesupport/regulation/ofr.page**]. This provides information on what the SRA Handbook contains, including a summary of the chapters in the Code of Conduct and a summary of the reporting requirements included throughout the Handbook.

The SRA have published a Handbook, which sets out all the SRA's regulatory requirements. It outlines the ethical standards that the SRA expects of practices and practitioners and the outcomes that the SRA expects them to achieve for their clients.

APPENDIX E

The SRA Handbook includes a Code of Conduct (the Code), which replaces the Solicitors' Code of Conduct 2007 (the 2007 Code). The Code establishes outcomes-focused conduct requirements and each chapter outlines outcomes and indicative behaviours (IBs).

The SRA Handbook and Code will be in force from 6 October 2011. The Solicitors' Code of Conduct 2007, and all of its rules and guidance, will not apply to conduct after that date and will cease to have any effect, save in respect of any review by the SRA of conduct taken prior to 6 October 2011 to which the 2007 Code will still be applied.

The Legal Services Act 2007 requires that a head of legal practice (HOLP) and head of finance and administration (HOFA) are appointed within each alternative business structure (ABS). The SRA have decided that all practices, including those which are not ABS should appoint someone to these positions. In their new regulatory framework, they have termed the roles compliance officer for legal practice (COLP) and compliance officer for finance and administration (COFA). It is the SRA Authorisation Rules for Legal Services Bodies and Licensable Bodies that outlines the requirements for these roles.

ABS will need to have individuals appointed to these roles when they are licensed by the SRA. All non-ABS will need to decide who they will appoint to these roles by 31 March 2012 and must provide details of their prospective COLPs and COFAs to the SRA for approval. The COLP and COFA will be authorised and will start to fulfill their obligations from 31 October 2012.

This practice note explains the roles of COLPs and COFAs.

1.3 Status of this practice note

Practice notes are issued by the Law Society for the use and benefit of its members. They represent the Law Society's view of good practice in a particular area. They are not intended to be the only standard of good practice that solicitors can follow. You are not required to follow them, but doing so will make it easier to account to oversight bodies for your actions.

Practice notes are not legal advice, nor do they necessarily provide a defence to complaints of misconduct or of inadequate professional service. While care has been taken to ensure that they are accurate, up to date and useful, the Law Society will not accept any legal liability in relation to them.

For queries or comments on this practice note, contact the Law Society's Practice Advice Service: **www.lawsociety.org.uk/practiceadvice**.

1.4 Terminology

Must – A specific requirement in legislation or of a principle, rule, outcome or other mandatory provision in the SRA Handbook. You must comply, unless there are specific exemptions or defences provided for in relevant legislation or the SRA Handbook.

Should

- Outside of a regulatory context, good practice for most situations in the Law Society's view.
- In the case of the SRA Handbook, an indicative behaviour or other non-mandatory provision (such as may be set out in notes or guidance).

These may not be the only means of complying with legislative or regulatory requirements and there may be situations where the suggested route is not the best possible route to meet the needs of your client. However, if you do not follow the suggested route, you should be able to justify to oversight bodies why the alternative approach you have taken is appropriate, either for your practice, or in the particular retainer.

May – A non-exhaustive list of options for meeting your obligations or running your practice. Which option you choose is determined by the profile of the individual practice, client or retainer. You may be required to justify why this was an appropriate option to oversight bodies.
SRA Code – SRA Code of Conduct 2011
OFR – Outcomes-focused regulation
SRA – Solicitors Regulation Authority
IB – indicative behaviour
COLP – Compliance officer for legal practice
HOLP – Head of legal practice
COFA – Compliance officer for finance and administration
HOFA – Head of finance and administration

A glossary of other terms used throughout this practice note is available on the SRA website [**www.sra.org.uk**].

2   SRA Principles

There are ten mandatory principles which apply to all those the SRA regulates and to all aspects of practice. The principles can be found in the SRA Handbook [**www.sra.org.uk/solicitors/handbook**].

When thinking about how to meet the outcomes in the Handbook, you must consider the principles which apply across the Handbook including the SRA Code. You should always bear in mind what the ten principles are and use them as your starting point when implementing the outcomes.

3   Who can be a COLP or COFA?

3.1   Who can be a COLP?

A COLP must be an individual who:

- is a lawyer of England or Wales; registered European lawyer (REL) or European lawyer regulated by the Bar Standards Board
- is an employee or manager of the firm
- is of sufficient seniority and in a position of sufficient responsibility to fulfil the role
- is approved by the SRA for that role
- has consented to undertake the role
- and is authorised to do one or more of the reserved activities specified in the firm's certificate of authorisation.

A person cannot be a COLP if they have been disqualified from acting as a HOLP.

There is no definition as to what sufficiently senior or responsible might mean. However guidance indicates that COLPs should have:

- clear reporting lines between themselves and the governing body of the firm ie the partners, members or directors
- access to all management systems and arrangements and all other relevant information.

There may be no one who is ideally positioned to take on the role within your practice. In many cases, those with sufficient seniority may not have detailed knowledge of the compliance systems.

APPENDIX E

One solution may be to appoint a more senior person who delegates some of the day-to-day functions (but not responsibility) to other members of staff. However, the COLP should monitor any work they delegate and there should be clear reporting lines between the COLP and those carrying out day-to-day functions on their behalf.

3.2 Who can be a COFA?

A COFA must an individual who:

- is an employee or manager of the firm
- is of sufficient seniority and in a position of sufficient responsibility to fulfil the role
- is approved by the SRA for that role and
- has consented to undertake the role.

A person cannot be a COFA if they have been disqualified from acting as a HOFA.

There is no definition as to what sufficiently senior or responsible might mean.

Unlike a COLP, the COFA does not need to be a lawyer. This gives organisations greater flexibility about who they can appoint. The role, as set out by the Authorisation Rules, relates to the SRA's Accounts Rules [**www.sra.org.uk/solicitors/handbook/accountsrules**].

Therefore the COFA will need a good understanding of the rules applying to solicitors, rather than just a general financial understanding.

The role of COLP and COFA can be carried out by the same person.

4 The role of compliance officers

The responsibilities placed on compliance officers are broad. While the SRA have highlighted that responsibility for compliance ultimately rests with the managers of a practice, compliance officers may also find regulatory action is taken against them where they fail to meet their responsibilities.

It will be important for a compliance officer to ensure they are in a position to carry out their role effectively. Even though compliance ultimately rests with the managers of a practice, there may be situations when a compliance officer reports issues to the SRA which may be against the wishes of the managers of the practice. A compliance officer will need to consider whether they have the authority to do this.

4.1 The role of the COLP

In essence, the role of the COLP is to:

- take all reasonable steps to ensure compliance with the terms and conditions of their firm's authorisation
- take all reasonable steps to ensure compliance with any statutory obligations for example, the duties imposed by the Legal Services Act 2007, the Solicitors Act 1974 and the Administration of Justice Act 1985
- to take all reasonable steps to record all failures to comply. Also to report any such failures to comply to the SRA as soon as reasonably practicable, although in the case of non-material breaches, the firm will still be deemed compliant if they are reported as part of the Information Report required under Rule 8.7 of the Authorisation Rules.

It is important to note that compliance with the conditions of the licence includes compliance with all the SRA's regulatory arrangements including those within the Handbook. The SRA regulatory arrangements include all rules and regulations set by the SRA in relation to:

- authorisation
- practice
- conduct
- discipline
- qualification of persons carrying on legal activities
- accounts and
- indemnification and compensation arrangements.

With the exception of the Accounts Rules, those designated as COLP will need to be in a position to be able to discharge these responsibilities.

General conditions will be applied to all practice's authorisation and the conditions are set out in Rule 8 of the Authorisation Rules. These include conditions in relation to:

- compliance with regulatory arrangements
- suitable arrangements for compliance
- management and control of a firm including approval of mangers and owners
- provision of information to the SRA

The range of general conditions placed on practice's authorisation means that a COLP's responsibilities relate to a broad range of requirements. COLPs should become familiar with the general conditions as well as any additional conditions placed on their licence.

The SRA's guidance has highlighted that the COLP will be responsible for ensuring systems are in place for compliance. The SRA have provided guidance [**www.sra.org.uk/solicitors/handbook/accountsrules**] on the systems they might expect to see practices put in place. They suggest that practices should consider the following:

- a system for ensuring that undertakings are given only when intended, and that compliance with them is monitored and enforced
- a system for ensuring appropriate checks on new staff or contractors
- a system for ensuring that basic regulatory deadlines are not missed e.g, submission of the firm's accountant's report, arranging indemnity cover, renewal of practising certificates and registrations, renewal of all lawyers' licences to practise and provision of regulatory information
- a system for monitoring, reviewing and managing risks
- ensuring that issues of conduct are given appropriate weight in decisions the firm takes, whether on client matters or firm-based issues such as funding
- file reviews
- appropriate systems for supporting the development and training of staff
- obtaining the necessary approvals of managers, owners and COLP/COFA
- arrangements to ensure that any duties to clients and others are fully met even when staff are absent.

The existence of the COLP does not detract from the practice's and managers' responsibilities and their obligations to comply with the SRA's regulatory arrangements.

Read the Authorisation Rules guidance on the SRA website [**www.sra.org.uk/solicitors/handbook**].

4.2 The role of the COFA

The role of the COFA is to:

- take all reasonable steps to ensure compliance with the SRA's accounts rules

APPENDIX E

- to record all failures to comply. Also to report any such failures to comply to the SRA as soon as reasonably practicable, although in the case of non-material breaches, the firm will still be deemed compliant if they are reported as part of the Information Report required under Rule 8.7 of the Authorisation Rules.

In order to be in a position to discharge their role fully, the COFA will need to consider whether they:

- have access to all accounting records
- carry out regular checks on the accounting systems
- carry out file and ledger reviews
- ensure that the reporting accountant has prompt access to all the information needed to complete the accountant's report
- take steps to ensure that breaches of the SRA Accounts Rules are remedied promptly
- can report all breaches, which are material either on their own or as part of a pattern, to the SRA and
- can monitor, review and manage risks to compliance with the SRA Accounts Rules.

While the rules highlight the COFA's role in relation to the SRA's Accounts Rules, the SRA's 'Quick guide to outcomes focused regulation' also implies that there is a role for the COFA in reporting when the practice is in serious financial difficulties. The COFA may therefore also need to consider whether they are able to access information on the practice's overall financial status and be in a position to make an assessment of that status.

Read the Accounts Rules on the SRA website [**www.sra.org.uk/solicitors/handbook/accountsrules**]

Read the Quick guide to outcomes-focused regulation [**www.sra.org.uk/solicitors/freedom-in-practice/OFR/ofr-quick-guide.page**]

The SRA's guidance has highlighted that the COFA will be responsible for implementing and overseeing systems for compliance in relation to the Accounts Rules. The SRA have provided guidance on the systems they might expect to see practices put in place. They suggest that practices should consider the following:

- a system for ensuring that only the appropriate people authorise payments from client account
- a system for ensuring that undertakings are given only when intended, and that compliance with them is monitored and enforced
- a system for ensuring appropriate checks on new staff or contractors
- a system for ensuring that basic regulatory deadlines are not missed e.g. submission of the firm's accountant's report, arranging indemnity cover, renewal of practising certificates and registrations, renewal of all lawyers' licences to practise and provision of regulatory information
- a system for monitoring, reviewing and managing risks
- ensuring that issues of conduct are given appropriate weight in decisions the firm takes, whether on client matters or firm-based issues such as funding
- file reviews
- appropriate systems for supporting the development and training of staff
- obtaining the necessary approvals of managers, owners and COLP/COFA
- arrangements to ensure that any duties to clients and others are fully met even when staff are absent.

Read the Authorisation Rules guidance on the SRA website [**www.sra.org.uk/solicitors/handbook**].

5 The role of the COLP and COFA in smaller practices

The roles of COLP and COFA can be fulfilled by one person and this may be appropriate in smaller practices. However, those managing smaller practices should also remember that non-lawyers can take on the role of COFA. This provides practices with greater flexibility over who they might appoint.

Smaller practices should consider carefully the guidance provided by the SRA on the systems and processes that practices may put in place.

The SRA highlights that 'what needs to be covered by a firm's compliance plan will depend on factors such as the size and nature of the firm, its work and its areas of risk'.

Smaller practices should consider carefully, where there are risks to compliance and how they can be mitigated. Systems and processes should be proportionate. Overly complex systems are often by-passed and thus become ineffective.

6 The reporting requirements

COLPs and COFAs will be required to report all breaches in compliances to the SRA as soon as reasonably practicable. However, as is noted in 4.1 and 4.2 above, in the case of non-material breaches, the firm will still be deemed compliant if they are reported as part of the Information Report required under Rule 8.7 of the Authorisation Rules.

6.1 What is 'material'

When deciding if a breach, or series of breaches are material the COLP or COFA will need to consider:

- the detriment, or risk of detriment, to clients
- the extent of any risk of loss of confidence in the practice or in the provision of legal services
- the scale of the issue
- the overall impact on the practice, its clients and third parties.

It is important to note that while a single breach may be trivial, if it part of series then it may be material. For this reason, a compliance officer will need systems to identify patterns of breaches.

Compliance officers will need to remember that the SRA Code covers a wide range of issues including business management and financial stability. Compliance officers will need to notify the SRA if they believe the practice is in serious financial difficulty.

6.2 Other reporting requirements

There are a series of other reporting requirements that are placed on the practice such as informing the SRA about changes to that practice. While these requirements are placed on the practice it is likely that in many cases the COLP will take on the role of reporting these issues to the SRA.

6.3 Keeping records

It is a requirement that COLPs and COFAs keep record of all breaches in compliance. Practices may consider putting in place a centralised reporting system to allow them to capture and record all breaches in compliance.

While data on all breaches may be difficult to collect, particularly in larger organisations, it can be valuable. The data may highlight area where the risk of non-compliance is higher and

APPENDIX E

allow the practice to put in place measures to mitigate against the risk of further non-compliance. The data can also be used to measure the effectiveness of interventions to improve compliance.

It will also be important that the data is captured in such a way that the COLP and COFA can identify any patterns of breaches which may be material. This will be easier in smaller practices, where there are likely to be fewer breaches reported. However, in larger practices there may need to be some system of categorisation of breaches e.g. by rule breached or area of law, to allow the COLP or COFA to identify patterns of breaches that may need to be reported to the SRA.

7 Contingency planning

The SRA guidance highlights the need to have in place arrangements to ensure that any duties to clients and others are fully met even when staff are absent. As with all areas of the business practices should give consideration to how they will manage the absence of a compliance officer. If the practice ceases to have a compliance officer they will need to:

- inform the SRA,
- designate another manager or employee to replace its previous compliance officer and
- make an application to the SRA for temporary approval of the new COLP or COFA, as appropriate.

This should be done immediately or in any event within seven days Where a compliance officer is likely to be absent for a significant length of time they may need to be replaced. The practice should discuss whether replacement is appropriate action with their supervision team at the SRA.

8 More information

8.1 Law Society

Practice Advice Service [**www.lawsociety.org.uk/productsandservices/services/practice advice.law**]

8.2 Other

Solicitors Regulation Authority's Professional Ethics Helpline [**www.sra.org.uk/contactus.page**] for advice on conduct issues.

Index

Access to justice 1.2, 4.3, 5.3, 5.8
Administration of oaths 2.2.6
Advice and assistance at a police station 2.5
Alternative business structure (ABS)
    benefits 1.2
    description 1.1
    impact of regulatory boundaries 2.8
    LSA 2007 and 1.2
    models 1.1
    nature 1.1
    origins 1.2
Appeals to SDT 3.1, 6.1, 6.7
    appellant's reply 6.7.2
    case management 6.7.1, 6.7.3
    consent order 6.7.5
    constitution of panels 6.7.1
    costs 6.7.6
    delegated authority 6.7.1
    disposal 6.7.5
    further appeals 6.7.7
    general powers 6.7.1
    hearings 6.7.4, 6.7.5
    notice of appeal 6.7.2
    preliminary steps 6.7.2
    re-hearing 6.7.5
    response to notice 6.7.2
    striking out 6.7.5
    time limit 6.7.2
    withdrawal 6.7.5
Association of Chartered Certified Accountants
    insolvency work 2.4.3
    probate activities 2.2.4
Association of Law Costs Draughtsmen 1.2
    probate activities 2.2.4
    reserved instrument activities 2.2.3

Audience *see* Right of audience
Authorisation
    access to justice objective 5.8
    application process 5.1
    approval of COLPs and COFAs 5.6
    approval of HOLPs and HOFAs 5.6
    approval of owners *see* Ownership tests
    assessing applications 5.3
    business systems and governance 5.4
    certificate 5.1
    conditions 5.1, 6.4
    decision period 5.1, 6.7
    enforcement of conditions 6.4
    extension notice 5.1
    fees 5.2
    grant 5.1
    insurance requirements 5.7
    notification of decision 5.1
    ownership tests *see* Ownership tests
    reasons for refusal 5.1
    register of authorised entities 5.1
    revocation 6.3
    SRA Authorisation Rules 2011 5.1–5.4
    suspension 6.3
    withdrawal 5.1
    see also Licensing

Bar Standard Board 1.2
Business systems and governance 5.4

Chartered Institute of Patent Attorneys 1.2, 2.2.4
Claims management services 2.4.2
Clementi, Sir David *see* Clementi report

INDEX

Clementi report 1.1, 1.2, 2.5, 3.5, 4.1
Co-op model 1.1
Competition in Professions (OFT report) 1.2
Competition and Regulation in the Legal Services Market (Department for Constitutional Affairs) 1.2
Compliance officer for finance and administration (COFA) 3.3
   disqualification 6.1
   obligations 3.3
   SRA approval 5.6
   see also Head of finance and administration
Compliance officer for legal practice (COLP) 3.3
   disqualification 6.1
   obligations 3.3
   SRA approval 5.6
   see also Head of legal practice
Conduct of litigation 2.2.2, 2.3
   ancillary activities 2.2.2
   continuity of rights 2.2.2
   definition 2.2.2
   immigration services and advice and 2.4.1
Consumer complaints 1.2, 3.5, 4.3
Conveyancing 1.2
Council for Licensed Conveyancers (CLC) 1.2
   conduct of litigation 2.1, 2.2.2
   reserved legal activities 2.1, 2.2.1, 2.2.2
   rights of audience 2.1, 2.2.1

Divestiture 6.5

Employees
   disqualification 6.1
   regulation of 3.2
   see also In-house lawyers
Enforcement 4.3
   appeals *see* Appeals to SDT
   divestiture 6.5
   firm-based approach 3.6, 6.1
   intervention powers 6.6
   investigatory powers 6.2
   of licence conditions 6.4
   restriction notice 6.5

   revocation of licence 6.3
   SRA strategy 6.1
   supervision 4.3.1, 4.3.2, 6.1
   suspension of licence 6.3
Entity regulation 3.6
External ownership 1.2
   co-op model 1.1
   conveyancing 1.2
   with more than one ring-fenced company 1.1
   regulation 1.1
   totally externally owned: owner has an interest in supply of ABSs' services 1.1
   totally externally owned: owner has no interest in supply of ABSs' services 1.1

Floated company model 1.1
Foreign ownership 5.5.1
Future of Legal Services: Putting Consumers First (White Paper) 1.2, 2.4.1

General Council of the Bar 1.2
   immigration advice and services 2.4.1
   separation of functions 1.2

Head of finance and administration (HOFA) 3.1, 3.3
   approval 5.6
   disqualification 6.1
   obligations 3.3
   requirement 3.3
   see also Compliance officer for finance and administration
Head of legal practice (HOLP) 3.1, 3.3
   approval 5.6
   disqualification 6.1
   duties 3.3, 5.5.1
   requirement 3.3
   see also Compliance officer for legal practice
Hub and spoke model 1.1

Immigration advice and services 2.4.1, 2.6
In-house lawyers 1.1
   pro bono work 2.3

reserved legal activities 2.3
see also Employees
Insolvency Practitioners Association 2.4.3
Insolvency work 2.4.3
Institute of Chartered Accountants in England and Wales 2.4.3
Institute of Chartered Accountants in Ireland 2.4.3
Institute of Chartered Accountants of Scotland
    insolvency work 2.4.3
    probate activities 2.2.4
Institute of Legal Executives 1.2
    conduct of litigation 2.2.2
    immigration advice and services 2.4.1
    probate activities 2.2.4
    reserved instrument activities 2.2.3
Institute of Trade Mark Attorneys 1.2, 2.2.4
Insurance requirements 5.7
Intervention powers 6.6

Land registration
    reserved instrument activities 2.2.3
Law Society 1.2, 3.2, 4.1
    as approved regulator 1.2, 4.1
    consumer complaints 3.5
    entity regulation 3.6
    immigration advice and services 2.4.1
    relationship with SRA 4.1
    role 4.1
    separation of functions 1.2, 4.1
    statutory powers 4.1
Law Society of Scotland
    insolvency work 2.4.3
LDP plus model 1.1
Legal Ombudsman (LeO) 1.2, 3.5
Legal Services Board (LSB) 1.2, 2.6, 4.2
    extension of reserved legal activities 2.7
    HOLPs and HOFAs 3.3
    immigration and advice services 2.4.1
    licensing 2.6, 3.3, 5.5.1
    outcomes-focused regulation 4.2
    separation of functions 4.1

Legal Services Institute 2.2
    reserved instrument activities 2.2.3
Licensing 1.2, 3.4
    conditions 3.4
    LSB consultation paper 2.6, 3.3, 5.5.1
    see also Authorisation
Litigation *see* Conduct of litigation

Managers
    definition 1.1, 3.2
    disqualification 6.1
    regulation of 3.2
Master of the Faculties 1.2
    conduct of litigation 2.2.2
    notarial activities 2.2.5
    rights of audience 2.2.1
Multi-disciplinary practices (MDPs) 1.1, 1.2, 2.6

Non-reserved legal activities 2.1
Not for profit organisations 1.1
Notarial activities 2.2.5
    definition 2.2.5
    exemptions 2.2.5

Oaths, administration of 2.2.6
Office of Fair Trading (OFT)
    Competition in Professions 1.2
Office of the Immigration Services Commissioner 2.4.1
Office for Legal Complaints (OLC) 1.2, 3.5
Ownership regulation 3.1
    associates 3.1
    conditions 3.1
    continuing notification requirements 5.5.1
    controlled interest 5.5.1
    foreign ownership 5.5.1
    material interest 3.1, 5.5.1
    restricted interest 3.1, 5.5.1
Ownership tests
    fitness to own test 5.5.1
    LSA 2007 tests 5.5.1
    regulated persons test 5.5.1
    regulatory objectives test 5.5.1
    SRA Suitability Test 3.1, 5.5.2
    see also Authorisation

INDEX

Permitted separate business 2.6
Police station
    advice and assistance at 2.5
Private equity investment model 1.1
Probate activities 2.2.4
    continuity of rights 2.2.4
    meaning 2.2.4
    scope 2.2.4
Professional indemnity insurance 5.7
Prohibited separate business activities 2.6

Regulation of Legal Services: Reserved Legal Activities – History and Rationale (2010) 2.2, 2.2.3
Regulated but not reserved legal activities 2.4
    claims management services 2.4.2
    immigration advice and services 2.4.1
    insolvency work 2.4.3
    see also Reserved legal activities; Unregulated legal activities
Reserved instrument activities 2.2.3
    continuity of rights 2.2.3
    exemptions 2.2.3
    meaning 2.2.3
Reserved legal activities 2.1, 2.2
    administration of oaths 2.2.6
    alterations to 2.7
    conduct of litigation 2.1, 2.2.2, 2.3
    controlling the perimeter 2.3
    employees 2.3
    exercise of a right of audience 2.1, 2.2.1
    extension 2.7
    importance 2.1
    in-house lawyers 2.3
    notarial activities 2.2.5
    pro bono work 2.3
    probate activities 2.2.4
    reserved instrument activities 2.2.3
    see also Regulated but not reserved legal activities; Unregulated legal activities
Restriction notice 6.5

Review of the Regulatory Framework for Legal Services in England and Wales – Final Report see Clementi report
Revocation of licence 6.3
Right of audience
    continuity of rights 2.2.1
    exemptions 2.2.1
    exercise of 2.2.1
    immigration services and advice and 2.4.1
    meaning 2.2.1
    refusal 2.2.1

Self-regulation 1.2
Separation of functions 1.2, 4.1
'Solicitor'
    use of title 2.1
Solicitors Disciplinary Tribunal 3.2, 6.1
    appeals *see* Appeals to SDT
Solicitors Regulation Authority (SRA) 4.1
    Authorisation Rules *see* SRA Authorisation Rules 2011
    description of ABS 1.1
    enforcement *see* Enforcement
    entity regulation 3.6
    establishment 1.2
    Indemnity Insurance Rules 2011 5.7
    insolvency work 2.4.3
    investigations 4.1
    investigatory powers 6.2
    models for ABSs 1.1
    nature 4.1
    new regulatory environment and 4.2
    outcomes-focused regulation 4.2, 5.5.2
    'Regulating Alternative Business Structures' 1.1
    relationship with Law Society 4.1
    reserved legal activities 2.1
    risk-based regulation 4.3
        risks inherent in individual firms 4.3.2
        risks presented by reported events 4.3.1
        thematic risks 4.3.3
        role 4.1–4.3.3
        supervision 4.3.1, 4.3.2, 6.1

SRA Authorisation Rules 2011
    access to justice 5.8
    appeals to SDT 6.7
    application 5.1
    approval of COLPs and COFAs 5.6
    approval of managers 3.2
    authorisation process 5.1–5.4
    COFAs 3.3, 5.6
    COLPs 3.3, 5.6
    ownership regulation 3.1
    SRA Suitability Test 3.1, 5.5.2
    suspension/revocation of authorisation 6.3

Supervision 4.3.1, 4.3.2, 6.1
    see also Enforcement

Suspension of licence 6.3

Unregulated legal activities
  2.5, 2.6
    see also Regulated but not reserved legal activities; Reserved legal activities